CULTURES OF THE CITY

PITT LATIN AMERICAN SERIES

John Charles Chasteen and Catherine M. Conaghan, Editors

Cultures of the City,

MEDIATING IDENTITIES IN URBAN LATIN/O AMERICA

edited by RICHARD YOUNG and AMANDA HOLMES

UNIVERSITY OF PITTSBURGH PRESS

Published by the University of Pittsburgh Press, Pittsburgh, Pa., 15260
Copyright © 2010, University of Pittsburgh Press
Manufactured in the United States of America
Printed on acid-free paper
10 9 8 7 6 5 4 3 2 1

Library of Congress Cataloging-in-Publication Data

Cultures of the city : mediating identities in urban Latin/o America / edited by Richard Young
and Amanda Holmes.
    p. cm. — (Pitt Latin American series)
  Includes bibliographical references and index.
  ISBN 978-0-8229-6120-8 (pbk. : acid-free paper)
    1. Latin America—Social conditions. 2. Hispanic Americans—Social conditions. 3. Sociology,
Urban—Latin America. 4. Group identity—Latin America.   I. Young, Richard A., Ph. D.
II. Holmes, Amanda, 1972–
  HN110.5.A8C85 2010
  307.76097—dc22   2010031725

Contents

V

Illustrations

CULTURES OF THE CITY

Introduction Mediating Urban Identities

RICHARD YOUNG and AMANDA HOLMES

> The street corner where, intrigued, I followed the changes for several weeks, is no longer a rundown corner in Buenos Aires. For a few days it was an old recycled corner, but once that phase was over it became a universal place that could easily be found anywhere because it no longer had any meaning.
>
> —Beatriz Sarlo, *Instantáneas*

Beatriz Sarlo's verbal snapshot of the installation of an advertising marquee on a building at the corner of a street in Buenos Aires is one in a book of snapshots (*Instantáneas*) that leaves little doubt about how much the city and everyday life at the end of the twentieth century were already part of a globalized urban experience. The ironic loss of meaning discovered in a street corner following its acquisition of a new role in communications is among several themes that permeate her book as she ponders how times have changed. Sexuality and morality in a new age, fast food, and the influence of mass media on the judiciary and politics are also among the topics that attract her attention. Yet, for all the universalization she finds, there is no mistaking the Argentine capital as a constant point of reference, or the location of the places and urban culture she describes in her book. The street corner may have changed its specificity, but it is still a part of Buenos Aires.

Sarlo's city corner and her reaction to its changes, as well as her reactions to other aspects of contemporary Buenos Aires, exemplify the dynamic relationships formed between individuals or groups and urban environments. The connections to place evoked by her experiences seem simple enough, but they are also a source for reflection on the complex interaction between people and familiar urban places, and how these places engage many aspects of identity and culture. Such, in effect, is the subject of this volume, which presents a series of contributions intended to explore aspects of that interaction in a number of major cities of Latin/o America.

Not every area or country in the region is represented. The primary centers of Mexico City and Buenos Aires figure significantly. The secondary capitals Havana, Bogotá, and Lima are also included, and there is space for Asunción, one of the lesser known capitals of South America, as well as Recife and Salvador, two of the smaller state capitals of Brazil. The inclusion of a chapter on Los Angeles to represent Latina/o North America requires no explanation, given the visibility of that city's Latina/o population, although a preference for Detroit over other cities, such as New York or Miami, is less obvious. Yet the Motor City is also a representative choice, a reminder that, regardless of size, whether in the United States or Canada, few cities in North America have remained impervious to the Latina/o diaspora.

Half the contributions included in this volume examine representations of urban worlds in music, art, film, writing, and photography, including some snapshots in the more conventional sense of the term. The other half are developed from consideration of particular events, conditions, and practices of urban life. In bringing this range of works together, we have sought to provide a group of reflections on how the relationship between cities and their inhabitants is culturally mediated in ways that contribute both to the construction of identities by urban dwellers and to the attribution of identity to the city. As a group, the chapters describe a heterogenous ensemble of urban phenomena, but they are connected by their common link to the representation or performance of urban identities and culture.

Given the spectrum of phenomena examined, the notion of culture invoked is broad enough to embrace the two kinds of contributions mentioned: those taking the lived urban experience as their source and those focused on symbolic representations of experience through different forms of cultural expression. Understood in this context, culture encompasses the full range of human behavior and its products, whether embodied in thought, language, actions, or material artifacts. It includes what are conventionally known as the arts, but also embraces social, economic, political, and religious practices and therefore touches on matters of ideology (in the broad sense of this term). Culture, that is, corresponds to the range that Abril Trigo has claimed for the objects forming the field of inquiry for cultural studies: "what can be read as a cultural text, what carries a sociohistorical symbolic meaning and is intertwined with various discursive formations, could become a legitimate object of inquiry, from art to literature, to sports and media, to social lifestyles, beliefs and feelings" (2004, 4). For Trigo, as for this volume, the study of "the cultural," to use his term, presupposes no a priori exclusion on what may be studied or on the disciplinary perspective from which it may be approached.

Placing this volume within a broad understanding of culture has opened it to urban life in general, as well as the representation of urban life in symbolic form. At the same time, the recognition that the urban is a field engaged by many academic disciplines has prompted inviting a wide array of perspectives. As Anthony D. King has remarked, interest in the city is no longer so confined as it once was: "The discourse of the city, at one time simply a privileged territory in the social sciences on which generally white, western, and usually male urban sociologists, geographers, anthropologists, or city planners inscribed their theoretical models, or where urban and architectural historians told their different stories, has increasingly become the happy-hunting-ground of film theorists, poets, art historians, writers, television producers, literary critics, and postmodern cultural connoisseurs of all kinds in the humanities" (1996, 2). Monographic studies in English of urban Latin/o America tend to focus on single cities and a limited range of issues or cultural phenomena. They also fall squarely on one side or other of the social sciences/humanities divide.[1] In comparison with such texts, our volume clearly benefits from the scope afforded by anthologies where discussion of a greater number of cities by specialists from a variety of disciplines is facilitated by a common theme.[2]

That the source of the chapters in this volume includes both the humanities and social sciences is reflected to some extent in the organization of our content in three clusters. The first of these combines discussions of the imagined city, representations of the urban in popular music, film, literature, and art. The second is concerned with peripheries in the form of images of peripheral cities and the condition of urban communities located on the social margins. The third cluster highlights aspects of the notion of performance: the (re)enactment of rituals and practices that organize and symbolically represent social beliefs, values, and traditions. Rather than constituting three mutually exclusive groups of contributions, these clusters primarily serve to sequence the chapters. The imagined city, for example, does not figure solely in the first cluster, and the concepts of the peripheral and performance recur across the entire collection, giving a measure of overlap that permits the chapters to dialogue regardless of where they are situated in the volume or of the disciplines they engage. However, variations in the volume resulting from the inclusion of chapters from different disciplinary perspectives is not smoothed over. Indeed, to echo King's comments concerning a book with a similarly multifarious content: "This book sets out to *be* uneven" (1996, 5; original emphasis). Rather than focus on a single urban phenomenon manifested in a variety of cities, our collection highlights urban diversity in order to exemplify the many contexts from which identities are constructed. At the same time, we have expressly sought to confront the reader with a range of urban topics that will satisfy both the disciplinary curiosity of Latin Americanists working from particular perspectives and the interests of those for whom the study of Latin/o America is a multidisciplinary activity.

The relation of the collection as a whole to the concept of identity and to its manifestation through consideration of contemporary urban Latin/o America is explored by Abril Trigo in the volume's concluding chapter. Taking the intensity with which the dialectics of identity unfold in urban milieus as his point of departure, Trigo responds to his reading of the contributions through drawing them into a theorization of identity. He shows how they exemplify urban practices in the formation of identity and the exercise of citizenship, whether through co-optation by, or through resistance to, the prevailing social imaginary. Consumption and commodification also underlie Trigo's consideration of identity in relation to history and memory, as well as his consideration of the formation of identity through the experience of urban space, a formation he finds expressed in all the chapters in the volume.

Just as this collection prompts a reflection on the thematics of identity, it is also concerned, like Beatriz Sarlo's snapshots, with particular places. Her anecdote about a street corner in Buenos Aires is a striking illustration of the ties between individuals and familiar locations. The changes to the corner erase former meanings so that it no longer speaks to her in the same way as before. It has ceased to embody for her what Tim Cresswell describes as "the most straightforward and common definition of place—a meaningful location" (2004, 7). Expressed differently, the new face and function of the corner disturb Sarlo's "sense of place," a term that refers to the subjective or affective and psychological connections people have with places (Cresswell 2004, 7–8). Such connections, as the now classic studies by Gaston Bachelard (1964) and Yi-Fu Tuan (1974 and 1977) have recognized, are especially strong with the places of one's origin, childhood, and adolescence, but are felt in relation to all the places known and frequented during a lifetime, including those known only through the mediation of forms of representation, such as film or literature. Place and the experience of place are thus among the elements that enter into constructions of identity. People feel themselves to be, or are thought of by others as being, *porteño*, *limeño* or *santiaguino*, with all that such attributions of urban identity entail, including feelings of association that derive both from individual experience and from collective meanings about cities and their spaces shared by nations and communities. In this respect, a sense of place is not only a reaction to material space, but an "idea, concept and way of being-in-the-world" (Cresswell 2004, 20).

In light of the intimate nature of sense of place, broad categorizations of the kind described by José Luis Romero (2001) in his history of urban Latin America, such as "criollo cities," "patrician cities," or "bourgeois cities," fall short of providing the multiple contexts from which identities are constructed. A similar observation might be made of Ángel Rama's *The Lettered City* (1996), which is centered on the relationship between the power of written discourse and the foundation and growth of cities in Latin America. His book drew attention to the humanistic dimension of urban space and has been very influential, but not without controversy.[3] Since 1996, the consideration of Latin American cities as sites of production of popular culture, with the wealth of phenomena they embrace, has moved writing on the city beyond the range of Rama's study. His lettered city is an instructive metaphor but misses much of the organic side of city life and growth, caught more fully in Carlos Monsiváis's images of urban chaos (1995). Nor does Rama's study catch the concept of the city as subjective experience, a concept described by Armando Silva (1992) and Néstor García Canclini (1997). The cultural complexity of the city has found fuller expression, in this respect, in Latin America's urban chronicles, a genre to which Sarlo's *Instantáneas* and some of her earlier publications belong (see Sarlo 1994).[4]

The precise issues tackled in this volume are confronted from the disciplinary perspectives and interests of each author and are theoretically contextualized in relation to positions prompted by consideration of these issues, without necessarily engaging discourses concerned with the theorization and analysis of place. Nevertheless, the collective focus on the urban, and the attention given to questions of culture and identity, inevitably draw place and its meanings into the equation, establishing in the process a territory where the chapters intersect and complement one another.

Humanistic representations of urban life offer some of the fullest explorations of the affective and psychological connections to place. As Angela Prysthon relates in her chapter, the emergence of a vibrant film industry in northeastern Brazil has created the opportunity to display cities such as Recife and Salvador on screens dominated by Rio de Janeiro and São Paulo, and to break with hitherto stereotypical conceptions of northeastern urban life and culture, in favor of self-representation and greater authenticity. Whether in the context of picturesque cityscapes or poverty-striken barrios, the dramas of individual *nordestinos*, often against a soundtrack of the region's popular musical cultures, reveal a close relationship between place and a sense of local identity.

In some cases, the intimate relationships formed with the city, as represented in the films described by Prysthon, are a source of conflict. As such, they have elements in common with films from postdictatorship, neoliberal Argentina of the late 1990s in which individuals find themselves adrift in Buenos Aires, striving to reconnect with familiar places. These characters experience an extreme form of the disaffection expressed in Sarlo's *Instantáneas*, to which (not coincidentally) Geoffrey Kantaris alludes in his commentary on three films set in the same city.

If questions of identity and individuals' sense of urban places loom large in symbolic representations of city life, it is because of these places' corresponding significance in lived experience. Thus, how city dwellers identify with their environment also figures significantly in contributions directly concerned with the practices of urban life. Gisela Cánepa's commentary on Andean festivals highlights, above all, the agency the festivals give to Andean migrants who claim a place in the city that corresponds to their origins and their sense of identity. The fact that their assertion is challenged by a criollo counterclaim does not diminish its legitimacy but serves only to emphasize how much a sense of place may be shaped in a field of competing interests. The two contributions to this volume on U.S. cities make a similar case for other migrant communities. The sense of place prevailing in the population of Los Angeles, when considered in light of the city's restaurant industry, described by Juan Buriel and Rodolfo Torres, sees Latinas/os cast as Others whose labor confines them to the service sector and whose culture is an object of consumption. Similarly, as Catherine Benamou argues in her chapter on media, dominant constructions of Detroit either exclude the Latina/o population from the public sphere or grant it only limited, not to say stereotypical, recognition, notwithstanding its historical presence and identification with the city.

As the preceding comments imply, a sense of place not only entails subjective attachments to particular locations such as Sarlo's street corner, but encompasses a range of phenomena that includes ethnicity, social and economic class, gender, cultural practices, and the practices of everyday life. Among these factors, whether in the form of historical events from the city's past or of historical meanings attached to locations or built structures, history is singularly significant. A sense of place and identity have strong connections to the past through memory, and are often symbolically represented through buildings whose prominence, architectural design, and continuing presence as tacit witnesses of the passage of time make them visible markers of history (see Cresswell 2004, 85–93). Hence, the historic center of a former colonial city may become the symbol of an official urban identity at the same time that it holds other meanings for contemporary communities, as the politics of ownership of the center of Lima exemplify. Similarly, contesting claims inform the representation of Havana in the lyrics of Gerardo Alfonso's songs, as Robin Moore discusses. Whereas the naming of buildings in some songs is consistent with an officially sanctioned identity, this identity is undercut by references to the everyday in the same or other songs, creating a tension in Alfonso's oeuvre between the monumental city that represents the past and a sense of place rooted in the contemporary lived experiences of people in the parks, streets, and buildings of Havana. By contrast, the relative lack of importance attached to contemporary life is a problem in the work of the two chroniclers of Asunción analyzed by Amanda Holmes. Although both writers are advocates of modernization, they are also inclined to nostalgia and to identify with a city that looks primarily to its past.

A different example of the effects of memory may be had from the occasion in 1999, analyzed by Andrea Noble, when members of the EZLN (Ejército Zapatista de Liberación Nacional [Zapatista Army of National Liberation]) brought their campaign to Mexico City. Their presence relives a moment in 1914 when the city was occupied by Zapatista and Villista troops during the Mexican Revolution, so that the new occupation engages the past and its inscription on urban places, subjecting it to a rereading or reconstruction. Noble's account of the EZLN in the Mexican capital also affirms the idea that sense of place does not emanate from the place itself, but rather from the meanings that people derive from or ascribe to it in light of how they use it. As Cresswell remarks, "Place is the raw material for the creative production of identity rather than an a priori label of identity" (2004, 39). His conclusion is reached after a survey of the work of several authors who have advanced the notion that places are constructions resulting from their occupation and use: "Seamon [1980], Pred [1984], Thrift [1983], de Certeau [1988,] and others show us how place is constituted through reiterative social practices—place is made and remade on a daily basis" (2004, 39).

The principle of the construction of place through iterative social practice is well exemplified in this volume by Héctor Fernández L'Hoeste's study of the public transportation system inaugurated in Bogotá at the beginning of the millenium and subsequently imitated in other urban centers in Colombia. The system is intended to solve problems of transportation but has also had considerable impact on the construction of spaces by the city's population. Above all, it is seen to embody the intention of a central government set on imprinting its presence, and therefore its authority and view of social order, on the cities where the system operates.

On a much smaller scale, the two novels by the Argentinean César Aira, as studied by Richard Young, focus on a particular barrio in Buenos Aires. In both works, the barrio is constructed as it is revealed and given meaning by the movements and activities of individuals whose discovery of the places they encounter is shaped by relationships formed with them. The process is akin to how other cities are discovered, as described in other contributions: the Havana the songwriter finds not just in its buildings but in the lived experiences of its inhabitants; the festivals and public processions that shape the meaning of Lima for Andean migrants; the view of Los Angeles obtained from a consideration of the preparation and consumption of restaurant food; and the image of Latina/o Detroit that emerges from its relationship to the media.

Among all these representations, the embodiment of Mexico City in the art of Teresa Margolles, analyzed by Anny Brooksbank-Jones, is especially note-worthy as an example of the city as a construction. The degree of abstraction possible through artistic practices and performance art allows Margolles to in-terpret the relationship of the human body, the urban environment, and lived experience in a highly dramatic form. Her treatment of human remains not only engages the traditional ethos of death associated with Mexico City, but also captures the city as a bodily experience lived for some of its inhabitants in the cultures of marginality and violence.

The idea that the identities of places are constructed in relation to how they are inhabited and what people do in them is often expressed through the con-cept of performance.[5] For Nigel Thrift, "performance is, at this moment, one of the most pervasive metaphors in the human sciences . . . precisely because it provides a way of understanding meaning as not residing in something but as generated through processes" (Thrift 2008, 124–25). When viewed from the per-spective of this metaphor, places and their meaning are works in progress, in a continuous process of becoming determined by the behavior or performance of those who occupy or inhabit them. The performative character of public spec-tacles has been compellingly described by Daniel M. Goldstein (2004), whose study of festive celebrations and vigilante violence in Villa Pagador, a barrio on the outskirts of the Bolivian city of Cochabamba, examines the two kinds of activity as spectacles involving representations of identity, claims for recog-nition, and assertions of belonging to inhabited places. The spectacles studied by Goldstein belong squarely within the concept of performance enunciated by Thrift, and refer to actions that give meaning to those who perform them and to the places where they are performed. Referring to people doing what they are, performance therefore embraces not only participation in the programmed rit-uals of iterative festivals, but also collective community actions that often have a deceptive air of spontaneity, as well as the individual practices of public and private life pursued in accordance with social convention (see Cresswell 2004, 35–37).

In one way or another, performance of the city figures in all the chapters in this collection. The spectacular city is notably on display in Lima in the religious processions of Andean migrants, and is also visible in Latina/o Detroiters' celebrations of national holidays, the festive occasions serving in both instances as assertions of claims for belonging and recognition. The annual book fair in Havana, as discussed by Antoni Kapcia and Par Kumaraswami, is a different kind of occasion for performing the city, one that spectacularizes a nationally sanctioned official culture. There is also something of the spectacle in the repetition of urban history in the appearances of members of the EZLN in Mexico City, but discussions of transportation in Bogotá and the consumption of Mexican culture by Angelinos have more to do with performances of the city in the practices of everyday life, notwithstanding their deeper political implications. In contrast to such collective activities, the city is performed on a smaller scale in the examples of film, literature, music, and art explored in the volume, explored with a greater focus on the activities of particular individuals and their symbolic representation of urban life.

The religious processions in Lima are not that city's only source of spectacle. As Gisela Cánepa notes, the processions are staged within an historic center that is a designated World Heritage site and is therefore a spectacle on its own merits. Such assets have, as in such other places around the world as London, Prague, and Jerusalem, also turned Lima into a tourist city (see Judd and Fainstein 1999) and made tourism an important resource in the national economy. The spectacularization of the city through promotion of both its historic architecture and its celebration of traditional cultural practices has consequently made objects of consumption of the city and its citizens, drawing them into a global market and contributing to a complex situation in which local interests and identities complement and compete with the demands of a society experiencing the effects of globalization. In this respect, the contemporary condition of Lima has much in common with other urban centers of Latin/o America.

Although globalization and its impacts on urban environments are not subjects of central concern for this volume, the relation between the global and the local surfaces either directly or implicitly in all of the chapters. The interaction between these two dimensions of contemporary urban life are experienced worldwide in a variety of ways, and in ways not easily disentangled (see Massey 2005, 177–85), with significant effects on how people construct the spaces they live in and the sense of identity such places create. The loss experienced by Beatriz Sarlo through changes at a familiar street corner, like many of the reactions recounted in *Instantáneas,* is a response to the cultural homogenization that accompanies globalization. It is not unlike the sense of uniformity and loss of urban specificity resulting from construction of the identical systems of urban transportation in different Colombian cities, documented in Fernández L'Hoeste's chapter.

The difficulty experienced by Latina/o communities in North American cities to compete locally against dominant global trends is described in two chapters. In globalized, multicultural Los Angeles, Mexicans constitute a low-income labor pool for the restaurant industry and their culture is consumed as the exotic Other, while Latina/o Detroiters struggle for visibility in a globalized media. Three chapters—on northeastern cinema in Brazil, the art of Teresa Margolles, and the presence of members of the EZLN in Mexico City—highlight specific endeavors to assert the presence of the local and the marginalized on a global stage; by contrast, discussions on Asunción and Havana reveal a tendency to shun contemporary global networks, the former through nostalgia for the past and the latter in response to economic and cultural isolation. Among all the cities discussed, however, the opposition between the local and the global is at its most conflictive in representations of Buenos Aires, a consequence in part of the impact of neoliberal economics during the postdictatorship period and the persistence of memories of the violence of recent history.

If global economic trends, cultural homogeneity, or the invisibility of cultural minorities are of interest for these chapters, it is because of their specific effects on local communities. These effects constitute a notable series within the complex of factors that give particular places their perceived character both for those who inhabit them and for those who visit or study them. Yet, although these chapters seek to describe particular cities and identities configured in light of the cultural practices and social phenomena associated with them, the idea of any permanent sense of place is elusive. Cities and how they are experienced are fluid spaces, as Beatriz Sarlo became only too keenly aware. We have already referred to urban spaces as works in progress, a condition that the era of globalization has merely exaggerated (see Massey 1997). How places are perceived depends above all on the angle from which they are seen. Reflecting on the role of tropology in urbanism and on the rhetorical basis of knowledge, James S. Duncan remarks, "Pre-given reality is thus not so much a transparently viewed object of representation as it is the material from which something new is fashioned" (1996, 254). The apparent predominance of some of this "material" may sometimes cause certain places to be viewed stereotypically, especially in the popular imagination. Yet even academic rhetoric of description entails a process of selection; whether in the form of artistic representation or in the form of a particular social practice, each contribution in this volume has taken a certain cultural phenomenon to serve as the lens through which to examine aspects of urban life. These phenomena are approached from the perspective of specific methodologies and are seen within the constraints of particular periods of time.

Thus the images presented here, and the identities constructed by citizens of themselves and their cities, are ephemeral, transient views. They may be thought of as snapshots that portray what for a given time and under given circumstances are some of the salient characteristics of urban life in Latin/o America. It is as such that they have their value and contribute to our overall understanding of the region and its cities.

IMAGINING URBAN IDENTITIES

Havana in the *Nueva Trova* Repertoire of Gerardo Alfonso

ROBIN MOORE

Havana represents a fascinating focus of study for considering notions of identity, uses of place, and processes of cultural formation. The city has always been a nexus of influences, developing along trade routes crossing the Atlantic, and serving as a site for the fusion of cultural influences from Europe, the Middle East, sub-Saharan Africa, the United States, and elsewhere. Havana's residents represent themselves musically in many ways that reflect this rich heritage. Some of the city's genres—for instance, its Afro-Cuban religious repertoire or political theater—have generated controversy for decades, even centuries. Yet one might argue that, with the onset of the revolution of 1959, the Cuban capital became a discursive battleground of representation to an even greater extent, with exiles and revolutionaries alike actively attempting through music and other cultural forms (as well as academic projects, news reports, etc.) to support or contest particular ideologies. Within this tense context, musicians tread on sensitive ground as they choose how to frame the complexities of their personal experience.

Cuba's geographic and political isolation, compounded by the difficulty of travel for most of the population, means that domestically produced music often circulates nationally more than internationally. For this reason, popular songs foreground local images markedly, perhaps to an even greater extent than those created in other places. And such references create palpable affective responses in listeners. Martin Stokes has noted that music has a special ability to evoke collective memories and experiences of place "with an intensity, power and simplicity unmatched by any other social activity" (1994, 3). He suggests that the places constructed through music may be influenced by numerous external forces (e.g., musical styles from abroad), that they frequently create or reinforce social boundaries of various kinds (generational, gendered, racial), and that they may emphasize difference, alternative ways of conceiving self and other. This final issue is especially relevant, since many younger artists experiment broadly with alternative representations of self and citizenship in the context of urban life. Their lyrical themes and musical choices often contrast with or even implicitly challenge those of official state discourses.

Many of these trends are evident in the work of artist Gerardo Alfonso, who serves as the focus of this chapter. An Afro-Cuban guitarist, pianist, and singer-songwriter, Alfonso grew up on the outskirts of Havana during the heyday of *nueva trova*, socially conscious protest song. He uses music as a means of commenting on life in the city, constantly presenting musical and textual references unique to that location. Lyrically, Alfonso's songs deal with themes such as vagrancy, prostitution, and the negative effects of the tourist trade, topics for the most part absent in the media. Musically, his clever reworkings and adaptations of traditional Afro-Cuban genres (the bolero, chachachá, *son*) create tensions between conceptions of localism and globalism, modernism and tradition. Central themes that characterize his compositions include a concern with race relations, a desire to broaden the notion of Cuban music through its fusion with foreign elements, and a tendency to use songs and musical styles from the past to comment on present-day realities.

HAVANA AS CULTURAL CONTEXT

The city of Havana, home to approximately one-third of Cuba's population of eleven million, has been the historical center of commercial music-making in that country and arguably in the Caribbean as a whole. Beginning as early as the late nineteenth century, with the international popularization of the habanera, Havana has influenced the world with its music. The vast majority of Cuban musicians and record labels have been based in this city, especially during the influential years of the 1940s and 1950s. Since the revolution of 1959 and the creation of centralized cultural institutions overseen by the state, Havana's national importance has if anything increased. The government's primary record company, EGREM, is based in Havana, as are its radio and television studios, its most prestigious cultural institutions (museums, theaters, libraries, symphony, and ballet), and its most advanced institutions of higher learning. The Ministry of Culture and related institutions are located in the same city, as are many other government organizations that support and patronize the arts.

The first stages of Havana's development after becoming a colony centrally involved music and dance, as well as another diversion. In the sixteenth and seventeenth centuries, the city catered to the pleasures of sailors of the Spanish armadas, with such abandon that it became known as the "Babylon of the Americas" (Iznaga 1986, xxiii). Black women known as *negras mondongueras* opened numerous small restaurants where sailors ate, drank, smoked, played cards, sang and danced, and slept with prostitutes. This tradition continued to a significant extent in later centuries, largely because of the city's ongoing importance as a center for maritime commerce. The long role of Havana as a tourist haven, most infamous during the mid-twentieth century, has contributed to a culture described by some as "ruled by pleasure and transgression" even today (Rojas 1998, 138). Certainly much of the city's music and performance continue to foreground pleasure, sensuality, double-entendre, parody, and humor.

Although it was one of the earliest Caribbean colonies established, Cuba soon lost its significance for Spanish authorities, after gold was discovered in Mexico and the Andes. As late as 1750, Cuba had only about 150,000 inhabitants, concentrated primarily in the cities of Havana, Matanzas, and Santiago. This situation changed dramatically toward the end of the eighteenth century, however. As a result of a rapidly expanding sugar industry and the creation of new trade relations with the United States, the political and economic center of activity shifted from Santiago to Havana. Havana grew in size and wealth at this time, and entered its second phase: that of transformation into an affluent colonial metropolis that could afford to support a variety of cultural activity. Dozens of private dance societies formed in Havana by the mid-nineteenth century (Castillo Faílde 1964, 105–10), as well as dozens of periodicals devoted to music and dance (Lapique Becali 1979, 11). Popular orchestras flourished, performing creolized *danzas*, *contradanzas*, and other forms of music derived from Europe. Composers of light classical music such as Ignacio Cervantes and Manuel Saumell popularized works for piano. Virtuoso orchestral performers such as Claudio Brindis de Salas traveled widely to international acclaim. At the same time, slaves and the free population of color perpetuated sub-Saharan African musical traditions in mutual aid societies known as *cabildos de nación*, and in massive street processions on January 6, Día de los Reyes (Feast of the Epiphany). In general, the Afro-Cuban population dominated all forms of professional music, beginning in the mid-nineteenth century, gradually infusing their European-derived repertoire with new aesthetic sensibilities. In cultural terms, the population remained divided; it represented itself through European-influenced traditions in broadly sanctioned public events (concerts, dances), and more clandestinely through African-influenced music and dance performed in private homes and marginal neighborhoods.

The turn of the twentieth century marked the onset of a third phase of Havana's development, that of independence from Spain and increasingly close ties with the United States. Cuba's Wars of Independence (1868–1898) ended with U.S. intervention in the hostilities, the occupation of the country by North American soldiers for four years, and the establishment of U.S. military bases in Guantánamo and on the Isle of Pines. Close, though sometimes strained, relations between the two countries continued to develop. Havana became a major tourist destination for North Americans, beginning in the 1910s, and the numbers of tourists continued to expand continuously up through the mid-1950s. Revenues from sugar production, gambling casinos, and taxes on foreign businesses helped support an ever-expanding economy and an array of new musical forms in Havana, including symphonic music, zarzuela (nationalist light opera), the bolero, salon music, and dance repertoire (son, mambo, chachachá). Cuban music gained tremendous international popularity in the 1950s, circulating globally in recorded form. Like those of the nineteenth century, most Cuban performers of the mid-twentieth century tended to be black or mulatto, and to come from the working class. North America's economic and political presence had its corollary in the realm of popular culture, with the popularization of the fox trot, jazz bands, and early rock and roll.

The overthrow of Fulgencio Batista by revolutionary forces in 1959 initiated a major change in the social and cultural milieu in Havana. Beginning in the 1960s, the government implemented a centralized, planned economy modeled after that of the USSR, and prohibited capitalist enterprise. Class disparities largely disappeared in the wake of state-mandated salary adjustments; the leadership guaranteed citizens a job, health care, and adequate housing. Musical activity shifted from a largely market-driven enterprise to one supported and regulated by government institutions. Publicly circulated music in Havana tended to foreground political themes to a greater extent than before; in institutional contexts, students of music were encouraged to study classical repertoire, often to the exclusion of other styles, since the leadership perceived popular music of the 1940s and 1950s as associated with the prerevolutionary period and thus did not consider its support a priority. The same could be said of music from the United States and Britain: because of ongoing political antagonisms with these countries, the performance of rock and other styles viewed as distorting or displacing local music was discouraged for many years.[1]

Musical life in Havana changed substantially once again in the 1990s. The collapse of the Soviet Union in 1989 and thus an end to foreign subsidies led to an immediate economic crisis. Without this support, the island's economy suffered a drop of over 40 percent in GNP. Extended blackouts, transportation crises, and severe rationing of all goods ensued. Responding to the situation as best they could, leaders slashed military spending and began to solicit foreign investment and visits from tourists for the first time in decades. Since then, and against the will of much of the top leadership, the country has moved toward a mixed capitalist economy. All of this has provoked a fundamental crisis of values among artists, and has provoked reflection about the future of socialism itself.

A liberalization of the centrally controlled economy, beginning in the mid-1990s, and Cuba's gradual opening to the capitalist world have created new opportunities for present-day performers. The legalization of foreign currency in 1993, the ability to negotiate recording contracts directly with foreign entrepreneurs, and greater freedom to travel have all proved a blessing, in this regard. The government's earlier ambivalence toward popular music (especially foreign) has been replaced with relative tolerance. This, with decreasing national control over recording, means that artists can express themselves in more varied ways as they seek to represent themselves and their urban experiences through song.

GERARDO ALFONSO AND NUEVA TROVA

Nueva trova is one of the most well-known forms of musical expression associated with revolutionary Cuba. The term *trova* derives from *trovador* (troubadour), a name given to early twentieth-century Cuban guitar player-composers who created a primarily romantic repertoire. Nueva trova, by contrast, is a form of socially engaged music incorporating stylistic influences from Cuban traditional and popular genres, jazz, rock, and other sources. It first became popular in the late 1960s among younger artists, primarily university students in Havana. Nueva trova represents part of a pan–Latin American song movement known as *nueva canción* and also has links to song traditions in the United States and Europe. Its best known performers internationally are Pablo Milanés (born in 1943) and Silvio Rodríguez (born in 1946). Far from being wholeheartedly embraced by the establishment, nueva trova artists, through the early 1970s, maintained a tense relationship with government officials, who considered their long hair, "hippie" clothing, and interest in rock a manifestation of "capitalist decadence." By the late 1970s, however, most of these musicians received at least some official support.

Gerardo Alfonso, who was born in 1958 in Guanabacoa, a district of Havana, is part of a second generation of nueva trova artists; he began his artistic career in 1980.[2] His musical influences are diverse, including traditional Cuban music of various sorts, and international bands and artists from Britain (Led Zeppelin, Deep Purple, Elton John), Puerto Rico (José Feliciano), and Brazil (Roberto Carlos). Like many aspiring musicians, Alfonso found it difficult to become a professional, given the small number of vacancies for music students relative to the numbers of applicants. Eventually he pursued a degree in the physical sciences, but continued to write songs. In 1984, at a concert in Casa de las Américas, one of the main state-sponsored cultural centers in Havana, he drew the attention of Pablo Milanés. With the latter's help, the young performer arranged additional concerts with Xiomara Laugart and Alberto Tosca. At about the same time, he began collaborating with rockers Santiago Feliú, Frank Delgado, and Carlos Varela in the Casa del Joven Creador cultural center. Despite these successes, Alfonso had little stable income as a musician, and worked at many jobs—bricklayer, political educator (*profesor de fundamentos políticos*), and even coffin carrier—to make ends meet. For the first thirteen years of his professional life (1980–1993), he was unable to make a recording.

In 1986, Milanés invited Alfonso to tour with him through Spain; this and subsequent invitations to perform abroad led to Alfonso's heightened public profile and to the formation of his own band in 1989. Since that time, he has had an active international career. His music has been performed by fellow artists, including Marta Campos, the bands Moncada and Mayohuacán, and the jazz fusion group Mezcla. He has consistently performed for left-leaning political organizations abroad (French communist youth organizations, the "Solidaridad Cuba Sí" association in Berlin), in addition to strictly commercial venues, reflecting through his career the same delicate balance that Cuba itself has struck between capitalism and socialism. Likewise, Alfonso participates in events within Cuba such as charity fundraisers for public health projects, libraries, and disaster aid.

The composer notes that he went through a profound process of self-reflection in the early 1990s regarding the socialist ideals he had been taught. He initially came to the conclusion that the revolution had failed, that he didn't believe in it any more. At that time he wrote several songs that were very critical of the state; the reaction of authorities to these pieces marginalized him from public performance, for a time. Slowly, Alfonso began to adopt a more nuanced stance, one of acceptance of and integration into revolutionary society while still writing music with a critical edge. This process of reconciliation, and his decision in 1996 to write "Son sueños todavía" (They Are Dreams Still), an award-winning song dedicated to Che Guevara, again opened many professional doorways at home. Quite possibly Alfonso has become, if anything, too well known for this piece, along with a handful of others: they receive heavy airplay nationally to the exclusion of other excellent and potentially more controversial works.

ALFONSO'S REPERTOIRE

To a greater extent than one might imagine, imagery of Havana's streets, architecture, and inhabitants appears constantly in the song lyrics of contemporary Cuban musicians. One must keep in mind that not only is this city diverse and complex in many senses (history, race/ethnicity, religion, architecture, etc.), and thus merits attention, but it is also the only reality that most Cuban nationals have known. Only the most successful singer-songwriters travel at all, which limits the ways they can meaningfully allude to other places. The constant referencing of local images and sounds also derives in part from the strong promotion of national culture by the revolutionary government. Evoking *lo cubano* through references to people, places, terminology, and musical styles from Havana is a technique immediately comprehensible to the public and one that gatekeepers of the state-controlled media support enthusiastically.

Of course, there are many ways to represent urban experience through music. Most popular songs that have been promoted as national patrimony in recent decades are accompanied by exclusively Cuban-derived styles of music and refer only to lovely women in Havana, romantic sites such as the *malecón* breakwater, or particular neighborhoods. Examples include "Dulce habanera" (Sweet Woman from Havana) by Rafael Ortiz, "A la loma de Belén" (To Belén Hill) by Ignacio Piñeiro, "El rumbón de Luyanó" (The Big Party in Luyanó) by Arsenio Rodríguez. Popular song can reference "blackness" to varying degrees through the adoption of particular styles of music associated with the Afro-Cuban community, through incorporation of slang, or through reference to areas of Havana populated mostly by Afro-Cuban residents. Popular song can foreground other ethnic/racial associations, religious affiliations, or distinct regional identities (and the like), or avoid such references entirely. In general, the music most frequently heard in state media tends to be the most all-encompassing, referencing "Cubanness" or "Havananess" in broad terms. However, performers make individual choices about such discourses and decide how to represent themselves and their city through song, creating a gamut of constructs. The songs of younger nueva trova artists incorporate nationalist tropes frequently, while also challenging official representations; for this reason some receive less airplay.

Gerardo Alfonso's compositions exemplify these trends. The lyrics of one of his best known pieces, "Sábanas blancas" (White Sheets 1992), consist almost exclusively of images of Havana and references to its neighborhoods:

Habana, mi vieja Habana	Havana, my old Havana
señora de historias de conquistadores	lady with a history of conquistadors
y gente, con sus religiones	and of people, with their religions
hermosa dama	beautiful matron
Habana, si mis ojos te abandonaran	Havana, if my eyes ever abandon you
si la vida me desterrara	if life takes me away
a un rincón de la tierra	to a different corner of earth
yo te juro que voy a morirme	I swear to you that I will be dying
de amor y de ganas	of love and of desire
de andar tus calles	to walk your streets
tus barrios y tus lugares	your parks and places
Cuatro Caminos, Virgen de Regla	Cuatro Caminos, the Virgen of Regla
puerto de mar, lugares vecinos	the ocean port, neighboring spots
el largo muro del litoral	the long sea wall of the breakwater
el Capitolio y Prado	the Capitol and El Prado
con sus leones, sus visiones	with its stone lions and visions
sábanas blancas colgadas en los balcones	white sheets hung out on the balconies

The metaphor of sheets drying on a balcony brings to mind multiple associations: the home, domestic labor, day-to-day economic struggles, intimate family life, and so on. In this piece, Alfonso creates a relatively uncontroversial representation of some of what it means to be habanero. His focus on white sheets personalizes and makes more poignant the less personal references to monuments, streets, and other public spaces of the city. Musical accompaniment to "Sábanas blancas" consists of solo guitar performed in an international folk-rock style, arguably the music that has influenced nueva trova artists most heavily since the mid-1960s.

Although Alfonso's lyrics are closely tied to place, they also foreground social problems or raise concerns that appear only rarely (if at all) in state-controlled media. Official news downplays critical commentary; attention focuses instead on improvements in social services, concern for the welfare of children, international politics, and so forth. One might characterize Alfonso's lyrics as both Havana-centric and nationalistic, on the one hand, and oppositional or subversive of orthodox discourse, on the other.

The Cuban government does not allow all groups to express their views on the radio, on television, or in the press. Afro-Cubans, for instance, have no programs dedicated to their unique concerns. The same is true of other ethnic minorities, of the gay community, and of religious associations. This means that popular music serves an even more important role as a source of commentary about current events, and as an alternative perspective to official pronouncements. Popular music, it appears, functions now much as noncommercial folklore has at certain moments for the Afro-Cuban community—as a "social chronicle of the dispossessed" (Acosta 1991, 54).

Alfonso's early musical experiments along these lines included a rhythm called *guayasón*, a mixture of the *clave* genre—an early-twentieth-century song form in 6/8 time—with the duple-meter dance rhythms of *guajira* and son. The resultant hybrid, in 6/4, is said to have been very influential among trovadores in the mid-1980s.[3] In fact, the vast majority of his compositions involve experimentation with established musical styles. This is true on the level of individual songs, in which sometimes decidedly incongruous elements frequently combine, and also on the level of entire albums, whether recorded on CD or on cassette. Releases such as *El ilustrado caballero de París* (The Illustrious Gentleman from Paris) (Alfonso 2001) present a dizzying number of musical genres back-to-back in each collection. International influences from pop, rock, and Brazilian music combine with local folkloric instruments or rhythms and traditional dance repertoire.

"No me mires tan extraño" (Don't Look at Me So Funny), one song that exemplifies this CD, is written in an international pop style, foregrounding electric bass and synthesizer. Much of the music consists of a repeated vamp over a four-chord keyboard progression (Amin7/E, Emin/D, C6, and Amin7). The texture is initially sparse, but the entry of each new verse brings additional instruments, notably electric guitar, horns, and percussion. Over the second verse, Cuban dance music instruments (bongo, congas, maracas) are heard as the song discusses "latin lovers." The last instrument to enter is a Brazilian *afoxê*.

Like those of "Sábanas blancas," the lyrics of this piece consist almost exclusively of images of Havana, especially the tourist-oriented Vedado neighborhood. Yet the representation of the city is distinct: Alfonso foregrounds themes such as food shortages and economic need, public masturbation, prostitution, gay street scenes he depicts as overly licentious, and so on. The city in this song appears dysfunctional and ridden with vices, something to be risen above rather than identified with. The foreign (or at least hybrid) orientation of the music contrasts with local textual references, perhaps as a means of underscoring the negative effects of foreign sex tourism and foreign currency:

Tomé 23 después de la 10	I took 23rd street after it crossed 10th
por la misma acera del Cine Riviera	on the same side as the Riviera Cinema
le compré maní a la gente allí	I bought peanuts from the people there
cada uno gana algo como pueda	everyone earning money however they can
llegué donde el Parque del Quijote	I arrived at Quijote Park
habían sus sayas y sus escotes	filled with skirts and cleavage

un tipo debajo de un bombillo	a guy under a light bulb
moviendo su mano en el bolsillo	moving his hand in his pocket
y yo intentando hablarte de mi amor	and me, trying to talk to you of my love
que me escuches cuando hablo de amor	listen to me when I speak of love
no me mires tan extraño	don't look at me so funny
El Coppelia es la estación central	Coppelia Park is the grand central station
de los pepes *gay*, de los *latin lovers*	of the gay pretty boys, the latin lovers
no es secreto ya, ni en el caminar	it's no longer a secret, in the way they walk
ni en el modo de llevar los pantalones	nor in the way they wear their pants
esquina de *Fresa y Chocolate*	street corner of *Strawberry and Chocolate*
los chulos, lástimas elegantes	the pimps, a shameful elegance
esquina de todas las ofertas	the place for any kind of offer
lujuria y placer a pierna suelta	lechery and pleasure walking all over
y yo intentando hablarte de mi amor	and me, trying to talk to you of love
que me escuches cuando hablo de amor	listen to me when I speak of love
no me mires tan extraño	don't look at me so funny

The third verse continues with what might be considered even harsher social critique, noting "the drool of old European men" smeared on the breasts of Cuban women from the provinces who have come to sell themselves for money. Despite the bite of Alonso's critique, the song has a strikingly tender quality that mediates its message. The ostensible interest of the protagonist is not in the sordid behavior he details at all, but rather a desire to ignore it and pursue true love. Alfonso is a master at this sort of softening of message; he has the ability to frame harsh appraisals of urban society in relatively innocuous terms.

Other songs on this album relate to the musical and lyrical themes under consideration. In "Barrio Chino" (Chinatown), Alfonso focuses on the experiences of Havana's Chinese minority, brought to the island as indentured servants in the late nineteenth century. A pentatonic scale outlining a B minor chord (B-D-E-F#-A) is used as the principal theme in the introduction, serving to reference "Asianness" along with use of a gong, woodblock, and metal idiophones. Lyrics discuss the harsh treatment of, and racist attitudes toward, these "coolies" for many years, as well as the food and customs they brought to the Caribbean. "Polaroid Havana Rock" is a major production number, performed by a group reminiscent of a U.S. band such as Chicago, and including prominent electric guitar. Lyrically, it revels in Havana's rock counterculture of long-haired "freaks" (*bichos y pelos largos*), noting that rock was a persecuted music in Cuba, but asserting that, even should rock represent "ideological penetration by the enemy," no one cares anymore. "Balada de John" (Ballad of John) takes as a musical point of departure the Beatles tune "Eleanor Rigby," using its principal melody and others to narrate the story of a bronze statue of John Lennon that now stands in Havana. Lyrics describe the significance of the statue to residents of the area; the piece ends with a chorus singing "Ah, look at all the lonely people" in English to the accompaniment of a George Martinesque violin section mixed with conga drums!

In all of these compositions, Alfonso's interest in subcultures is evident. Through the use of particular sonic and lyrical elements, he depicts marginal perspectives or experiences and presents them in ways that problematize existing social relations. Without trying to determine whether Alfonso's representations are more or less accurate than others—though they clearly resonate with many listeners—one may underscore the nature of his compositional process, the elements he incorporates into his work to accomplish such goals, and the extent to which his views contradict orthodox notions of lo cubano.

Three other songs on the *Ilustrado Caballero de París* release deserve more extended commentary, given that they are especially effective at evoking meaningful images of the city and of playing with foreign and local symbolic elements in inventive ways. The first is "Lo que me atrapa aquí" (What Traps Me Here). Musically and lyrically it plays with the connotations of being trapped in and/or captivated by Havana. The musical genre Alfonso chooses as the basis for this composition is the chachachá, first popularized in the early 1950s. It thus represents "older" music, bringing to mind the prerevolutionary era and, by extension, a feeling of stasis, a lack of innovation or movement. The instrumentation of the song is that of a *charanga* band, a traditional dance orchestra of the early twentieth century featuring piano, multiple violins, acoustic bass, timbales, and cowbell. However, the author plays with this instrumental format, adding nonstandard touches of jazzy electric guitar under the chorus sections.

Lyrically, many images evoked by this song are also associated with a sense of timelessness, such as that of an old car from the 1950s that is still in use. Others, however, are simply typical of Havana neighborhoods: the smell of food coming out of an open window, old men playing dominos, a single bicycle with extra seats attached used to transport a family of four, a semiclandestine *paladar* or home restaurant:

Este carro es un Chevrolet de los años 50	This car is a Chevrolet from the 1950s
que al final se puede mover	that in the end still works
porque la gente inventa	because people are inventive
cuando te sientas un poco apretado	if you feel a little short of money
convierte tu casa en un restaurant	convert your house into a restaurant[4]
que aquí de una bicicleta	here one can make a bicycle
se hace una nave espacial	into a space ship[5]

Esos viejos del dominó	Those old guys
son campeones mundiales	are world champs at dominos
los romances del malecón	the romances on the breakwater
no he visto otros iguales	I've never seen anything like them
y esos sazones en cada ventana	and those smells from every window
la radio sonando a todo lo que da	the radio blaring at full volume
la vida es como una aldea	life here is a village
con leyes de una ciudad	with the laws of a city

Although the tone is playful, one wonders exactly what the author means by *atrapado*. Certainly his choice of wording is provocative, given that most Cubans cannot travel easily and that many wish to leave the island. Being trapped in Havana seems to have both positive and negative connotations, in this song. Does Alfonso feel trapped technologically, artistically, economically, or politically, or is he referring only to social bonds? As before, the appeal of his compositions derives in part from his ability to evoke pithy and somewhat critical images of daily life in innovative ways, yet to couch his commentary in humorous and/or ambivalent terms.

The second song, "Suave, suave" (roughly, Easy Does It), brings additional issues into focus, notably racial tensions and stereotyping, as well as how Afro-Cuban culture is perceived on and off the island. The song tells the story of a Swedish couple visiting Havana. The woman is obsessed with finding "real rumba" and spends her time walking into tenement buildings (*solares*) and poor neighborhoods, asking where to find drummers, while her husband heads off to buy rum and cigars. Eventually the woman finds a conga player; he refuses her offer of money for lessons and offers to simply spend the afternoon playing with her for fun—a surprising twist, given the economic need of most residents. Musically, the piece combines influences from traditional Cuban rumba and son with international pop, rock, and rap, nicely complementing the Europe-meets-Cuba theme of the text.

The introduction to "Suave, suave" begins with an acoustic bass solo, behind which sounds from a working-class neighborhood party slowly emerge. One hears the clinking of glass (rum bottles?), then a high *quinto* conga drum playing a solo. Suddenly a synthesizer and trumpets enter; this is followed by a solo bongo drum over a repeated melodic vamp. As the verse begins, a maraca and the bongo fall into standard rhythmic patterns associated with dance music. But the harmonies and the timbre of the synthesizer, more characteristic of Santana-esque pop or rock than of Cuban music, continue to contrast with these instruments and create stylistic tension.

Modern dance repertoire, *timba*, is also referenced aurally in the piece through the incorporation of high, virtuosic unison horn lines, salsa-style vamping on the keyboard against the chorus, and a *bomba* or "breakdown" section in which melody instruments drop out but the percussion continues to play. Timba music iconically links the composition to tourism, entertainment for foreigners, and more broadly an entire subculture of *jineterismo* or hustling in which habaneros offer services of various kinds (material, sexual) to visitors in return for money. The chorus vocal is performed in a rapped style, reminiscent of some timba yet resonating with the foreign stylistic elements. Other notable sounds in the piece include an electric guitar solo near the end, and a trumpet break between verses in which the performer quotes Ernesto Lecuona's 1912 melody "La comparsa." This melody is a complex, ambivalent musical sign in its own right: it was originally a stylized piano composition written by a white classically trained Cuban in imitation of Afro-Cuban carnival bands; this context brings to mind again one central theme of the composition, white fascination with black culture:

Una sueca vino al país	A Swedish woman came to our country
a aprender la rumba como se toca aquí	to learn rumba as it's played here
Su marido fue al malecón	Her husband went to the breakwater
a comprar tabacos y botellas de ron	to buy cigars and bottles of rum
En La Habana todo se intenta	In Havana you can try anything
lo que no se puede se inventa	what can't be done is managed somehow
todo el mundo quiere salir de su derrotero	everyone wants a break from their routine
Ella caminó toda la ciudad	She walked through the whole city
ella se metió en cualquier lugar	she wasn't afraid to go anywhere
ella preguntó en cada solar	she asked in every tenement building
y en un patio descubrió	and in one patio discovered
un negrón tocando tambor	a black man playing a drum
con los brazos fuertes	with his arms big and strong
como de un gladiador	like a gladiator's
En los hombros brillos de sol	On his shoulders the sun glistened
casi encandilaban	almost like fire
y la sueca que lo miraba	and the Swede stared at him
cuando no reía sudaba	she laughed, she started to sweat
Todo el mundo quiere salir de su derrotero	Everyone wants a break from their routine

A final example of Alfonso's reworkings of the sounds and images of Havana through song can be found in "El ilustrado caballero de París," the title track of the album examined here. The "caballero" himself, José M. López Lledín (1899–1985), was an educated but deranged immigrant turned vagrant from Spain who wandered the streets of Havana for many decades.[6] Virtually everyone who lived in the city, from the 1940s through the 1980s, remembers him. Alfonso makes López Lledín the centerpiece of the text, depicting him as a Christ-like mendicant, noble of spirit but wearing tattered clothing and eating out of trash cans. This caballero, like a good revolutionary, rejects the importance of money, but he is also delusional. His persona is thus semiotically loaded; he supports Castro and the revolutionary government, but his very existence and the extent of his mental instability raises questions about not only his judgment but, by extension, the revolutionary endeavor itself.

Musically, the composition is a bolero, the genre par excellence of romance and apolitical sentimentality. Its instrumentation is traditional, drawing a stark contrast between the relatively mainstream (though tasteful) plane of sound and the song's rather daring and experimental text. Two classical-style acoustic guitars are heard, one playing lead melodies and the other arpeggiated chords; they are complemented by bass, bongo, and maracas. The song's introduction is in an unmetered rubato; metered time enters at the first iteration of the phrase "Pero yo lo recuerdo muy bien" (But I remember him well). The decidedly sweet sound of the composition and the adoption of the bolero format create an ambience of nostalgia and tenderness into which the textual images are inserted. As in previous examples, Alfonso's approach to the material diffuses what would otherwise be a decidedly controversial topic. Rather than focusing directly on the homeless man's dire physical or mental condition, or what they may imply about revolutionary Cuba, Alfonso's sentimental rendering encourages us instead to think of the caballero as an endearing old man, a colorful, harmless oddity, a relatively neutral marker of the experiences common to all of Havana's residents, and one that evokes the melancholy of our own past at least as much as any sociopolitical message:

Pero yo lo recuerdo muy bien	But I remember him very well
comiendo sobras de un plato	eating leftover food on a plate
y escribiendo "que viva Fidel"	and writing "long live Fidel"
en recortes de las servilletas	on strips of napkin
y lo hacía con amor	and doing it with love
venerable luz en su cabeza	a venerable light around his head
Y así nació en esta capital	And so was born in this capital
esa leyenda de un viejo singular	the legend of a singular old man
tan gloriosa como casas coloniales	as glorious as colonial houses
y así vivió y murió en este país	and thus he lived and died in this country
el Ilustrado Caballero de París	the Illustrious Gentleman from Paris
sobre La Habana un ángel se cayó	over Havana an angel has fallen
un Cristo ya vencido	a defeated Christ

Pero yo lo recuerdo muy bien	But I remember him well
durmiendo en los portales	sleeping in doorways
y los niños riéndose de él	and the children laughing at him
y su melena tan larga y tan dura	and his hair, so long and tough
como la que tuve yo	like the hair I once had[7]
cuántos años, cuántos sueños rotos	how many years, how many broken dreams
cuánta historia, cuántos años locos	how much history, how many crazy years

MULTIPLE MEANINGS, MULTIPLE PURPOSES

Gerardo Alfonso's evocations of Havana through song, his re-creations of social space, present images very different from those in the official media. Reading the news in *Granma*—the newspaper of the Cuban Communist Party and the only nationally circulating daily—or listening to the nightly news on one of two or three state-operated television stations, one will hear little of vagrants, sex tourism, racial stereotyping, or any number of subjects found in the repertoire analyzed here. In the highly regulated environment of the Cuban media, popular song is one of the few means by which subjects outside the boundaries enter public discourse.

Well-crafted works of art are complex; rather than conveying a single message, they lend themselves to varied interpretations. The compositions of Gerardo Alfonso exemplify this trend perfectly. Alfonso chooses subject matter that is socially significant and politically charged, yet treats it in a manner that avoids dogmatism and suggests multiple readings. By the same token, the composer wants his music to be at least somewhat controversial; he has suggested that artists should push the boundaries of the acceptable and make people confront issues they may be avoiding or feel uncomfortable with: "It is important that the trovador, a type of artist who for good reason is called a protest singer or committed singer, tries to reach people's consciences, their opinions, and introduces debates into society in order to transform it, revolutionize it. It's not enough that we have accomplished a revolution, we need to continue with that revolution, it is a wheel that moves forward. And it is important to debate themes that are not discussed . . . what appears to be the most banal can be profoundly interesting" (Alfonso, cited in Rodríguez Sotomayor [n.d.]).

One of the most effective ways that Alfonso creates or shapes lyrical meaning is by contrasting it with sound. Music and its socially derived associations may be used to underscore or complement lyrical meaning, as in the case of the chachachá beat in "Lo que me atrapa aquí" or the timba dance rhythms in "Suave, suave." Alternately, the use of sound may problematize lyrical meanings, as in the incorporation of foreign, non-Cuban elements into a song discussing a traditional folkloric genre such as rumba. Music may be used intertextually, by quoting older local melodies (laden with their particular social meanings) within new compositions to draw parallels or make inferences. Finally, music may be used to change the tone of a lyrical message or to help evoke particular emotional states in the listener, as in the case of the bolero and "El ilustrado caballero de París." The close associations between music and particular stages of life, periods, places, and states of mind makes music an especially useful vehicle for the manipulation of emotion.

The meanings of cities such as Havana are invariably embedded in preexisting historical narratives. Artists such as Alfonso position themselves within such narratives and actively respond to them, reinterpreting and reframing the discourses of reality as presented by others. Alfonso's repertoire might be viewed as an attempt to assert symbolic control (Stokes 1994, 8) over urban space "from below," reconfiguring the constructs, sounds, and images that Havana's residents use to think about their city. His music is socially relevant precisely because of its nuanced incorporation of local meanings, its engagement with little-discussed aspects of day-to-day reality, and its attempts to reconfigure urban Cuban music making in a more inclusive way, using a broad palette of sounds to comment on the Cuban present.

Last Snapshots / Take 2
Personal and Collective Shipwrecks in Buenos Aires

GEOFFREY KANTARIS

n 1989, seven years after the collapse of the military dictatorship, a film with an evocative title was made in Argentina: *Últimas imágenes del naufragio* (Last Images of the Shipwreck), directed by Eliseo Subiela. Set in 1982 or 1983, but also reflecting the uncertainties and crises of Raúl Alfonsín's mandate, it is a stylized film that links the sense of social dissolution of the years of hyperinflation and political uncertainty to the collapsing narratives of a failed author cum insurance salesman who finds himself unable to make sense of the entangled threads of poverty, crime, and dissolution of family relationships in the midst of a dark city whose boundaries are as uncertain as the lives of its shipwrecked inhabitants. The shipwreck metaphor proved prophetic, although the idea that these would be the "last" images of this social wreck was premature—which is why the title of this chapter is "Last Snapshots / Take 2." Through this title, I want to suggest a temporal paradox of belatedness and repetition, a paradox that will send us fast-forwarding to the end of the millennium, to films made with a radically different aesthetic to Subiela's but that repeat the sense of a personal and collective shipwreck that Argentina was still experiencing even through its most recent social and economic crises.

I have argued elsewhere that *Últimas imágenes* and its more famous contemporary, *Sur* by Fernando Solanas (1988), were emblematic of the loss of the dreams of Argentine national modernity—put on hold since the fall of Perón's government in 1955 and condensed in the intensely nostalgic images of the "table of dreams" and the Proyecto Nacional Sur in Solanas's film (Kantaris 1996). More recently, Idelber Avelar's book *The Untimely Present* (1999) argued compellingly, via an interpretation of the work of Ricardo Piglia and others, that the dictatorship from 1976 to 1982 forcefully shifted Argentina from a social and economic paradigm of statism and national modernization to the neoliberal paradigm of postmodern, globalized market economics. Thus, in the spirit of Beatriz Sarlo's studies of end-of-millennium postmodernity in Argentina, *Escenas de la vida posmoderna* (1994) and *Instantáneas* (1996), the three urban films I shall focus on here might be collectively called snapshots ("instantáneas") of *post*modernity. These films are: *Buenos Aires vice versa* (Agresti 1996), *Pizza, birra, faso* (Caetano and Stagnaro 1997), and *Mundo grúa* (Trapero 1999). It is true that none of these films have what one might call a pro-postmodern aesthetic: their relationship to the loss of temporal depth, to the erasure of memory, to the failure of grand social narratives in the globalized megalopolis is more resistive than reflective. However, one obvious difference from the films of the 1980s is that these films are no longer steeped in the mode of nostalgia for the contained narratives of the modernizing nation. Although they do not *celebrate* the rise of mass-mediatization and the dissolution of temporal paradigms into spatial ones, they illustrate dramatically the social effects of such processes, of the interpenetration of place with global flows of power and money, of the personal and collective shipwrecks that these seismic flows and currents engender.

In many ways, the space of the city becomes the privileged canvas for the filmic exploration of these geological shifts in personal and collective identity at the end of the 1990s. The urban paradigm that emerges in a cluster of films from this period suggests a spatialization of identities, a loss of historical depth and of personal histories which nevertheless are rendered spatially, often through a series of paradoxical visual metaphors. Discussion of globalization and its social effects is inseparable from understanding the global city at the end of the second Christian millennium. In fact, the Marxist critic of postmodernism and globalization Fredric Jameson claims that the new modalities of time and space emerging in the global interlinking of economies "ha[ve] everything to do with the urban, . . . its postnaturality to technologies of communication as well as of production and . . . the decentered, well-nigh global, scale on which what used to be the city is deployed" (1994, 11). David Harvey puts this point in a more pessimistic vein when he talks, in a single breath, about the urbanization of capital and the urbanization of consciousness: "The urbanization of capital on a global scale charts a path toward a total but also violently unstable urbanization of civil society. The urbanization of consciousness intoxicates and befuddles us with fetishisms, rendering us powerless to understand let alone intervene coherently in that trajectory" (quoted in Gregory 1994, 362).

The films examined here question the befuddling fetishisms produced by the urbanization of consciousness, which have now become generalized within the globalization of the urban condition. These films do this through multiple techniques that resist the fetishization tendency inherent in film itself since film can never be considered an innocent bystander or observer in urbanization processes but is itself complicit with what French urban philosopher Henri Lefebvre called (1991, 33) the violent "representation of space," which is to say its reduction to a visual grid of fetishisms. Thus in its focus on representation, contemporary Argentine filmic culture is critically responding to the grid of representations generated by the structural transformations of global capitalism; in this, it parallels a vigorous intellectual debate within Argentina, which also focuses on representational practices in the context of an intensifying polarization of social inequality and cultural homogenization. The two noted volumes by Beatriz Sarlo can be taken as paradigmatic of this debate. Both offer impressionistic "scenes" or "snapshots," miming the loss of *durée* implied by technologically mediated cultural practices such as "zapping" (Sarlo 1994, 57–73), which nevertheless confront the dissolution of temporal depth, the fragmentation of space, and the simulation of imagined communities in the virtual spaces of the mass media with precisely what is discarded from the homogenizing field of vision (from, that is, both the "scene" and the "seen"). On the one hand, "postmodernity has no centre. It flows and carries everything along in its wake: past and future are comfortably intertwined, because the past has lost its density and the future has lost its certainty" (1996: 59); on the other, "capitalism is undergoing its third techno-scientific revolution in the context of societies which are fractured by poverty and disjointed by the sprouting of individualist ideologies. . . . In peripheral countries, the convulsions of the end of the century show, more than cultural and social diversity, the intolerable difference between the miserable and the rich" (1994, 180). In this context, the ways in which these films portray the dissolution of the urban social fabric—their focus on the cuts, gashes and absences in the (smoke)screen of globalization—seem designed to suggest that their urban micro-narratives lie at the intersection points of much wider, unrepresentable, or unmappable systems and processes. Although made before the major Argentine economic crisis that broke in 2001, these films nevertheless bring to the fore the social tensions and contradictions that had remained unresolved since the dictatorship and were intensifying during the Menem years of trade liberalization, deregulation of labor, and privatization.

BUENOS AIRES VICE VERSA (1996)

Buenos Aires vice versa is the most complex and challenging film to date by the prolific Argentine director Alejandro Agresti, both in the way that it yokes together the gaps or absences of post-dictatorship Argentine history with a sense of narrative disintegration in the globalizing metropolis, and in the way it self-consciously interrogates the relationship of the aesthetic to a disavowal of politics in the neoliberal Argentina of the 1990s. The diegesis concerns a series of interwoven and interconnecting stories, all circling in one way or another around absences and gaps, the unhealed wounds left by the military dictatorship, the hypocrisy of the fictive, televisual construction of a present that has forgotten time, memory, and history. The film begins with an on-screen dedication to the children of the disappeared, the adopted orphans of contemporary Buenos Aires who had to grow up not knowing the true identity of their parents, and the principal characters are two unrelated teenage orphans, Daniela and Damián, who do not meet until the end of the film but whose paths cross earlier, since Damián works as an employee in a motel where Daniela goes to have sex with her boyfriend. Other narrative threads in the film concern a couple of television engineers, one of whom starts a relationship with a TV addict (who believes herself to be in a televisual relationship with a TV chat-show presenter) when her television breaks down, and a pair of blind lovers who separate at the beginning of the film and spend the rest of it trying to find each other again in the immensity of Buenos Aires. The interweaving of these, and other, apparently unrelated, stories suggests societal fragmentation but also the potential for new forms of connection to emerge in the interstitial spaces of the megalopolis, such as the brief relationship between Daniela and the street orphan Bocha (before he is shot for petty thievery in a shopping mall). The interweaving of unrelated stories has since become a common one in Latin American urban film, with the Mexican *Amores perros* (2000) perhaps providing the best-known example of the potential for allying the very procedures of cinematic editing (découpage and montage) with the fragmenting and recombining processes at work within megapolitan society.

The metaphor of blindness in this film is an extremely powerful one, and the blind couple who separate near the beginning act as a foil for the blind (urban) spaces that the film seeks to illuminate. In a work intimately concerned with intervening in the ways that the city is represented, in questioning the dominant representation of the contemporary, globalized urban existence of Argentineans, blindness must in many ways represent what has been left out of that representation. This idea is consonant with Michel de Certeau's exploration of those everyday practices of urban life that slip into the interstices of the panoptic, visual regimes of the modern city: "The ordinary practitioners of the city live 'down below,' below the thresholds at which visibility begins. . . . These practitioners make use of spaces that cannot be seen; their knowledge of them is as blind as that of lovers in each other's arms. The paths that correspond in this intertwining, unrecognized poems in which each body is an element signed by many others, elude legibility. It is as though the practices organizing a bustling city were characterized by their blindness" (1988, 93).

The first sequence that establishes the function of this strand is especially telling, in particular a long take in which the blind couple are seated at the bar of a café with their backs to the camera, which is positioned in the street outside the café so that the take consists of an immobile long shot filmed through the glass doors, interrupted only by two hand-held shots of the couple from the side, their faces still mostly obscured. This mise en scène emphasizes a complex process of splitting: the sound is recorded inside the café (so that we hear the dialogue between the couple), but the camera is voyeuristically situated outside and so the viewer's gaze is frustrated since only the backs of the blind couple are seen: while they talk about the particular difficulties for blind people of making or reestablishing relationships in a big city, the spectator is also subjected to an experience of temporary metaphorical blindness. Further, a subtle screen effect is created by the procedure of filming through the glass doors of the café, since from time to time the reflected lights of passing traffic are clearly visible moving across the frame. Self-consciously drawing our attention to the insertion of this location within an urban "space of flows" (Castells 1996), the effect also highlights splitting and the duality of vision, the dual quality of veiling and displaying (or displaying through veiling) that is intrinsic to the concept of the screen in cinema. This effect functions through the tension created between not seeing (the theme of blindness, the frustration of the spectator's desire to see the faces of the interlocutors) and the insertion of these blind bodies within an audiovisual spectrum that overflows and exceeds any one person or place, which threatens to engulf and drown the haptic spaces that the couple talk about and inhabit differentially ("'Mondays were white, Tuesdays were green, and Wednesdays . . . what were Wednesdays?' 'Yellow'").[1]

If this problematic gap between the visual and the haptic is mapped onto urban space through the brilliant device of imagining the "blind spots" of the city, its points of disconnection and disaggregation, then the film extends this self-reflexive theme to the wider sphere of the constitutive relationship of image capitalism to urbanization and to globalization. It does this through its focus on the media and mediatization, introduced in comic fashion through the peculiar relationship of one character, Cristina, to the television persona of her former (or imaginary) husband. The narrative strands surrounding Cristina's relationship to the televisual provide a comic focus in a film that elsewhere deals with extremely harrowing issues, and in fact this ability to handle differing and apparently incompatible filmic registers within a single film is a unique feature of Agresti's filmmaking style, marking his work as perhaps the most experimental of the approaches examined here. The function of this televisual relationship is clearly parodic, pointing to the absurdity of the mass media's breeding of simulacra, and to the proliferation of these as the key mediating, or screening, device between the political and the social. During one episodic sequence, we see Cristina serving dinner to her television set, having placed it at the end of the table, with cutlery and crockery laid out for it. The camera cuts back and forth between the scene of spectatorship and the program, "América noticias," with its dramatic theme tune and video snippets of world events and personalities: Bill Clinton, warplanes taking off for Iraq, mad cows, Chirac, a group of hooded extremists. There follows a "dialogue" between the very laid-back news presenter (played by Lorenzo Quinteros and parodying a contemporary television journalist) and Cristina, who mockingly replies to his TV image throughout his absurd presentation, in which he uses exaggerated hand flourishes: "Let's begin at home. Astiz. Voluntary retirement, on account of his conduct in the dirty war. Slight rise on the markets. The upward curve continues. The index rose by 0.88 percent. Argentina, one of the best perform-ing economies this year, eh? Our country is in the top four. . . . What do you think about that?"

The almost telegraphic reference to the Argentine navy lieutenant Alfredo Astiz in this sequence, with the presenter clearly more interested in the financial indices, is highly significant. Astiz was the notorious navy torturer who surrendered to the British in the Malvinas war and who in 1987 served five months pending sentence for the murder of ten women, but was released under the amnesty for "due obedience." He was subsequently convicted and sentenced in absentia by a French court to life imprisonment for the murder of two French nuns, but in 2001 the Argentine judiciary decided not to extradite him. Astiz is described in this sequence as having voluntarily retired (due to questions raised about his conduct in the Dirty War); his resignation occurred in 1995 after massive public pressure following an attempt by the navy to promote him. This passing reference cleverly yokes together the events of the dictatorship, failed military nationalism, and the fictive nature of Argentine neoliberal market-oriented economics. If television and the mass media act as the screen of globalization, as cheerleaders for the ideology of the market (and Cristina ironically cheers "Argentina, Argentina" when the presenter mentions the stock-market performance), then this sequence, as a cameo for the processes at work in the entire film, exposes the gashes and cuts in the screen, albeit here with humor and heavy irony.

Buenos Aires vice versa is heavily concerned with televisual mediation and mediatization, and it is this more than anything else that marks it as a transition film between the classic, modernist, post-dictatorship concerns with failed national narratives, concealed truths, official and nonofficial histories (e.g., *La historia oficial, Sur, Camila, Hombre mirando al sudeste*), and the more recent postmodern preoccupation with urban micro-histories and the dissolution of national paradigms—the preoccupation that we see in all three of the films discussed here, and that we see even in later internationally successful productions such as *Nueve reinas* (Bielinsky 2001). Daniela herself gains employment making short home-video films of Buenos Aires for an elderly bourgeois couple who, since the disappearance of their granddaughter and their daughter's exile in Europe, have been too afraid to emerge from their apartment. They ask Daniela to bring them images of the city, offering to pay her two hundred dollars per cassette, an arrangement that provides a self-reflexive focus in the film on modes of urban representation. At first, the old couple do not like what she films for them: images of the homeless, the destitute, ordinary people in a time of growing crisis. They want beauty, they say, not the ugliness of poverty and squalor, and Daniela is forced to find or construct some "beauty" in the decaying social fabric of the city: "Tell me where the hell I can find any beauty in this bloody city?" she cries in frustration at one point. The (Baudelairean) theme of beauty and the city,[2] of how to represent the city, which is dwelt on at some length, is aimed at underlining the complicity of the aesthetic (and of televisual regimes in particular) with the erasure and fabrication of the real, and it necessarily implicates the filmic medium itself, since so much of the film is about Daniela's filming of Buenos Aires. She eventually finds beauty, at Bocha's suggestion, in shots of empty rooftops, still-life compositions of the Buenos Aires skyscape from which social interaction is entirely absented. These rooftop views, to use de Certeau's conceit, "transform the bewitching world by which one was 'possessed' into a text that lies before one's eyes. [They] allow one to read it, to be a solar Eye. . . . The fiction of knowledge is related to this lust to be a viewpoint and nothing more" (92). The elderly couple are, unsurprisingly, much more pleased with this sanitized, "artistic" representation, and unwittingly reveal the masquerading function of aesthetics in its relationship to politics, a function that this film is so concerned to critique, whether in traditional concepts of beauty, in the fiction of an empty and legible city, or in the simulacra generated by the mass media.

Despite this questioning of the masquerading function of the aesthetic, the interwovenness of the otherwise separate stories within the filmic/televisual screen we are watching nevertheless aims to establish the film's own aesthetic space as revelatory of hidden connections and disavowed dependencies, even as the film critiques this very idea in its self-reflexive questioning of televisually constructed identities and landscapes. These latencies come to a head toward the end, when Damián's supposed uncle is revealed to be an ex-torturer still obsessed with "leftists" and, further, the protagonist, while working as a security guard in a shopping mall, of the shooting of Bocha. In many ways, this is the crux of the film: the exposure of the effects, some fifteen years after the end of the dictatorship, of the continuation of this unspoken and unacknowledged violence into the present. This is Agresti's reading of the "personal shipwreck" and the "collective shipwreck" that is contemporary Argentina, of the latent violence and the refusal of the state to deal with it, of financial mismanagement, urban decay, unemployment, the reappearance of street children, the absurdity of the media's enthrallment to globalization, and above all of fear. This is summed up in a poetic soliloquy by one of the television engineers who has lost his job, providing a philosophical summary of Agresti's approach in this film: "As far as I know, a *mate* cannot induce amnesia. I wish I had amnesia to forget all this. Forget recent memories. Dissolve them like a bunch of flowers, throw it into the street, launch it one evening into the sunset. . . . Definitively, sometimes, the everyday shipwreck in which we are embroiled. . . . There is always someone worse off, damn it. Now I'm reminded of Baudelaire, the captives, the vanquished, people all alone on islands, shipwrecks. Personal shipwreck, and collective shipwreck."

Yet, for all its acute self-reflexivity and questioning of visual representational practices, *Buenos Aires vice versa* clings to a certain aestheticism in its desire for an ethical metanarrative. Its moving use of classical music to knit together disparate stories over two extensive sequences recalls the high modernism and portentous moral messages of a Subiela as much as it looks forward to the decentred and arrhythmic visual style of the new urban genres that subsequently emerged in Argentine cinema.

PIZZA, BIRRA, FASO (1997)

Pizza, birra, faso ("Pizza, Beer, Fags")[3] was made in Argentina in 1997 by a couple of young, virtually unknown directors, Bruno Stagnaro and Adrián Caetano, on the shoestring budget (for a feature film) of US$400,000 (Ravaschino 2002), and has been credited by the influential film review *El amante cine* with having substantially changed the course of contemporary Argentine cinema (Noriega 2001). Its frantic, in-your-face filming style, made possible by lightweight highly mobile cameras, did indeed come as something of a revolution in Argentine cinema, inaugurating a new mode of seeing the city that is signalled heavily in the opening sequences: instead of the immobile establishing shots of traditional filmic discourse (such as those parodied in the documentary prologue to Buñuel's *Los olvidados* [1950], for instance), we are presented with a frenetically speeding camera, a rush of movement in a fragmented cityscape where the durée of place has been replaced by velocity, smeared into a blur along lines of transportation and displacement. The credit sequence sets the scene for the violent mugging of a businessman in a Buenos Aires taxi by two adolescent boys (the subjects of the film) working in league with a corrupt taxi driver. The camera is hypermobile to the point of disorientation, showing snippets of city bustle, either filmed from some fast-moving mode of transport or jerkily hand-held, twisting this way and that as if time itself had gone into overdrive, while the audio track is overlain with police radio transmissions and by radio news reports about city violence, unemployment, and crime.

The audio and visual representation of transport and (electronic) communications systems, key components of time-space compression, creates an overwhelming effect: not only is the camera almost always travelling in the opening sequences, but at least six different types of transport are signalled: cars, buses, taxis, coaches, trains, aeroplanes, all in rapid movement. That such transport signifies velocity and time-space compression is obvious, but that velocity and rate substitute for temporal depth in the global megalopolis is, I think, carefully signalled by a close-up of the taxi-driver's taximeter in the roof of his car at the beginning of the taxi-mugging sequence: the taximeter represents, after all, the most basic form of the reification of time as a commodity to be bought and sold. Fredric Jameson argues that time can indeed no longer be perceived as a depth formation, something that accrues slowly in great geological strata, in the era of postmodernity. Time is now "a function of speed, and evidently perceptible only in terms of its rate, or velocity as such: as though the old . . . opposition between measurement and life, clock time and lived time, had dropped out" (1994, 8). If time has become velocity, the rate of change of fashion designs on the storefront or Web page, or the rate of change of locales in the shopping mall, of the built environment itself, then time thereby "instantaneously" fizzles out, since velocity measures displacement *over* time.

Pizza, birra, faso, is a film about the rebellious, youthful, criminal underworld of Buenos Aires; it follows the violent lives of a group of teenage boys and a pregnant teenage girl who resort to crime to supply their basic necessities, the pizza, beer, and fags of the title. They live the lives of the teenage youths analyzed in Mario Margulis's fascinating study of Buenos Aires nightlife, *La cultura de la noche*, youths for whom: "in the refuge offered by the night, the city is resignified and power appears to recede. It is an illusion of independence which encourages a playing with time; uncolonized time in which they are released from control; time not used up in economic production, industry or banking. If all the spaces are colonized, there remains the shelter of time, time as a refuge" (1994, 12).

In one particular sequence, this attempt to lay claim to urban topography, indeed to the very iconicity of urban space, is potently symbolized when the lads break into the famous obelisk in the center of Buenos Aires at night. One of them had already expressed the libidinal character of this urban icon, its relationship to the nocturnal eroticization of urban space, and in particular to a masculine economy of competing claims on urban territory, so often played out as fear of violence and violation in the nocturnal cityscape:

> PABLO: You know, this girl once told me that the Obelisk got her hot.
> CÓRDOBA: What do you mean, got her hot?
> PABLO: I dunno, she said it was a kind of penis which . . . which captured all the hollows [*las zonas porongóticas*] circulating around the city nowadays.
> CÓRDOBA: She was a bit of a whore, that girl, eh?

The imagery provides an intriguing metaphor: a *porongo* is a hollow container (often made from a gourd), most commonly used as the container in which *mate* is brewed and drunk. Here the unusual adjective (*porongóticas*) seems to signify the hollow spaces with which the city has become infused, the circulating empty spaces, the interstices, which are attracted to the icon of the obelisk as to a phallic illusion of plenitude and fulfilment. This sense of urban flow reduced to a pure circulation of hollow signs, generating empty temporalities and spatialities, is a moving metaphor for urban impoverishment and the wider processes of deterritorialization at work in the globalized megalopolis, akin to the haptic blind spots of *Buenos Aires vice versa*.[4] Sure enough, the lads make a symbolic raid on the obelisk to take possession of its phallic status and iconic, imaginary plenitude. Ironically, the film crew had to break into the obelisk to film this sequence, because they were unable to obtain official permission, and the actress who plays Sandra (Pamela Jordán) was close to giving birth (Sandrós 1998). Sandra herself, heavily pregnant with Córdoba's child, is unable to climb over the barrier; Córdoba leaves her behind and is left to watch from on high as she is dragged off by the police. This gendering of space as well as of modes of circulation through the city becomes a core dilemma for the protagonist.

Indeed, Córdoba finds himself increasingly caught between his carefree criminal existence and the growing responsibilities demanded by Sandra, who comes to represent locatedness, home, and a more anchored mode of inhabiting space. But the tensions seem unresolvable; unable, despite trying, to hold down a regular job, Córdoba resorts to increasingly audacious robberies in order to be seen as providing for his future family. Increasingly desperate, the lads in the end mount a raid on a glitzy nightclub from which they are barred by their social status: their bodies must remain invisible, slinking in the dark and dangerous corners of the city; violence is the only way for them to transgress the spatial lines of power governing the right of access to public visibility. The raid, which fails disastrously, is aimed at getting enough money for Córdoba to take Sandra to Uruguay to start a new life. It is significant that the film projects the only mode of emplacement that the characters can imagine onto another form of *dis*placement, a journey across (national) frontiers.

Although not the first urban film of the post-dictatorship period in Argentina, *Pizza, birra, faso* is the first such film to return to the use of largely nonprofessional actors, to engage uncompromisingly with the idiolect of the street, and to avoid any kind of moralizing metacommentary, whether in voiceover as in *Sur* by Fernando Solanas (1988), or in portentous narrative development and cinematic self-reflexivity, as in *Buenos Aires vice versa*. My main conjecture, however, is that the film is linking the temporal dysphasia of these teenagers, their sense of no past and no tomorrow, of the cheapness and emptiness of life, to the new instantaneous temporality of the globalized megalopolis, and their spatial dysphasia to a wider set of systemic dislocations. What is sure is that the film's politics are no longer bound up with ethical rights and wrongs or with representations of truth and fiction. These are lives lived out in the interstices of some unimaginable spatiotemporal grid, smeared out along lines of velocity and transport. The representation of social politics can no longer be thought outside of this representation of space-as-displacement.

MUNDO GRÚA (1999)

The final film under discussion was directed by Pablo Trapero in 1999, and, although it takes a representational approach that, in its durée, would seem diametrically opposed to the arrhythmic velocity of *Pizza, birra, faso*, it shares many of the latter film's concerns.

Mundo grúa ("Crane World") follows the fortunes of a middle-aged construction worker nicknamed Rulo as he searches for work in Buenos Aires and subsequently in Comodoro Rivadavia, two thousand kilometers to the south. His full name is Luis Margani, which happens also to be the name of the nonprofessional actor who plays him. At the beginning of the film, Rulo starts a new job as a high-rise crane operator, and at the same time falls in love with Adriana, who owns a little shop near the construction site. Life seems to be looking up, literally, when, two months into Rulo's new job, his medical report arrives: he has been refused cover by the company's insurers due to being overweight, and he is unceremoniously sacked. Told of a job down south in Comodoro Rivadavia, he reluctantly undertakes the trip.

The entire film was shot in black and white, and no night illumination was used: instead 200ASA film stock was forced sometimes as high as 800ASA, giving the night shots a heavily grained quality. According to the director, "Being shot in black and white, the idea was to work with the lines and the textures of the machines and, in interior shots, with contrast."[5] The use of black-and-white photography is on the one hand a defetishizing device, since color in cinematic representation is so strongly associated with illusionism, depth, and the deep libidinal attraction of color's play on surface and depth. Yet black-and-white photography, in the era of color, is a stylized choice, associated with nostalgia in cinema and with the play of light, dark, and form in photography. In other words, the aesthetic choice is not an innocent one, but becomes a marker of the film's ideology.

In many places, the film has an almost documentary feel, and the director is clearly working with the visual language and themes of Italian neorealism: "One of my ideas was to create this doubt in the spectator: how much of all this is documentary? Is Rulo an actor or a worker? The film walks this particular tightrope." The film even teases us with a couple of Dickensian references: Rulo is suffering from the medical condition known as Pickwickian Syndrome (a condition, that is, first portrayed in the Dickens novel *Pickwick Papers*), and one of the characters is described as "David Copperfield." In situating itself in an ambiguous space between fiction and documentary, *Mundo grúa* seeks to render ambiguous the very urban materiality it strives to represent. The more we delve into the material world of bricks, cement, and machines (what a different episteme would term the "real" world of labor) the more that world seems to dissolve into a shadow play of light and dark, of white and black. The night scenes, with their intensities of light and dark, seem to illuminate a *world* (rather than a representation) that remains inaccessible to the televisual gaze.

Similarly, the more the camera lingers over the machines, their imposing size, and their power, the more poetic the machines become. The most poignant shots are, paradoxically, of machines that no longer work—for instance, the still-life shots of immobile cranes after Rulo's sacking.

The material world (the "mundo grúa") is not given; it is constructed. What does this mean in a post-Marxist episteme where we can no longer equate labor with the origin of social meaning, the basic doing that makes "culture" possible? Trapero himself gives one answer: "The cranes are like a thermometer measuring the state of the city. They are a symbol of progress. From this perspective, the film is somewhat paradoxical. The protagonist, who slowly loses everything that he has, works in an apparatus which represents the opposite of what happens to him." The cranes represent the globalized economy of high-rise office blocks, their height a measure of the overheating of an economy of fictions that dictates and controls the very material world on which they operate. From this perspective, the Marxian formula is reversed, and the material space of the city loses substance, is emptied out even as the film attempts to capture its weight and density: that which resists, like Rulo's own inertia-ridden body, which cannot keep pace with the velocities of this new world. As Rulo begins his downward curve, so the materiality of place dissolves. He is forced on the move, subject to the whims of an economic system that lays off workers at will in one place and hires them in another, transferring its power to shape the material world. It is no wonder that the spaces inhabited by Rulo are frequently juxtaposed with the high-tech video-game parlors inhabited by his son—no wonder, either, that the urban condition seems to have invaded every space within the film: even on Rulo's long trip south we are mostly given shots of asphalt and passing road lights, suggesting an infinite extension of the urban condition across huge geographical distances.

The film, in its allegorical juxtapositions, could be a case study for Fredric Jameson's dictum, in his book *The Geopolitical Aesthetic,* that: "all thinking today is also, whatever else it is, an attempt to think the world system as such. . . . On the global scale, allegory allows the most random, minute, or isolated landscapes to function as a figurative machinery in which questions about the system and its control over the local ceaselessly rise and fall" (Jameson 1992, 3–5). In this regard, it is worth noticing that when Rulo is first sacked, the foreman who gives him the news is himself disempowered; neither worker is in control of the economic forces structuring their lives. The foreman claims he is just following rules made elsewhere, as it is the insurance company that prevents Rulo from working: agency has been emptied of personal connotations and handed over to an anonymous, financial elsewhere, to depersonalized corporations and systems.

It is no surprise to learn that what is sacrificed in this bleak scenario is time, memory, and history. In his youth, Rulo, it emerges, used to be Paco Camora, a member of a famous rock band called the "Séptimo Regimiento," and his son is trying to start up his own rock band. In a poignant speech at the end, after his second sacking, Rulo declares that, although his head is full of stories from the past, he would rather forget them. Rulo, in one sense, is also Argentina, caught at the vague and violent periphery of a global system that erases history as easily as it dissolves the materiality of place: "This country has a *Paco Camorra* in its history. This country could have been better, it had its five minutes of fame and now has to live with this memory in the same way that Rulo lives with his bass and his wrinkled photos. The mothers of the Plaza de Mayo are the *Paco Camorra* of this county, if you like. It's all you have left in the present which helps you to intuit a different past" (Trapero, quoted in Acuña 1999).

"LAST" SNAPSHOTS?

To conclude, each of these films tells stories of personal disintegration that are also stories of collective disintegration. Yet each also attempts to recover what is violently erased within the televisual regimes of postmodernity and its dematerialization of urban space. One of the last sequences of *Buenos Aires vice versa* shows the blind couple from the beginning of the film sitting at opposite ends of a busy central café, each destitute, and unable to reestablish contact despite the small physical distance that separates them; this sequence suggests extreme pessimism concerning the survival of the haptic within the aggressive visuality of the megalopolis. Conversely, it is when the blatant hypocrisy of the news media is revealed in the absurd report of the circumstances surrounding the shooting of Bocha that Cristina realizes the fictive nature of her TV romance, and the film ends with a shot of her embracing the television engineer she has now fallen in love with. In *Pizza, birra, faso*, the camera delves into the "zonas porongóticas" and provides us with a genuinely new vision of the urban underbelly, a vision that, though structured by the urban forces of velocity and exchange, illuminates the invisible interstices of that system. The film's final shot is an extremely long take of the departing ferry carrying Sandra and the booty from the botched robbery to Uruguay: it is as if the mad velocity of these teenagers' lives has come to a full stop, stemming the space of flows even as the blood seeps from the lifeless body of Córdoba on the ferry quay. And, finally, in *Mundo grúa*, Rulo's lingering gazes, like the film's nostalgic shots over stopped machinery after each of his sackings, attempt to recover a temporal dimension at the very moment of its erasure. By definition, postmodernity will always produce new images to replace the old. Yet, like still lives, these frozen gazes, "instantáneas," paradoxically stem the televisual flow of globalization, like the last fleeting snapshots of a postindustrial desert.

Buenos Aires and the Literary Construction of Urban Space

RICHARD YOUNG

The Buenos Aires locations presented in the novels *El sueño* (The Dream; 1998) and *La villa* (Shantytown; 2001) by César Aira—streets, buildings, businesses, and public spaces—are identifiable both by native *porteños* and by literary tourists finding their way with street maps in hand. However, the geography of Aira's barrios and city streets cannot be understood solely in light of conventional maps. The familiar places of his fiction are constructed according to a complex geography that embodies the status of Buenos Aires as a social space and derives from a dynamic between his characters' knowledge of the physical city and the practices of their daily lives. Since Aira's project is literary, the city he builds is imaginary, but the process his characters engage in to create it provides a context for exploring how such cities are perceived and understood by those who frequent them in reality.

The idea of "constructing" urban space involves the creation of the built spaces of urban environments, on the one hand, and, on the other, the attribution of social meaning to city spaces and their contents. Like signifier and signified in semiotic systems, the built spaces and their meanings are inseparable, although the relationship is not simple. As Ángel Rama notes with respect to the first Spanish settlements in the Americas, an intention or meaning precedes the material foundation of cities: "Before becoming a material reality of houses, streets, and plazas, which could be constructed only gradually over decades or centuries, Latin American cities sprang forth in signs and plans, already complete, in the documents that laid their statutory foundations and in the charts and plans that established their ideal designs" (Rama 1996, 8–9). The imagined city, then, is not the exclusive preserve of literary or artistic creation, but is first expressed in the texts that project the eventual shape of the real place and, therefore, to some extent, underlie all subsequent textualizations regardless of their form. Literature and the arts, notwithstanding their importance as means for constructing and circulating urban imaginaries, are among many forms of textualization.

The imagined city is as broad and complex as its counterpart in reality. Consisting of the collective and individualized idea of the city carried in the mind and memory, it is drawn from a knowledge of the past and present of the city, personal experiences, and the meanings derived from these sources. Speaking of the construction of an image of Rome, Rob Shields writes, "This means fully locating it in the different emotional geographies of people as different as tourists and city dwellers, building up an image of the place through the events and activities it attracts and repels, mapping its function in language and its role as a pole in the gestalt field of Western historical culture" (Shields 1991, 6). The same may be said of other places, even if they lack the centrality of a city such as Rome. In the potential scope and immense diversity of the image that this process suggests, however, regardless of the size of the city in question, the sheer scale of things seems overwhelming. What strategies, then, do urban subjects deploy to negotiate a phenomenon as huge and varied as a modern metropolis?

Burton Pike could well have been anticipating that question when he remarked, in *The Image of the City in Modern Literature* (1981), "The city is . . . incomprehensive for its inhabitants; as a whole it is inaccessible to the imagination unless it can be reduced and simplified" (Pike 1996, 245). With respect to Buenos Aires, the collective reduction of the city to a comprehensible image is already evident in the expression of its history through a series of labels, each of which encapsulates a specific period of time: the colonial backwater elevated to viceregal capital in 1776; the *gran aldea*, or big village, of the 1800s transformed between 1880 and 1930, during Argentina's early industrialization, into "the Paris of the South" and the city of immigrants; the modern metropolis of 1930 to 1983 dominated by military governments, Peronism, and further industrialization; and, finally, the post-dictatorship city from 1983 to the present under globalization and neoliberal economics.

As James Scobie (1964) has long since recognized in the case of Buenos Aires and Argentina, the city and the nation are highly integrated constructions. Cities cover wide areas containing many geographies, not only the topography of natural landscapes but the varied urban habitats and districts that result from differences in economic status, ethnic and cultural diversity, and political allegiances. In many instances, especially with capital cities, the metropolis embodies the character of a national region or the nation itself and may be envisaged in the same way as Benedict Anderson's "imagined community" (1983). As Anderson has argued, once communities grow beyond a certain size they become, in a sense, unknowable. The idea of a national community does not derive from full knowledge of it, but from the simplification that results from the imposition of dominant cultures and ideologies that make the part stand for the whole.

The reduction that takes place when a community views a city or the nation as a whole has its counterpart, perhaps even some of its origin, in the kind of limitations imposed on the point of view of every urban inhabitant. The citizen's view of the city has at least two real restrictions. Most citizens do not know their city as a whole, only those areas with which their daily life brings them into contact. There are districts of which they may remain forever ignorant, or know of only through hearsay, because they have no need, desire, or opportunity to enter there. Or they may feel themselves excluded from such areas by social restrictions. At the same time, urban horizons are closed, limited by the rows of buildings along streets that most citizens frequent in a normal day, imposing a sort of blinkered vision. As Edward Relph remarks in *Place and Placelessness* (1976): "For the city-dweller the space of the city is only spread out and extensive on those rare occasions when he looks down on it from some vantage point. More commonly his experience of cities is that of his home, his place of work, and the space of the street in all its variety of views, sounds and smells" (Relph 1976, 17). And he adds a comment from Eric Dardel to endorse his point: "The town as geographical reality is the street—the street as the centre and realm of everyday life" (qtd. in Relph 1976, 17).

The implications of the view from an elevated vantage point were considered by Roland Barthes in an essay on the Eiffel Tower (1997), in which he describes how the viewer organizes the urban panorama seen from the platform at the top of the tower. More famously, perhaps, in "Walking in the City" Michel de Certeau dwells on meanings generated by walking through the streets of New York and the view of that city from the 110th floor of the former World Trade Center. As with Barthe's Paris, the view from above changes New York for the viewer: "It transforms the bewitching world by which one was 'possessed' into a text that lies before one's eyes" (de Certeau 1988, 92). By contrast, the city dwellers at ground level have no such broad perspective. They "follow the thicks and thins of an urban 'text' they write without being able to read it" (93), existing in a space to which they are partially blind because they cannot see it overall. However, there is more to seeing a city than the view from the ground and the one from above, making a critique of how Barthes and de Certeau read Paris and New York respectively, in some sense, necessary.

It is largely the view from the ground in Buenos Aires that has figured in representations of the city in Argentinean literature. There are many such representations, in texts by Manual Gálvez or Roberto Arlt, for example, showing the conflictive side of the relation between the urban subject and city streets, but Jorge Luis Borges's *Fervor de Buenos Aires* (1923) stands out as an essential paradigm. His poems convey the city through a series of details: a quiet street, a row of houses, an architectural feature, a garden, or a plaza at sunset, facets of the urban setting all readily discernible to a pedestrian. The details not only stand in for the city as a whole but serve as a point of departure from which to convey a sense of belonging and identification and to reflect on the place of the individual in the world at large, in a movement that takes us from the particular to the universal. The city is reduced, but the simple images that represent it have, in the end, enormously complex meanings.

A similar process is found in the products of popular culture. The connection between Buenos Aires and tango hardly needs explanation. Its origin and history in the growth of the densely populated, cosmopolitan city of the early twentieth century turned tango into a medium of expression of the ethos of the city itself. The number of songs with lyrics that dwell on the city are legion, but they all employ forms of reduction that allow them to embrace the city within their own small space. In "Mi Buenos Aires querido" ("My Beloved Buenos Aires"; 1934), a widely known anthem, Alfredo Le Pera's lyrics simplify the city in at least two ways. As in Borges's poems, the material city is a matter of a few details, mainly familiar images of neighborhood streets, as if to reinforce Eric Dardel's contention that they are "the centre and realm of everyday life" and to underline the idea that cities are seen mainly from street level. This view is coupled to an emotional attachment formed by a sense of nostalgia and longing for the streets of Buenos Aires expressed through reference to music, desire, and lost loves. Through identification with particular urban places and the activities they embrace, combined with a sense of fidelity and belonging, feelings are created for an ideal space where all wrongs can be righted. Not only is the physical city represented minimalistically, but all its diversity and contradictions are smoothed over into several simple images.

Although *Fervor de Buenos Aires* and "Mi Buenos Aires querido" belong to the 1920s and 1930s, respectively, the idea of the city they convey has not disappeared. Borges's poems are still read and the old tangos still figure in contemporary repertoires. Thus, when an author such as César Aira writes about the city today, he does so in the context of a cultural archive surrounding its representation. Aira was born in 1949 and has published many books, most of them novels. Some of his fiction shows the qualities of magic realism, although not in the style of García Márquez and his followers. The magic in his realism arises not from a mythologized view of reality but from a focus on hitherto unrevealed or unnoticed details of the everyday world, which occasionally take him into improbable plots. However, his novels are not detached from beliefs about the qualities of reality. The two novels of his discussed here refer to the material city and its streets quite precisely, but they also consider the urban world as a social construction and, at least in one case, highlight the material and economic differences between the marginalized poor and the middle class, even as they emphasize the ideologies that give social meaning to those differences. Aira also engages processes of reduction and simplification, but the scope of the novel as a genre allows him to explore his images of the city more extensively than poetry or song lyrics in order to show how they are formed and how the gulf is bridged between what the city is objectively and how it is subjectively imagined.

The central figure of *El sueño* is a newspaper vendor named Mario who works at a street corner kiosk with his father. His life is spatially contained within the few city blocks of the kiosk's domain and controlled by a regime set by the early morning opening and midday closing, the daily round of home deliveries, and the coming and going of regular customers. On one particular day, he is led to explore hitherto unknown territories within his otherwise familiar corner of the city when he searches for Lidia, last seen entering a shelter for single mothers that is located on the same corner as the kiosk. When his quest takes him into an underground labyrinth beneath La Misericordia, a convent located in the next block, he is led into encounters more gothic than everyday.

As this summary suggests, *El sueno* offers an interplay between the mundane and the unexpected, between surface meanings and hidden depths. The story belongs to the real city, however. It is located in the barrio of Flores, an area on the northern side of the 25 de Mayo Freeway at a point just before the road divides and continues north and west into the suburbs of greater Buenos Aires. Within this area, the events narrated unfold in a rectangular space bounded by the Calles Bonorino and Lautaro on two sides and by the Avenida Bilbao and the Avenida José Bonifacio on the other two. The names of the streets and avenues and their spatial relationships are real and figure on street maps of Buenos Aires. Such a map would not show the kiosk on the corner, or Divanlito, the bed-and-sofa shop further along the street, although La Misericorida, a religious institution, might be marked, as might also the Plaza de la Misericordia occupying the city block immediately south of it. These landmarks are part of the everyday landscape for the inhabitants of the barrio and are easily discovered by a transient visitor. Yet, although the location of the kiosk and the convent may be identified precisely on a street map, where they would appear as contiguous, the spaces they construct are worlds apart. The kiosk is small, open to the street and the elements. Like a temporary structure, it is set against the building housing the women's shelter, with which it is said to have a symbiotic relationship (Aira 1998, 44). By contrast, La Misericordia is large and imposing, closed to the street but with an architectural and structural autonomy related to an institutionalized social function that endows it with solidity and permanence.

Not only is this relationship lost on most conventional maps, but it takes a certain type of urban geography to recognize it. As postmodern geographers have emphasized, maps are neither objective nor comprehensive with respect to the reality they represent. They respond to ideology, politics, and economics and are drawn in light of their intended function (see Harvey 1990, 340–59). Although images of spaces created by urban societies, city maps are also rationalizations that show only what their makers decide to show, and refer principally to built environments to provide a key to the labyrinth of the material city. They reveal little of the lived environment, the social space that embodies the kind of contrast represented in the difference between the newspaper kiosk and La Misericordia.

The geography of Mario, his father Natalio, and others at the kiosk has some similarity to a city map. The characters' conversation, like the narrator's discourse, is punctuated by references to streets and buildings from which a conventional map might be constructed, and which affirm the spatial character of their vision of the world and their relationship to it. Nevertheless, the characters' knowledge of spaces is limited, defined by their social interaction with other city inhabitants. Mario's knowledge of the barrio is confined to its morning activities. His routine is spelled out clearly and, like the references to location, also anchors the narrative; it amounts to an iterative practice, the negotiation of a given set of actions within a determined period of time and a particular space. Mario's routine also interacts with those of others. His practice is social, such as the one sustaining the symbiotic relationship of the kiosk to the also-mentioned shelter for single mothers. The connection between kiosk and shelter is not solely a matter of spatial contiguity, the physical attachment of one to the other, but also of the intersecting routines observed by those who frequent each place. Beyond the shelter, Mario's practices engage an entire community through the distribution of newspapers to homes and the interaction with customers at the kiosk, whether they buy a newspaper or simply pass the time of day.

Through representation of the activity associated with the newspaper kiosk, Aira's novel affirms that knowledge of space is a function of its use and perception. The text of the practice underlying this knowledge is inscribed primarily in the memory, in the minds and gestures of the inhabitants of the city. The characters in *El sueño*, for instance, have a map of sorts, consisting of a notebook kept by Natalio with the names, addresses, and orders of customers on home delivery. It is not easily deciphered, as Natalio realizes when looking for a particular entry. Yet, paradoxically, the notebook is more lucid than a street map. Although the latter seeks to provide an unequivocal guide, it suppresses the ambiguity inherent in any social space. By contrast, Natalio's notebook is filled with uncertainty. It shows spatial relationships in the material city as an effect of how people belong to the spaces they occupy, and it introduces an historical dimension by also encompassing those who occupied these spaces in the past. The identity of spaces and the processes of their configuration are therefore mediated by memory, and owe as much to perceptions and experiences of the past as to the present.

Mario and Natalio map familiar urban spaces in accordance with their knowledge, and prepare the daily newspaper routes from memory. Their familiarity with urban space and its social dimension is notably incomplete, however, limited to the places they service. There are buildings they have never entered and potential customers of whom they know nothing. Mario, for example, has never been inside La Misericordia before. Its space, as Natalio reflects, is "a black hole on the surface of his business" (Aira 1998, 63), not only because Mario sells no newspapers there, but because he knows no more of the shelter than the rumors that circulate in the street, just as he knows little of the customers at the kiosk, even those with whom he has daily contact.

Although *El sueño* is grounded in a recognizable urban reality, the figures who inhabit it struggle with ambiguity and the elusiveness of the certainty of knowledge. Their condition is most clearly illustrated when events take a new turn in the second half of the novel. The pivotal moment comes one morning when Mario, about to enter La Misericordia for a second time in his search for Lida, decides to reconnoiter before attempting entry again, by viewing the terrain from the roof of a nearby apartment tower where his friend Horacio works as a porter. Once on the roof and looking out over the ground he knows so well from below, his perceptions are challenged, calling to mind de Certeau's transformation that turns "the bewitching world by which one was 'possessed' into a text that lies before one's eyes" (de Certeau 1988, 92). Mario's view from above, along with his reaction to it, removes some of the ambiguity of spatial and social relations on the ground, as if his everyday view of space had been replaced by the rationalization of a conventional street map:

> It was so different he had to translate mentally what he was seeing. He spent a significant part of his life there, at the end of the block, and he had difficulty recognizing it. . . . Yes, he found his bearings, but the strangeness persisted because all those apartment blocks he knew from memory from the outside stretched out at the back into patios, gardens, and vacant lots that no-one ever saw. It had never occurred to him that houses on different streets were actually joined at the back; perhaps because of his work, the home deliveries, the houses were all in a line, a line with many twists and turns, but a line none the less. (Aira 1998, 114–15)

Moreover, it is not only a sense of space that is challenged in Mario. His friend Horacio attempts to persuade him that the distance to the ground from the top of a tall building makes it possible to see what is happening below moments before it happens. Horacio's contention is based on an ingenious deduction derived from the notion that, when we look up at the stars, we are looking into the past because of the distance that light has traveled; therefore, when he looks down over a great distance, the opposite effect obtains and he is able to see into the future. It is an intriguing popular extrapolation of a partially understood scientific theory, but it also serves to reinforce the lesson that Mario has just learned with respect to space—there are no absolute perspectives. From above, he sees what the mapmakers see, the contiguity of objects in material space; from the ground, he sees and experiences these objects as social space. What he sees from the ground is also a text, but a vastly different one.

Through its representation of city streets as the focus of urban life, and by its account of how individuals accommodate to the material city through the subjective relationships they form with it, *El sueño* echoes Borges's verses and the lyrics of tango. At the same time, it anticipates *La villa*, the second of Aira's novels we are considering; in this novel, too, characters explore unknown areas of the city or struggle to see beyond the façade of urban reality. The story told in *La villa* is complicated, one where many hidden connections gradually come to light. Its structure may be taken to reflect the rhizomatic interconnectedness of elements of the urban environment, although many connections either remain invisible to individual characters in the story or are misinterpreted when noticed. It is only the reader, who sits like a watcher in a tower with an unimpeded prospect above the streets, who has an Olympian view and can piece things together to create a coherent text.

The protagonist of *La villa* is identified only as Maxi (a name that shows some affinity with Mario in *El sueño*). He is a middle-class high school dropout who spends his mornings working out at the gym and in the late afternoons helps the *cartoneros* or *cirujas* (scavengers) who frequent the barrio where he lives, the same barrio featured in *El sueño*. The cartoneros are among the city's marginalized poor, including recent immigrants and many who suffered economic displacement in the fallout from the neoliberal policies of the 1990s and now survive by retrieving what they can from the garbage put out for collection daily in middle-class neighborhoods. Putting the muscle he has developed at the gym to good use, Maxi helps the cartoneros carry their loads back to their *villa miseria* (shantytown) in an area adjacent to middle-class residential zones. Maxi is drawn to the villa, but initially knows only its periphery and the entries to its alleyways. Although he eventually enters one of the dwellings and spends a night there, he never comes to know the villa fully. His view of the city is therefore limited, and not just because there are areas he cannot enter or building façades behind which he cannot see. Maxi suffers from *ceguera nocturna*, or night blindness: he has poor vision at night or in artificial light. With the onset of darkness, after the exertion of helping the cartoneros, he hurriedly turns homeward to sleep. He only goes more deeply into the villa (at the end of the novel) on an occasion when, exhausted and caught in torrential rain, the cartoneros he has been helping take him to a place they have prepared for him.

Maxi's ceguera nocturna is a real affliction and also a metaphor for his relationship to his environment, his blindness with respect to several aspects of his surroundings. He is unaware of how much his conduct intersects with that of others and places him at the center of an intrigue. He does not "see" the people he helps as others of his social class might see them, but recognizes them only as individuals in need of assistance. He is blind to the middle-class prejudices that marginalize the poor and disadvantaged economically, socially, and ethnically. Finally, he does not share common preconceptions about the villa that make it a hotbed of drug trafficking and criminal violence. Arriving at the fringes of the villa at nightfall, Maxi is unable to see into it or make sense of it, but he does not surrender to ignorance by yielding to a tacit acceptance of the negative social values conventionally attributed to it. On the contrary, he confronts and questions those aspects of the configuration of urban space in the villa that puzzle him because of their difference from the rest of the city.

Maxi's attention is first drawn to the dazzling array of electric lights around the perimeter of the villa and along the alleyways separating the dwellings, but soon realizes that the number and design of the array differ for each alleyway, and serve to identify it in the same way as a street name or number would in the ordered city. He also understands that the extravagant display of lights, which at first seems surprising because of the poverty of the villa, is possible thanks to a free electricity supply obtained by illegally tapping into the grid. This realization draws his attention to other features of the villa and its relation to the city and society at large. The villa is a peripheral space, both within and beyond the spaces encompassed by the urban area; although within the greater Buenos Aires region, it is excluded from the city's formal economy, as exemplified by the cartoneros whose survival depends on scavenging in the city garbage, or by the absence of urban infrastructure that results in the *villeros* hooking into the electricity supply illegally. Above all, the use of shapes outlined in illuminated lights as a way to identify the streets, in contrast to the convention of street names or numbers, points to a different way of configuring urban space.

From Maxi's perspective, the organization of the streets in the villa "was outside rational geography" (Aira 2001, 35), where "rational" means conformity to established patterns, which the villa appears to ignore at every turn. It is not just that the villa appears circular and that its streets lie at unusual angles in relation to its perimeter. There are no cross-streets, so that the villa's layout dispenses with the standard checkerboard design characteristic of Buenos Aires— a design at the basis of urban development in Latin America since the earliest European foundations. Maxi's dilemma thus is that the organization of the villa escapes the conventional organization of most urban centers. He cannot imagine it because it does not conform to traditional configurations of urban space. Nor, however, can he reduce or simplify it, because his curiosity about this new urban order does not lead him to impose on it a model of understanding founded on middle-class ideology, a model that would cause him to judge the organic structure of the villa, given its lack of conformity to any kind of city ordinance, as something akin to urban chaos. Seen from such a perspective, the villa would become another version of what at the time of the transformation of Buenos Aires from *gran aldea* to metropolis was thought of as the "grotesque city," the ill-formed territory of immigrants, the working class, the poor, and the marginalized (see Bergero 2008, 46–48 and *passim*).

Maxi's freedom from ideological containment is also shown in his broader relationship to urban landscape. In the first instance, he recognizes the limitations of his horizons. Much like Mario's in *El sueño* before seeing his neighborhood from the roof of an apartment building, or that of de Certeau's walkers in the city who are unable to read the urban text of which they are part, Maxi's essential view of the city is of the street. He does not see behind the façades that line the sidewalks and can only imagine what lies there, rarely feeling any disappointment when he catches an occasional glimpse through an open door-way or surveys the view from the top of a tall building. The attitude of curiosity and enchantment he shows towards the formal city is, however, also extended to the villa. He understands that a villa miseria contains none of the hidden wealth that might lie behind the façade of a middle-class house, but the villeros' creative use of electricity leads him to suspect hidden talents: "no-one knew what creative abilities people who came from very different places might have, who mostly had no steady jobs and a lot of time on their hands" (Aira 2001, 35). Evidently the villa cannot be envisaged in the same terms as those applied to a middle-class urban landscape, but should be configured or imagined in ways corresponding to its own personality and structure.

Maxi is not the only character in the novel who contends with the unknown in urban space and attempts to give it meaning. In one case, the configuration of central Buenos Aires as a city of high-rises plays a part in the relationship between two teenage girls, Vanessa and Jessica (the former is Maxi's sister). The two girls live in buildings that are identical in every respect and stand opposite each other, producing a complex interplay of reflections for anyone looking out the window of one at the windows of the other. On one occasion, as Jessica looks down at the building opposite her, she sees her friend Vanessa framed in a win-dow. In another window, Jessica makes out a different person and realizes this is a reflection of someone in her own building on a floor below her. From what she sees, and from the actions of the two figures she can make out, she derives a full narrative to explain, albeit incorrectly, what they are doing. Coincidentally, in the mirror in his bedroom, angled so that he can see the building opposite, Maxi watches a reflection of the second figure seen by Jessica. In both these cases, the images reflected between the buildings have an impact on the actions of the characters who see them and on events in the story. Whether or not any of the characters read the images they see correctly is a different matter, but their attempts to do so offer interesting examples of interaction with the urban environment and of how individuals construct their understanding of reality. These attempts also affirm the capacity of the material city to mediate in the communication of messages and the progress of human lives.

A different example of the construction of urban space in *La villa* serves to emphasize the gulf between Maxi's unfettered imagination and the closed mind behind other, more conventional images of the villa miseria. Santiago Cabezas is a corrupt detective, currently under investigation by his superiors, but hoping to save his skin by breaking open a drug ring in the villa. His knowledge of the shantytown shows all the cultural and social prejudices of his class. Equating poverty with illegality, he sees the villa as the source of Buenos Aires's major crime and drug problems. He reduces and simplifies the city to make it understandable, but the code he uses is ideologically determined in a way that leads to error and confusion rather than understanding.

Having seen Maxi accompany the cartoneros through the streets, Cabezas assumes that his involvement with them can only have something to do with drug trafficking. His conclusion is the trigger to a complicated series of events, all based on misunderstandings by himself and others. On a day of torrential rain, when Cabezas is ready to enter the villa, seize the contraband goods, and arrest Maxi, the detective really has no idea where to go, although he has received a cryptic clue: "diecisiete patito" (seventeen duckling). The clue tells him nothing until he catches an aerial view of the villa broadcast on television from a news helicopter and he realizes the meaning. He grasps, in effect, what Maxi already understood: that the configuration of the lights at the entrance to the alleys is a means of identifying them, so that the *patito* in question is the sign for a street and the number the location of a dwelling. But, in the end, Cabezas's newfound knowledge does not serve him well. The villeros are tipped off that he is coming and they hide Maxi, who by this time is asleep in the villa, not by changing his location but by changing all the lights at the entrance to the alleys, moving each shape along six places, as if it were possible to spin the villa like a roulette wheel within its illuminated periphery. Thus Cabezas finds nothing where he expects to find Maxi and a cache of drugs. Instead, he runs headlong to his doom in an ambush set by his superiors, who are hunting him in the belief that he is a renegade police officer.

When confronted with the aerial view of the villa, Cabezas reads it in the only way his imagination will allow and therefore thinks of the lines on the Plains of Nazca, whose secret is revealed by seeing them from above. Yet, although he sees the urban text as he might see a city map, he cannot fully read it. His mistake is his ignorance of the villa as a dynamic structure whose design escapes the fixed, ordered control in which he and his class imagine the world. As a phenomenon outside rational geography, the villa, as Maxi realizes, cannot be understood according to preconceived notions. It would escape even the designs proposed by Rama, Barthes, or de Certeau, and is an organic structure, capable of mutation, not at all as the inhabitants of the ordered city imagine urban space to be. In this respect, Aira's novel is not only a vindication of the villa and the villeros but an exploration of the construction of urban space that takes into account both the material organization of the villa and the formal city and their place in urban imaginaries.

The experiences of the city and the forms of identification with Buenos

Aires narrated in *La villa* reveal a cultural heterogeneity not unlike that revealed in *El sueño*. The strategies deployed by characters in the two novels to negotiate the urban environment include reference to a combination of both formal and informal maps—that is, reference to constructions of urban spaces derived from varying social imaginaries as well as of those derived from subjective experience. Whether in combination or separately, however, neither construction is entirely satisfactory. The city harbors a constant capacity to suprise, whether in the newspaper vendor Mario's new perspective on the streets when he sees them from above, Maxi's discovery that not all districts or barrios are similarly laid out, or the detective Santiago Cabezas's new vision of the villa, even though he fails to understand it. Such discoveries offer some illumination yet give only a partial insight to the urban world, which otherwise remains highly unknowable. It is not only that horizons are limited to certain familiar streets and are circumscribed by the impenetrable façades of buildings, but that in the material environment known to city dwellers a person also encounters the limits of his or her cognition. In this respect, the city in Aira's novels is not just a space of potential confusion, but a paradigm for the unknowability of configurations of the city in the modern world.

Body Art and the Remaking of Mexico City

ANNY BROOKSBANK-JONES

Dedicated with love and thanks to Colin Greensmith
(October 11, 1942–May 2, 2008).

The place of the city, and visions of the city, in the construction and projection of identities has a long and periodically violent history in Mexico. This chapter uses key stages in that history to approach work by Teresa Margolles, an artist who has grounded her critique of Mexico's failed modernization in the heart of its capital. From her base in Mexico City's Central Morgue, she has expressed this critique in terms that recast the nation's conventionally mystical and heroic identification with death—at a time when its art has never been more bankable, nor its death traditions more resonant in the global imaginary.

Margolles's work radically reaffirms the age-old imbrication of visuality, death, and the city in Mexico. As Claudio Lomnitz recalls, the combined effects of the "violence, new modes of labour organization (including enslavement), resettlement, forced migrations, and devastating contagion" set in train by the Conquest led to the decimation of the native population; and this Great Dying would have "radical implications for politics, economics, and the metaphysical history of humanity" (Lomnitz 2005, 68–70). These intersected with the rise of the city during the post-Conquest period. Since the Conquest, Angel Rama observes, "Latin American cities have ever been the creations of the human mind . . . organized to meet increasingly stringent requirements of colonization, administration, commerce, defense and religion" (1996, 1). Something of this tendency predates colonization, however. Two hundred years before

Hernán Cortés's arrival, there was no trace of any "hierarchical design of urban space" (Rama 1996, 3) in which the Aztec social order would later be inscribed: Tenochtitlán was "a miserable collection of mud huts" (Clendinnen 2002, 62). From these arose the vision that, in 1519, would meet his men's astonished gaze; sophisticated canal networks, floating islands, and ceremonial architecture designed to manifest and sustain the power of a warrior empire, to be a theater for the ritual propitiation of its gods, and to strike awe into surrounding townships (Díaz del Castillo 1963). Two years later, the empire's warriors would be dead, and colonial Mexico City would begin to rise from its ruins, a new city for a new age built on the *disjecta membra* of an old one.

That was a founding moment in more than one sense. Cultures here have continued to proceed by displacement, Gonzalo Celorio suggests, rather than accumulation: Tenochtitlán was displaced by the colonial center, the viceroy's city by the independent one, the nineteenth-century capital by the postrevolutionary one. Mexico City is *una ciudad de papel* (city of paper), where those lost cities linger in the words of those who described, calibrated, liberated, or redefined them (Celorio 2005, 41). But it is not only paper that remains: pre-Columbian motifs incorporated by indigenous stonemasons in the capital's Catholic Cathedral endure today, even as the cathedral itself sinks back into the clay of Tenochtitlán's lake bed; in Mexico City and other Latin American capitals, "antagonistic urban and social structures have coexisted in a conflictive relation that continues today" (Hernández 2005, xiv). Carlos Monsiváis, one of Mexico City's most perceptive cultural critics, affirms a certain will to coexistence that keeps this conflict within manageable limits most of the time. He reads the capital as a site of new seductions and anxieties, linked to fresh understandings of its material and imaginative construction, its dynamic role in sociocultural and economic change, and its potential as a creative actor in national dramas (Monsiváis 1995). But he is equally sensitive to its repeated failure effectively to mediate and renovate the public sphere of which it has become a privileged stage.

Mexico's modern capital emerges from Monsiváis's account as a city built on the still vital bones of earlier cities, violently but creatively conflictual, magnetic, dynamic, and repeatedly falling short of its potential. For French cultural historian Serge Gruzinski, these qualities are associated with the role of the visual in the construction of Mexico and its capital. Where Rama focuses on the "lettered city" constructed by educated elites, Gruzinski explores how colonial imaginaries in the Baroque period placed art and other visual forms at the center of strategies for conforming the city and the nation. He examines how these visual forms decontextualized and reused images to educate indigenous and other groups, deliberately blurring references and confusing ethnic and cultural registers (Gruzinski 2001, 226). Most importantly here, he traces the resurgence or persistence of these tactics in the postrevolutionary period. Between the 1920s and 1940s, he observes, and particularly during José Vasconcelos's term as education minister (1920–1924), muralists Diego Rivera, José Clemente Orozco, and David Siqueiros helped to channel the creative dynamism unleashed by Mexico's bloody revolution. Encouraged by a program of sponsorship and commissions, their projects would aid the embedding of a particular, state-sanctioned vision of the new Mexico among the largely illiterate masses. This vision was fueled by a cultural mythology that stressed national unity by idealizing certain previously marginal or abjected elements—aspects of indigenous and pre-Columbian (especially Aztec) culture, for example—and by sublimating a lengthy history of violence and exclusions. Gruzinski underlines the didactic aspect of these huge frescoes and their location in key public buildings; in this respect, he argues, (as well as in their "redemptive and militant" intent, their utopian tendencies, and their "repeated borrowings" of imagery from earlier sources), murals produced between the 1920s and the 1950s "were an echo of the walls of images expressly addressing the Indians during the sixteenth-century" and forerunners of commercial television images in the "neo-Baroque," or postmodern, period (Gruzinski 2001, 221).

Gruzinski presents a powerfully continuist account of the imbrication of city and image, identity and imposition, from the Baroque to the neo-Baroque. One influential study of Mexico City in the early 1990s serves as a useful, anthropologically informed counterbalance to his analysis. It explores how the capital's residents themselves draw creatively on images to construct the city in their imagination and make its vast, disorderly spaces more hospitable (García Canclini, Rosas Mantecón, and Castellano 1996).[1] These images are drawn from the most diverse, formal and informal, sources: from the output of architects and planners, advertisements and *telenovelas,* press stories, photographs, and films. Cinema images of the 1930s, for example, played their part in helping Mexico City residents recognize, and adjust to, the accelerating of the urbanization begun in the nineteenth century under Porfirio Díaz. And from the 1920s to the 1950s, the photographs and photo essays of Enrique Díaz, Nacho López, Héctor García and others played their part in the capital's imaginative construction through the pages of the illustrated press (Monroy Nasr 2003; Mraz 2003; Kismaric 2004). García Canclini and his coauthors conclude that the visual configuring and reconfiguring of the city in the neo-Baroque period is a diffuse and ubiquitous affair. For Gruzinski, however, the visual strategies of the Mexican multimedia corporation Televisa lie at the heart of these processes; they are geared toward the production of a consumer capitalist consensus, he argues, and count on the complicity of their audiences.

Anxieties concerning the seductive or coercive power of visuality have a long history, but they have reached a new intensity with the viral proliferation of images via televisual, Internet, and other global networks.[2] Critical intellectuals like Román de la Campa have noted the tendency of these networks to reconfigure space: to weaken the authority of the nation-state, incidentally easing certain large cities to global prominence, while "absorb[ing] spaces of contestation and resistance" (cited in Trigo 2002, xvii). In the first half of the twentieth century, visual forms such as murals, films, and photographs were crucial in the imaginary construction of the modern Mexico City. Today, by contrast, when the flaws in successive governments' modernization strategies seem glaringly evident, the rise of what might be called global visuality is widely seen as emptying contemporary urban experience of its materiality and specificity (Buck-Morss 2005; Sarlo 1996). The city vanishes, apparently, in the fiction of media images (Conley 2003). But Monsiváis (1995, 2004) repeatedly foregrounds the life pulsing behind these images. Mexico City, he insists, has always been more vital, dynamic, and heterogeneous than is recognized in those images, or in the official strategies and discourses used to impose order on it. His analysis registers a wider discrediting of such ordering strategies. Philosophical and theoretical critiques of the Cartesian subject have eroded faith in the notion of the centered, disembodied, and self-present individual and in narratives of progress. And in Mexico this erosion has conspired with globalizing processes to bring to crisis (after decades of decline) a postrevolutionary project predicated on the nation's social progress. It is thus not surprising to find that commuters interviewed by García Canclini and his colleagues in the mid-1990s saw little they could identify with in Nacho López's 1950s images of a Mexico City being constructed through the solidary labor of residents; totalizing visions of the city and its inhabitants have lost their cohesive power for many of today's *capitalinos* (Gallo 2004).

The work of Teresa Margolles (and other contemporary artists) is produced and circulated in circumstances shaped by the processes outlined here: the changing role of the visual in configuring Mexico's urban spaces and identities; the decline of twentieth-century visions of modernity, progress, and "the national project"; the perceived draining of materiality from the experience of the city within globalization. And cross-cutting them is the cultural resonance of death in Mexico as tradition, metaphor, and quotidian reality. From the bones of Aztec warriors and their human sacrifices, through Posada's *ca-*

laveras, the sugar skulls and Days of the Dead rituals, it seems that death has seeped obsessively into the heart of everyday life. "Connections between death and community" in today's Mexico are so complexly embedded that "they resist any attempt to locate the origin of the phenomenon either squarely in 'the state' or in a pristine and unpolluted 'popular culture'"(Lomnitz 2005, 26). It is chiefly for her controversial attempts to disembed and reconfigure these connections that Margolles's work figures in global art networks as characteristically Mexican.

It is only in the last ten to fifteen years that new art from Mexico has been able to access those networks. Decades of state-sponsored nationalism made Mexican artists less ready than some of their Latin American counterparts to engage with the early signs of globalization. By the 1990s, however, the emergence of new aesthetic contexts was helping to stimulate radical new art practices, educating and encouraging practitioners to remobilize the cultural and social tensions arising from their position "in the line of fire of expanding global capitalism" (Medina 2005b, 353).[3] But globalization has also helped to complicate these tensions. The processes by which it has dynamized and pluralized cultural circulation have tended to reinforce existing economic power asymmetries; we are all now more or less fluent in the language of globalism, whether or not we are able to take advantage of it. Globalization involves "an intricate, conflictive articulation of forces," complex cultural entanglements and "multiple contaminations, mixtures and contradictions" (Mosquera and Fisher 2004, 6). On the one hand, this enables information to circulate "through transcontinental links forged not only along migratory routes, but also ideological or special-interest identifications that traverse the old traditional affiliations of nationality, ethnicity, class, [and] gender" (4–5). On the other, by reinforcing persistent imbalances in economic and cultural capital, it has ensured that the circulation of art through global contemporary networks remains highly restricted.

Margolles is one of a select group that has been able to access those networks. This is no doubt partly because she foregrounds the unmetaphorized, socially unprocessed deaths of victims of street violence. But it is chiefly because of how she does so. In 1990, after studying art in Sinaloa and communication sciences at the National Autonomous University in Mexico City, she founded a music collective with a group of university friends. From 1993, it turned increasingly to performance art, making installations and interventions in public places under the name "SeMeFo"—acronym of Servicio Médico Forense, the state agency that deals with the capital's unclaimed bodies and from which Margolles had earlier obtained a diploma in forensic medicine. By 1997, however, the collective project had faltered and Margolles, by now an assistant in the capital's central morgue, was producing individual work. These video, photographic, and neoconceptual pieces were based on plaster casts, body parts, fluids, and other organic material derived from corpses.

Unsurprisingly, responses to this work have been polarized. Solo exhibitions in Mexico, Spain, Guatemala, the United States, France, Austria, Switzerland, and Germany have led some international critics to hail Margolles as "the most radical artist of the new Mexican vanguard" (Hartmann 2002, 1). But the "shocking directness" (Kilchmann 2005, 2) that dynamizes her work has led others to condemn it as "heavy-handed" and wilfully sensationalist (Lomnitz 2005, 25).[4] Closer to home, she has been charged with reinforcing stereotypical visions of the capital as postapocalyptic, thrilling chiefly for its failures and abject excesses. As Monsiváis notes in another context, Mexico City emerges from these visions in "the configuration of nightmare . . . : overcrowding, dreadful contrasts between wealth and poverty, unemployment, urban violence, transportation problems, pollution, shortage of water, housing and food production" (Monsiváis 2004, 271–72). For decades, Monsiváis has been a passionate spokesperson for the capital's multitudes; like Gruzinski, however, he is acutely aware of the extent to which their visual environment is conformed by economic and institutional forces. In Mexico City,

> architecture made for the gratitude of future contemporaries is not profitable, and what rules is the method that razes, builds hurriedly, pleases the tastes of the entrepreneurs . . . and scorns the consensus in matters of urban aesthetics. And as ambitions for durability come to nothing, the vainglorious official architecture cracks—that which in every country is the product of homage to the State as a sacred end, to crush the insignificant (the individual) with visions of the monumental (that can only be measured on the scale of King Kong or Godzilla). "Kneel, poor human being. Before your eyes the majesty of the institutions arises, made clear by the concrete and grand empty spaces in buildings adverse to economy." (271–72)

Undermining the capital's pretensions to grandeur, Monsiváis insists, is residents' lack of the necessary time, space and security to lose themselves in the contemplation of their surroundings. Even the monumental old heart of the city is now largely reduced to a focus for tourism's hurried and half-distracted gaze. And everywhere there is visual pollution, expressed in chaotic architectural styles, the folkloric reworking of North American kitsch, the brash insistence of shopping malls and advertising material (2004, 287).

What is not immediately evident here is the affection that underpins Monsiváis's projection of his home city.[5] For he typifies those Latin American writers who use the media "to launch attacks against their own cities in order to express how much they love them and how much they wish they would be different" (Silva 2004, 299). And it could be argued that similar impulses motivate Margolles's own hyperbolic account of the drama of the capital, while helping to explain the divergent responses to it. For she uses death and its organic residue to challenge not only the chaotic urban visuality described by Monsiváis but also the violence and crime that coexist with it, as well as the official complicity, neglect, and indifference that help to sustain them (Medina 2005b). Although crime and corruption are certainly not limited to Mexico, the nation's end of millennium was ushered in by what was widely experienced as an exceptional surge of violence. The year 1994 saw the Zapatista uprising, at first brutally suppressed on the orders of President Carlos Salinas de Gortari, and later the assassination of presidential candidate Donaldo Colosio. This was followed by the murders of indigenous Mexicans by paramilitary groups at Aguas Blancas in 1995 and, two years later, at Acteal. By 1997, when Margolles began working independently, the capital was reportedly gripped in the worst crime wave in living memory (Preston 1997). As Peter Ward and Elizabeth Durden note (2002), the situation was probably less critical and unprecedented than is sometimes suggested; the rising tide of public concern nevertheless underlined the foregrounding of violence-related risk in Mexican (and especially metropolitan) imaginaries.

Margolles initially focused her critique on drug-related crime. In Mexico City, as in most metropolises, the great majority of crime falls into this category. Yet when drug-users and dealers assault each other they do not habitually seek help from the capital's (relatively small and radically underpaid) police force, or press charges. As a consequence, one of the most common sources of street violence remains underrecorded, while producing a high proportion of the (mostly young, male) victims whose corpses Margolles prepared for autopsy in the morgue. The fact that she was able routinely to produce plaster casts of these corpses, to obtain and informally remobilize their body parts, and that mothers could be found who were desperate enough to exchange parts of a son's dead body for a coffin to bury him in highlights the legal and ethical ambivalence that enabled and energized her early work (Roca 2003).[6] In the process, the work reinforced its critique, underlining the *padecimiento de un cuerpo social*, the suffering of the social body whose morbidity she memorializes and challenges (Medina 2005a, 15).

In its most general form, this critique connects with recent studies of violence in and outside Latin America that underline the founding violence of the imposition of the state, of its consolidation of juridical and institutional power, and the interactions of this regulatory or "socializing" violence with other forms that serve actively to corrode civil society. Like Margolles's work, these studies foreground the links between violent subcultures energized by frustration, social exclusion, and conflict, and the corruption and complicity of those charged with enforcing laws and keeping peace. This (largely, but not exclusively, metropolitan) violence is interpreted as "one of the clearest and most worrying of the identity-related pathologies emerging from societies that are exclusive, hierarchical and authoritarian, and that deny 'first-class' citizenship to those who do not follow liberalism's traditional paths of 'order', consumption, and social progress" (Moraña 2002, 10).

It is from this perspective that Monsiváis notes how, in Mexico's capital, *los rituales del caos* (the rituals of chaos) may also be a liberating force (1995, 16). U.S.-based critic Rubén Gallo goes further, aligning this liberating movement with Julia Kristeva's insistence on the psychic and social productivity of eruptions of affect within a body politic that depends for its maintenance on repressing them (Gallo n.d.). There is undoubtedly something reductive in this generalization and naturalization of complex processes that could, and should, be otherwise. Yet the French psychoanalytic tradition is by no means alien to Margolles. She has been interested since her student days in Georges Bataille's writings on erotism and death, while explicitly distancing herself from the "florido, místico y heroico" (florid, mystical, and heroic) conception of death in Mexico that Octavio Paz helped to institutionalize in *El laberinto de la soledad* (1950).[7] But she is closer to Paz than she acknowledges. He contrasts the homeliness of death among Mexico's *clases populares* with its sequestration among less traditional social groups: "the modern world functions as though death didn't exist. . . . For residents of New York, Paris or London, death is the word that's never spoken, because it burns their lips" (Paz 1973, 51). Recent years have seen a striking reversal of this sequestration, as Western societies have struggled to assimilate death within secular paradigms.[8] Among Mexico's metropolitan elites, however, isolated in security-guarded and cosmetically enhanced mini-versions of Los Angeles or New York, the desire to ward off death (and aging, the premonition of its inevitability) has lost little of its intensity.

The implications of this, and of death's place in the architecture of a city constructed on the relics of its predecessor, are made disturbingly clear in the first piece I encountered by Margolles. It is a small gray block of concrete, left, as if by builders, on the gallery floor. Its first referent here, the "visual codes of minimalism," are at once radically recontextualized, for, encased in this block, the catalogue tells us, is the foetus of an indigenous child donated to the artist by a mother who could not afford to bury it (Beausse 2005, 108). By such harrowing tactics, Margolles works to re-suture death and life, to open a wound the better to heal the breach that a certain vision of modernity has opened up between them, to abolish death's distance and its metaphorization. And she does so, in part, by forcing *la gente bien*, the well-to-do patrons of contemporary art galleries, to confront what they seek to defer or conceal, bringing death back onto the scene as something other than folkloric caricature or the unassimilably alien (*La grasa de los muertos mexicanos* 2005, 1). The cauterizing effect of this tactic rests on her insistence not on a tame and orderly passing, "chosen, dignified, well orchestrated, surrounded by companions" but on "death, brutal, degrading and solitary" (Lomnitz 2005, 16). By reenacting that brutal and degrading end in this rarified environment, it seems, Margolles exploits the impoverished mother—and visitors' sensibilities—for socially therapeutic ends. The voyeuristic aspect of this strategy is inflamed by the fact that we see the foetus only in imagination. Like the exploitation embodied in that grim, gray block, it can arguably be vindicated only by the realization of her transformative intent.

But that intent has itself undergone transformation since the 1990s. Lomnitz has suggested that Margolles uses death as a brutal signifier or invocation of the Real (2005, 25). He is right, but the converse is also true, and surely more significant. It is her insistence on the Real in death, on the unsymbolized materiality of death as it is lived in the city's streets as well as its galleries, that matters here and that promises to redeem the exploitative dimension of her work. But it is also what has led her to seek out the most explicitly sensational channels in a bid to short-circuit viewers' cognitive defenses via "death's violent penetration by the senses" (Jauregui 2004, 157). *Dermis* (1996), for example, comprises ten sheets on which corpses have been laid; not (as with the Turin shroud) as witness to the material base of spirit but to underscore, through the persistence of organic traces post mortem, the continuity of the body's past in its present.[9] The source of these traces are "non-identifiable tramps" who died on the capital's streets, and the smell of the chemicals used to inhibit decomposition is reportedly overpowering (Nungesser 2003, 3). Once again, Margolles's challenge to a city that does not bury its poor, anonymous dead with dignity is galvanized by the form, and the site, in which she is able to frame it.

More recently, however, this challenge has expanded to include the ritual and broader symbolic possibilities of the post mortem cleansing of the body. In *Vaporización* (2000), for example, as if to conjure a nonrepresentational *mirar háptico* (haptic gaze), she uses a humidifier to circulate, in a gallery room, water previously used to wash corpses prior to autopsy (Paulo Herkenhoff, cited in

Roca n.d.). The corpse's physical traces insinuate themselves onto and into the skin and the lungs of visitors who, at first unaware of its source, experience only a slight damp shiver as they move through the mist. Only later do we discover that this water has been disinfected. In *Llorado* (Deceased/Wept; 2004), water from the same source is heard dripping down walls; in *En el aire* (2003), it is used to create a play of bubbles, their conventionally frivolous and barely material character transformed by an awareness of its grim organic base. It has also been used in the production of *Banco* (2004), a cement bench on which unwitting visitors sit to recover from the impact of more graphic work. In *Trepanaciones* (2003), the gallery walls echo with the sounds of (we later discover) the mortuarial sawing of skulls.

Margolles is obliquely making us *desire* to see, by foregrounding smell, touch, and hearing in a place conventionally reserved for heavily symbolized visual encounters. Unsurprisingly, perhaps, taste does not figure here. The tongue does, however, in one of two pieces that mark the limits of the challenge she throws out to the city and its symbolizations. It is the pierced and silver-studded tongue of a teenage heroin addict killed in a street fight in the capital.[10] His mother, we are told, could not afford to bury him and, at the artist's request, gave Margolles his tongue in exchange for a coffin.[11] Abstracted here in language, this plastinated tongue, on its slim support, might be said to conjure before the gallery's visitors an almost literal invocation to the dead to speak. It recalls the use, in popular religious practice, of votive representations of the ailing body part offered as thanks, or an anticipation of thanks—in this case perhaps for the recovery of a dead man's ability to articulate the violence and indignities he suffered. But the tongue does not "speak": it is not a representation. Margolles has worked to put representation in check in order to talk, not about a young man's life, but about the material life of his corpse, with all its sociocultural and political implications. The process of decomposition dynamizes the organ excised from a subject-who-never-really-was, deferring, if only temporarily, its fetishization in the gallery setting as a sensationalized consumer art object.

This perverse dynamism recurs in what may be Margolles's most challenging work. It lies somewhere between the earlier recontextualizing of organic material and her more recent emphasis on the ritual cleansing of objects. This emphasis on the washing, displaying, and presenting of the body is the starting point for a harrowing photograph of Margolles in the central morgue. Dressed in white coat and rubber gloves, she stares into the camera; in her arms, she supports the livid body of a child after autopsy. The image is a world away from the Mexican tradition of post mortem portraiture, exemplified by, for example,

Frida Kahlo's folklorically stylized (1937) painting of the deceased Dimas child, and is tellingly described as *Autorretrato* (Self-portrait; 1998). In this perverse Pietà, the body of a girl child is offered up by a woman whose gaze, a chilling combination of incitement and blame, has very little of the maternal about it. The child, it says, is not hers but ours; this dark place and this dead child embody all that is suppressed, with our collusion, in newspaper statistics, televisual politics, necrophiliac fantasy. If this image has any of the Pietà's redemptive power it arguably derives from Margolles's reading of Bataille. In his theorization of the "economy of excess," societies produce excess (rather than scarcity, as Marx contends), and they dispose of it in different ways. They might incinerate it, for example, or (as here) where it is human, they might sacrifice it, standing back as young men and women who seem to have no future die on the capital's streets. In this sense, Bataille contends, we should love the dead: "the scream of the one that is killed is the supreme affirmation of life," for death "constantly leaves the necessary room for the coming of the newborn, and we are wrong to curse *the one without whom we would not exist*" (Bataille 34).[12] It is this excessive love that aligns the image with a Pietà. But there is also a more unholy transfiguration at work here. It can be glimpsed in the accusation that dynamizes the ritual offering up of the dead child; in the contrast between the limp pathos of the body, its macabre grimace, and the almost decorative re-suturing of the skull; in the artist's brutally penetrating gaze; and in the universe that separates the grainy industrial monochrome of her mortuary clothing from the iconic blues and reds of the Virgin's robes. The result is a charged negativity. There is nothing triumphalist about it: the victim here is not a trophy, and nor is she returned to the public sphere only to be effaced from it once again. The artist's harrowing expression seems designed to galvanize spectators, to block their intellectual acquiescence and to check the slide into banality or spectacle so often associated with shocking images (Gallo n.d.). The love and horror fused there seem as resistant as any photograph can be to art or critical, or any other, symbolization.

The reference to the Pietà is nonetheless a reminder that Margolles's social critique is firmly embedded in her art historical training. In *Secreciones en el muro* (Secretions on the Wall; 2002), for example, she smears a gallery wall with seven kilos of fat extracted during the course of liposuction operations in the capital. Niklas Maak describes the result as *un espejo* (a mirror) in which the "first world rediscovers its ideals of beauty (Maak 2005, 1). But the scale, its organic dimension, and the visibility of the brush strokes all remind him of the abstract expressionism of Pollock, the "piss painting" of Warhol, or the experimentalism of Rothko. Once again, it is this tension between its beauty and *el asco*, or revulsion, aroused by the circumstances of its production that gives her work its disturbing power (2). This tension lies at the heart of what Cuauhtémoc Medina characterizes as an emerging *estética del modernizado*, an aesthetically mediated response to Mexico's failed engagements with modernity (2005a: 14). Margolles sets out to saturate an environment perceived as sterile or sterilized (the white gallery walls, but also smart city pavements frequented by the *burguesía*) with the organic residue of that failure. By insisting on the sources of this residue, and the circumstances of its production, she works to make the metropolis a necropolis for those who have suffered most by the decline and decathection of Mexico's postrevolutionary national project—by its failure to maximize social justice and to counter social and cultural fragmentation (Jauregui 2004). In this sense, too, her strategies arise directly from the experience of late modernity in a capital city conceived as metaphor, repository, and stage for the nation, and play their part in its imaginary reconfiguring.

Margolles's strategies also work to jolt viewers into a fuller bodily experience of the processes she foregrounds, a time when the urban sensorium seems so dominated by visuality that nonvisual dimensions of the body can appear almost inhuman. As the reference to trepanning underlines, older anatomical practices resonate in her work. At the same time, however, its located and embedded character chimes with contemporary efforts to foreground the body as matter at a time when visual culture is routinely represented as colluding with globalization to neutralize the materiality of lived experience (Hopenhayn; Buck-Morss).

By a familiar irony, it is precisely this located quality that has helped to make Margolles's work attractive to curators in global art networks, and above all to those who, as public funding for the arts continues to decline, are scouring the world for novel material with mass commercial appeal. I began by noting that her critique of Mexico's failed modernity comes when its art has never seemed more bankable, nor its death traditions more culturally resonant. And like many other cultural producers since colonial times, she has found that a certain profile outside of Mexico, confirmed in exhibitions across Europe and the Americas, is one of the surest routes to recognition within. In a tradition that goes back to post-Independence portraiture, she now finds her work co-opted for the official construction of new versions of Mexican identity (Ades 1989). I have addressed her work through its relationship with the city that has helped to conform it; yet as Mexican contemporary art centers promote and package selected artists for international consumption, Margolles is finding her radical aesthetic co-opted as representative of a new, globalizing tendency in Mexican art.[13]

FIGURE 1. Teresa Margolles, *Secreciones en el muro*, 2002. Installation. Exhibition view, "Mexiko-Stadt: Eine Ausstellung über den Tauschwert von Körpern und Werten," Kunst-Werke, Berlin, 2002 (Courtesy Teresa Margolles and Galerie Peter Kilchmann, Zurich)

However it is defined, globalization is widely assumed to reduce the national character of aesthetic production.[14] At the same time, local singularities that are often seen as potentially vulnerable or especially resistant to globalization have proved magnetically attractive to it. Influential Mexican critics have been scathing about the appropriation of art produced in Mexico by the curators of extranational contemporary art institutions. Circulating in exhibitions and museum networks, they contend, in international art fairs and their media coverage, Mexican art becomes an exotic supplement used to refresh otherwise lackluster programs (García Canclini 1999; Debroise 2005). Because its international framing tends to focus relentlessly on the problems confronting Mexicans, rather than on their achievements in challenging circumstances, this process has been likened to a cultural voyeurism or *pornomiseria* (Debroise 2005; Roca 2003).

The select group of Mexican artists who are benefiting from this new global profile tends, perhaps unsurprisingly, to be more pragmatic. Their increased mobility in global art networks eases a loosening of ties with the local contexts that shaped their work. Partly as a consequence, the capital, focus of so much radical work in the 1990s, is now less likely to engage their attention. Today,

Minerva Cuevas rather sweepingly argues, Mexican artists are more "interested in producing art for international shows . . . very clean stuff with contemporary codes," in which context appears either transparent or, by virtue of the work's self-referentiality, irrelevant (cited in Obrist 2001, np; Shaw 2002). This charge has been levelled, above all, at conceptual artists. When art that is encoded as conceptual goes global, argues Alberto López Cuenca, everything in it remains communicable across borders, for conceptual art is global art par excellence, circulating freely by virtue of its instant accessibility and political blandness; in Mexico, he contends, its producers have become the first generation of *maquiladora* artists, conforming to late-capitalist models of production and consumption by assembling interchangeable elements, to order, for transnational clients. The end result is volatile, dematerialized, readily transportable to the next Biennale and "intelligible wherever it is exhibited" (2005, 20–21).

There are clear parallels between Margolles's neoconceptual work and international developments in contemporary art.[15] Even when its theme is cleansing rituals associated with the body, however, she explicitly resists the clean and transparent intelligibility criticized by López Cuenca. Her dynamic, grainy, presentation of the life of the corpse bears little relation to tame death expressed in spare transnational abstractions. It is the organic residue of chaotic, sacrificial, megapolitan excess, the limit point of a theme consecrated in Mexican self-projections. Margolles values her privacy and is not a globe-trotter; if her work has nevertheless gained a certain profile in new, transnational contexts, it is because it retains this particularistic, embedded quality. And, not being abstract or transparent, it has accrued new (and invariably more hyperbolic) resonances there. From her base in Mexico City, however, Margolles continues to probe the underside of identity, challenging the conventionally radical alterity that has inhibited critical engagement with the dead body, working to keep the life of the corpse nonpathologically in play and to make strange again aspects of late megapolitan modernity that have become troublingly normalized. By reintegrating the morgue into the public sphere, her radical art practice is helping to reconfigure the capital. And by re-embodying the transnational processes and discourses—modernity, capitalism, globalization—in which its citizens are implicated, she shows that they need not figure there only as objects or victims.

URBAN IDENTITIES AND CULTURES OF THE PERIPHERY

Feasting on Latina/o Labor in Multicultural Los Angeles

RUDOLFO D. TORRES and JUAN R. BURIEL

> It is by eating the Other . . . that one asserts power and privilege.
>
> —bell hooks, *Black Looks*

The symbolic production and consumption of the Other[1]—of minority and historically disenfranchised cultures—is perhaps most rampantly, yet inconspicuously, perpetuated in Los Angeles by style-setting nouvelle restaurants that cater to elite surveyors of multicultural cuisine. Such restaurants embody those spaces where the critical infrastructure[2] and largely immigrant Latino service workforce converge in a stark pairing to market and produce the multicultural cuisine that unassumingly defines Los Angeles as a global city.

That nouvelle restaurants help manufacture the edible multicultural symbols upon which a global city's pluralistic self-image is constructed is not surprising. The metropolis of the industrial age has long been identified as the style center that generates cultural models emulated in the suburban and rural periphery. In the postindustrial global city of today, moreover, that function has intensified as cultural production has become a chief economic activity. The formation of the ubiquitous field of cultural studies and the study of what Pierre Bourdieu once called "cultural capital" (243) indicates the emerging implications, scholarly and otherwise, of this postindustrial phenomenon. Studies abound in cultural scholarship that assess (to name only a few subjects) cultural iconography, culture industries, popular culture, and the commodification of culture. Yet, as Mike Davis claims in *Magical Urbanism*, a certain invisibility of Latinas/os persists in high-end urban studies charged with examining such cultural phenomena from the vantage of the world economy's impact on the metropolis. Davis contends that "for more than a decade urban theory has been intensely focused on trying to understand how the new world economy is reshaping the metropolis. . . . Yet most of the literature on 'globalization' has paradoxically ignored its most spectacular U.S. expression" (Davis 2000, 9). The present chapter purposes not only to bring visibility upon Latinas/os within urban studies, but also to speculate on the implications of having the labor of a largely immigrant Latina/o workforce support nouvelle multicultural restaurants in a postindustrial, and equally postcolonial, urban landscape like Los Angeles. For in Los Angeles the marketing and availability of multicultural cuisine has, to be sure, also become symptomatic of a certain postcolonial desire of the elite to possess the Other by symbolic measures in lieu of territorial and geopolitical expansion.

Building upon her earlier studies of gentrification, Sharon Zukin advances the concept of the "symbolic economy" in *The Culture of Cities* to more thoroughly explain this postindustrial and postcolonial transformation of the metropolis. She argues that urban elites appropriate the images, narratives, and symbols of multiculturalism and then inscribe these into the built environment to communicate their tastes, values, and desires to their cultural peers and to the citizenry at large. These signs of multiculturalism, which circulate in its symbolic economy, are meant to uphold the misguided assumption that one can have unmediated access to the world of the cultural Other. That is, these signs are intended to establish the illusion of cultural transparency. Homi K. Bhabha in *The Location of Culture* characterizes such instances of transparency as taking place when "the semantic seems to prevail over the syntactic, the signified over the signifier" (109).

This prevalence can come about since texts do not merely reflect reality; rather, and perhaps more significantly, texts create reality. A text, says Fredric Jameson in *The Political Unconscious*, "articulates its own situation and textualizes it, thereby encouraging and perpetuating the illusion that the situation itself did not exist before it, that there is nothing but a text, that there never was any extra- or con-textual reality before the text itself generated it in the form of a mirage" (1981, 82). Therefore, as should be clear, the texts woven by the symbolic economy of multiculturalism in effect perpetuate the illusion that certain timely signs (though, to the conscious minds of surveyors of multicultural cuisine, they appear as anything but signs) paradoxically provide for unmediated passage into the world of the cultural Other. And in the context of multicultural nouvelle restaurants, the texts of cuisine, with all their ethnic flare and flavor, unproblematically signal access to this different world.

Restaurants function as important gateways and clearinghouses, as well, for global labor recruitment. The size of a city's restaurant workforce, "the countries of origin of participants, and the volume of monetary transactions that pass through" them, Zukin writes, "make restaurant work an important transnational activity—and one that is mainly undocumented" (1995, 180). In Los Angeles, multicultural nouvelle restaurants straddle a paradox. Throughout the restaurant industry, but especially in style-setting nouvelle restaurants, Latina/o immigrants exercise the role of unskilled physical labor while college- and academy-trained chefs exhibit the role of culinary artists. In such an intellectual division of labor, a cadre of mostly non-Latino elite chefs appropriates and reinterprets the Latina/o ingredients and recipes their Latina/o staffs assemble into nouvelle creations; the restaurant's intellectual division of labor ghettoizes unskilled Latina/o workers, many of whom remain employed in the same positions indefinitely. Tens of thousands of Latina/o immigrant workers ensure that these places operate profitably and smoothly. That these ubiquitous contradictions of multicultural commodification in Los Angeles do not seem more jarring is due in part to the very idealism germane to the multicultural discourses that obscure them. As Rey Chow contends in *Ethics after Idealism*: "In the problematic of cultural otherness, the two senses of idealism come together: idealism in the sense of idealization, of valorization; but also in the sense of turning-into-an-idea. Often, in the valorization of non-Western 'others,' we witness a kind of tendency to see all such 'others' as equivalent, as a mere positive idea devoid of material embeddedness and contradiction" (xxi).

There is indeed a contemporary repression of contradiction from public knowledge about the intellectual division of labor present in style-setting nouvelle restaurants catering to a multicultural palate. This repression can be partly attributed to a vigorous anti-immigrant discourse that seeks to silence any consideration of the complexities and compromises that permeate the daily lives of individual Latina/o immigrants. Any of the proposed resolutions to the ongoing immigration issue in the United States imply a vacuous program of assimilation that, in the long term, would only maintain the current division of labor and preserve control of the symbolic economy for those in power. Even in the most humane legislative proposals, this immigrant Latina/o workforce would be permitted into the United States on the condition of, as the saying now goes, "filling the jobs Americans don't want." The immigrants would, in effect, occupy a silent, expendable, and exploited niche within the symbolic economy, confirming Herbert Marcuse's noteworthy forty-year-old claim that, in the technological work world of the twentieth (and now the twenty-first) century, the working class no longer appear "to be the living contradiction to the established society" (31). This potentially critical social agent has, in the postindustrial era, continued to be silenced—in part by the discursive efforts of urban elites trying to remarket urban landscapes like Los Angeles as unequivocally "multicultural." Such efforts, when in the service of the multicultural nouvelle restaurant industry, have attempted to accomplish simultaneously the incorporation of Latina/o cuisine *and* the marginalization of its low-wage culinary workers. The fact that new digital technologies now encourage the proliferation of industries based solely upon the commodification of cultural artifacts spurs local critical media, particularly dependent on and identified with their audiences, to continue to normalize elite culinary representations by translating them into popular vernaculars, and to negotiate a city's "look and feel," designating which cultures "should be visible" and which should remain invisible (Zukin 1995, 7). As Latinas/os emerge as the Los Angeles area's majority population and workforce, particularly in the growing service sector, the discursive juncture conjoining the representation and production of multicultural cuisine offers a critical site for gauging Latina/o cultural power, or, more precisely, relative lack of such power.

To be sure, immigrants have their reasons for seeking out the industry's low-paying, often dead-end jobs. Lack of English-language skills and U.S. educational credentials, willingness to work unusual and long hours at subminimum wages, "and the restaurant industry's traditional barriers to unionization" make immigrants "a pliable" labor force, preferred by employers (Zukin 1995, 159). In her ethnographic survey of New York restaurants, Zukin also found that those immigrant workers who were permitted direct contact with the public were more European in appearance and had mastered English and middle-class manners. By contrast, Mexicans dominated "the lowest-skill kitchen positions," a fact that she attributes to the rural origins of immigrant workers who had not yet acquired "urban job skills" (Zukin 1995, 173).

Several structural factors explain why style-setting restaurants prefer to employ Latina/o immigrants in unskilled and less visible positions. First, the celebrity chef and assisting sous chefs and line chefs represent the greatest part of style-setting restaurants' kitchen labor costs. Industry insiders note that restaurant owners do not spend money to increase the education or training of immigrant Latina/o workers beyond on-the-job training. And the language barrier between the skilled, generally non-Latina/o chefs and the unskilled Latina/o dishwashers, busboys, and busgirls reinforces the social distance that separates these groups. Moreover, a recent trend has further heightened the social bifurcation of skilled and unskilled restaurant workers: traditionally, even skilled restaurant employees received their training and experience on the job; today,

FIGURE 2. Line cooks behind the scenes at Taco Rosa, January 2007 (photo by Juan R. Buriel)

however, the preferred pathway to becoming a style-setting chef begins with a university degree, followed by vocational training in one of many European-styled culinary academies and an apprenticeship in a chic kitchen (LaGanga 1997, sect. A). Few Latinas/os receive elite professional training, although they represent the majority of Southern California's restaurant workforce. Rather, the majority of immigrant Latina/o workers enter the restaurant industry by the back door, through referrals or recommendations from other Latina/o immigrant workers; they get their on-the-job training at middle- to low-end restaurants, whether full-service or fast-food—a career path that does not prepare them for work in a chic restaurant. Also, the high restaurant failure rate and the undocumented status of many immigrant workers increase their vulnerability. From the immigrant worker's perspective, obstacles to advancement are indeed discouraging.

Near exclusion from the critical infrastructure, along with structural subordination in the workplace, articulate Latina/o restaurant workers' functional relationships to the symbolic economy. The social relations of restaurant production and the representation of Mexican cuisine mutually constitute Latina/o immigrants as a subordinated workforce while normalizing the commercial and aesthetic appropriation of Mexican culture. Inadequate educational preparation discourages these workers from effectively contesting the representation of their labor and their cuisine inside the restaurant, and racialized media representations of Mexican culture devalue immigrant restaurant workers in society at large. This structural-cultural symbiosis explains why the Latina/o flavor of Los Angeles—a city with a Mexican population second only to Mexico City, with more than thirty thousand restaurants where Latino cooks prepare myriad cuisines, and with a Latina/o workforce large enough to shut down the city's restaurants if it stayed home—remains marginalized in the city's culture wars (Meyer 1997).

Despite their seeming pluralism and populist disdain for class snobbery, multicultural nouvelle restaurants of Los Angeles are its most representative elite institutions. Once inside the restaurant, the tourist or overseas business person experiences a safe and highly aestheticized encounter with the multicultural city before heading off to an evening at the Dorothy Chandler Pavilion, a private screening on the Universal Studios lot, or an afternoon at the Museum of Contemporary Art. In other cases, dinner at Patina Restaurant is the evening's theatrical event. The multicultural style-setting nouvelle restaurant thus functions as an entertainment niche in its own right or as a prelude to another cultural experience. The largely Latina/o immigrant workforce, however, operating silently behind the scenes in such scenarios, serves as the very condition for the functioning of this city's multicultural experience. Latina/o immigrants are overrepresented, in comparison to Anglos, in Los Angeles County's food services industry by a ratio of more than two to one, and make up as much as 70 percent of this workforce (Dear 1996, 13; Watson 1992). Their sheer numbers behind the scenes of the leisurely multicultural experiences taking place in the public venue of the restaurant's seating and dining area suggests the kinds of serious economic disruptions that would take place without this workforce.

It must be noted that this neglect to acknowledge the critical role of the largely Latina/o immigrant workforce sustaining multicultural dining has been an ongoing historical blind spot extending from past efforts by elites to invent a cosmopolitan identity for Los Angeles through a very selective Hispanic fantasy discourse. A process of selective inclusion and exclusion allowed for the incorporation of a mestizo Mexican culture into a generic and romanticized conception of Spanish culture; ultimately, this created a sophisticated origin myth to be exploited by the patrician class of Los Angeles as a means of symbolic conquest.

While walking west from Ohio in 1884, writing about his journey in installments for the *Los Angeles Daily Times* (as the paper was then called), Charles Fletcher Lummis, California's most influential booster-journalist, delivered accounts of Mexicans and Indians that reiterated a well-established anti-Mexican and anti-Indian discourse. Throughout the Southwest, publishers of dime novels, travelogues, and newspapers used culinary imagery to illustrate Mexican "savagery" and "depravity" to mark this community (along with Native Indians) as racial Others. Similarly, implicitly referring to the effects of Mexican cooking, Lummis once remarked that "not even a coyote will touch a dead Greaser, the flesh is so seasoned with the red pepper they ram into their food in howling profusion" (xxxvi).

However, less than a decade later, Lummis excused himself for his "silly" Anglo-Saxon prejudices in his 1892 travelogue *Tramp across the Continent* (xxxvii). His ideological transformation began a personal and professional campaign to produce the narratives and symbols with which Mexican Los Angeles could be revalorized as a fantasy landscape of Spanish romance. In contrast to the blatantly anti-Mexican discourse of the mid-nineteenth century to which he had once subscribed, Lummis's more subtle Hispanic fantasy appropriated those Mexican cultural images that could be interpreted as "Spanish" (read: white and European) or as dependent on Anglo leadership and protection, while excluding others. Los Angeles area restaurateurs and cookbook writers, swept up in Lummis's mission revival movement, thus made their enchiladas and tamales more palatable for non-Mexican diners by affixing a "Spanish" label.

Lummis, however, cannot take all the credit for the symbolic reinvention of California. In 1884, Helen Hunt Jackson published *Ramona*, a novel she wrote to denounce exploitation of Native Americans; *Ramona* became, in the hands of D. W. Griffith, the perfect libretto for selling his vision of Spanish California; Griffith's 1910 film version of the novel deployed the standard Hispanic fantasy discourse to elevate *Ramona* to the level of respectable art for middle-class audiences. Jackson had originally made her protagonist, whom she identified as Mexican, the offspring of a Scottish father and an Indian mother, which Europeanized the character for readers who perceived mestizos as degraded "half-breeds." Griffith transformed the novel's half-white "Mexican" protagonist into the "daughter of the noble Spanish house of Moreno." And with Mary Pickford cast as Ramona, Griffith encouraged the male members of the audience to fantasize about a "Spanish" beauty, yet still portrayed Mexicans and Native Americans as innately inferior beings too powerless to impede progress, represented as white conquest and capital expansion (Noriega 1996, 206). By 1916, the novel had generated as much as $50 million in publishing, stage, and screen revenues (equivalent to the amount generated by a Spielberg blockbuster today), as well as providing the mythic rationale for landscape transformations already in progress.

That picture would change after the 1940s, when Mexican American activists would begin to win important social victories in the Los Angeles area's labor movement, as well as a few local elections during the 1950s. After the 1960s, these modest gains would be bolstered by the emergence of Chicana/o political activism, a burst of mainstream and grassroots book and magazine publishing by and about Chicanas/os, and rapid expansion of Spanish-language television, along with the grudging admittance of a handful of Mexican journalists into the mainstream English-language media. In East L.A., a resurgence of Mexican cultural pride hastened the disappearance of "Spanish" restaurants. The numerous *puestos* (food stalls) of the First Street Mercado, the introduction of pescaderías or seafood restaurants serving steaming bowls of *siete mares*, Mexico City–style taquerías serving *tacos al pastor*, and *birrierías* serving slow-roasted kid would offer new spaces for the social construction and expression of Chicano and Mexican identity. Neighborhood eateries such as Manuel's Tepeyac in East L.A., La Golondrina in Olvera Street, Lucy's El Adobe across the street from Paramount Studios, and Barragan's and La Villa Taxco on Sunset Boulevard continued to serve as third places for political discussion and deal making between an emerging Mexican American middle-class political leadership and the Democratic machine. Meanwhile, the spread of Mexican restaurants followed the movement of Mexican Americans into the suburbs. Central and South American restaurants would continue a slow but steady acquisition of cultural space in the Pico-Union/Westlake area, Hollywood, and Echo Park. Incremental increases in Latino political, economic, and media empowerment accompanied these conquests.

But after the 1970s, the government and media diluted these gains by reviving the term *Hispanic* and other aspects of the fantasy legacy. Suzanne Oboler points out, in *Ethnic Labels, Latino Lives,* the reductive leveling of the complex and diverse histories under colonialism and postcolonialism by this term:

> The ethnic label Hispanic began to be widely disseminated by state agencies after 1970. . . . The adoption of the ethnic designator Hispanic is commonly understood in terms of Spain's presence in the hemisphere for over three hundred years. . . . Thus, it is important to ask to what extent the appeal to the legacy of the Spanish colonial rule can justify the homogenization under the label Hispanic of the subsequent experiences of at least 23 million citizens, residents, and immigrants of Latin American descent. Can this appeal account, for example, for the legacies of Mexican Americans/Chicanos and Puerto Ricans, whose respective post-Spanish colonial histories and cultures have since been differentially shaped by their experiences in the United States? . . . And is

it rooted in an accurate perception of the diversity of Latin American populations in their *own* countries of origin? . . . It is important to note that contact and relations among Latin Americans and between them and the United States have historically been limited primarily to the interactions between and among their state representatives. (xiii; original emphasis)

Beginning in the San Francisco Bay Area in the 1970s, and then later in Los Angeles, the West Coast staged a culinary revolution called "California cuisine." The new label acknowledged recipes and ingredients from European and Pacific Rim culinary sources. Soon afterward, Los Angeles began to emphasize its Mexican and Native American influences. But, despite its international scope, this explosion in culinary innovation was dominated by a single culinary aesthetic, nouvelle cuisine. The new cuisine perfectly suited such emergent global cities as Los Angeles in their transition to economies of cultural production.

Like the European modernists of previous decades, the elite French chefs who initiated the nouvelle revolution in the early 1970s utilized the images, flavors, and associations of the exotic Other to critique a preceding generation of French haute chefs. Like the nouvelle chefs, who had rediscovered and reinvented France's regional cuisine, the American nouvelle disciples applied their techniques and aesthetic to local ingredients and recipes, a gentrifying impulse that explains an initial interest in regional culinary history. The practitioners and promoters of California cuisine, nouvelle cuisine mexique, and Cal-Mex, Southwest, and Tex-Mex cuisines, as well as of other variants of the new American cuisine, mined the past to feed a commodifying aesthetic, but few of these chefs felt compelled to engage in a critical dialogue with Mexican and other so-called Third World cuisines. The appropriation and rejection of local ingredients and recipes gathered from around the world represented, at a symbolic level, the rhetorical assertions and counterassertions of an argument occurring within a culinary tradition. The haute and nouvelle partisans did not seriously attempt to engage the practitioners and advocates of non-European, non-nouvelle culinary discourses in their dialogue.

This was true, of course, for Los Angeles, which emerged as a hotbed of nouvelle experimentation in the 1980s. With rare exceptions, the city's nouvelle disciples were not interested in incorporating Mexican cuisine as a fully realized cultural or aesthetic subject. Instead, the poststructuralism of the nouvelle style appeared to vanquish historical memory and freed chefs to fill their tamales with smoked salmon or caviar without having to worry too much about the cultural ramifications of how they had appropriated recipes or combined ingredients. The nouvelle chefs also discovered that they could make Mexican cuisine more palatable to their upscale clientele if they called it southwestern, a

FIGURE 3. Tortilla maker on display in the dining area at Taco Rosa, January 2007 (photo by Juan R. Buriel)

term that simultaneously evoked New Age appropriations of Native American mysticism and the Hispanic fantasy legacy, and de-emphasized overtly Mexican influences.

The food writers who fussed about "exotic" new ingredients and the ingenious ways nouvelle chefs painted on plates legitimated the chefs' cultural appropriations. Few of the critical infrastructure's members noted the imperial way a new generation of European-trained chefs had detached Mexican and so-called Third World cuisines from their social and cultural histories. More important, the one-way conversation of a postmodern French aesthetic imposing itself upon New World foods and ingredients was held up as a sophisticated urban metaphor of "salad bowl" multiculturalism, or, more technically, "liberal multiculturalism" (McLaren 1994, 51).[3] David Rieff, the New York writer and son of Susan Sontag, takes the culinary metaphor quite literally when he writes:

> Indeed, it was on the . . . far more basic level of what people ate that this multiculturalization of the Southland had progressed the farthest. Ethnic restaurants and fast-food restaurants, only recently . . . confined to particular neighborhoods or immigrant-owned minimals, seemed to be sprouting up everywhere. . . . A generation of Anglo

kids whose parents had been raised on steak and baked potatoes could comfortably tell the difference at a glance between Thai and Cantonese food. A previously exotic prospect like, say, a Szechuan dinner now seemed almost tame, a Mexican burrito as American as a hamburger. In other words, their bellies were growing up multicultural. (230)

The city's hosting of the 1984 Olympic Games, preceded and followed by two Los Angeles Arts Festivals that included artists from the Pacific Rim, and redevelopment projects rationalized as cultural improvement, drew upon multicultural motifs to engender wider public support. A "liberal multiculturalism," as defined by McLaren, emerged from the cultural events taking place in Los Angeles during the mid-1980s and early 1990s. "'Los Angeles'" writes Lisa Lowe, "was represented as a postmodern multicultural cornucopia, an international patchwork quilt, a global department store; although the 'signifiers' were the very uneven, irreducible differences between these diverse acts [cultural festivals], the important 'signified' was a notion of Los Angeles as multicultural spectacle. In the process, each performance tradition was equated with every other, and its meaning was reduced and generalized to a common denominator whose significance was the exotic, colorful advertisement of Los Angeles" (89).

The city's style-setting restaurants, and the food writers who reviewed them, played a prominent role in the "revalorization" of L.A. culture. The critical infrastructure fostered the convergence of Hollywood-style glamour with poststructuralist "multicultural delectation." Restaurateurs, chefs, architects, and interior designers marshaled music, lighting, celebrities, and "attractive" waiters and waitresses, as well as tastes and aromas to stimulate and normalize the experience of consuming the multicultural Other. These new culinary spaces, in other words, symbolically fetishized a kind of cultural cannibalism. The style-setting restaurants' mode of cultural production ran on more than symbolic appropriation, however; as has already been stated, commodification of multicultural cuisine reinforced and relied upon a division of labor that trapped Latina/o immigrant workers in the role of brute physical laborers.

Some scholars see a growing Latina/o middle class as the solution to the cultural silence of Latinas/os in the city they will soon dominate numerically. These scholars expect upward social mobility, which they confuse with the ability to earn middle incomes, to resolve this paradox: either Latino/a assimilation will reinforce the current hegemonic order or majority political and consumer buying power will allow Latinas/os to construct a mainstream version of Latina/o culture.

But if Latina/o majority numbers are to lead to the formation of a cultural class, the core of that class will emerge from the community of working-class immigrants and the popular culture they create and consume. There are a few reasons for this projection. First, Spanish remains the language of the service sector; behind restaurant kitchen doors, immigrant workers relying upon well-established social networks that maintain their access to restaurant jobs ensure the dominance of Spanish in the workplace. Second, the purchasing power of a growing immigrant population has expanded Spanish-language media and provided the Latina/o community the resources to satisfy its cultural appetites; an expanding economy of nostalgia supplies these immigrants with the raw ingredients to maintain and elaborate upon a vibrant culinary culture within the home and in the neighborhood. The memory-driven side of the market is sustained by the region's indigenous Latino cultures, new immigrant arrivals, and the second- or third-generation retro-Latinas/os trying to recover what they have forgotten.

Developing unions as cultural institutions would begin to invest the immigrant majority of restaurant workers with the intellectual authority to represent their own cuisines. Although such a future may seem far off, a variant of this model already exists. In France, the best chefs come from the working class and acquire mastery through on-the-job apprenticeship. Such a system cannot work here as long as the service sector divides workers into first- and second-class wage earners. But the unions could pursue their own institution-building strategy to make service sector work more economically and culturally rewarding. The unions, while increasing their Latina/o and Asian memberships, could assume more of the responsibility for cultural training and draw upon the expertise of neighborhood arts organizations. At the same time, these Latina/o-led unions could mobilize voters to both strengthen and reorient their local educational institutions. The schools would have the task of building a worker-oriented culture class that, on the one hand, challenges and opens the local critical infrastructure and, on the other, democratizes the restaurants' social organization and allocation of representational power.

Los Angeles, a veritable tangle of culture industries, exemplifies the global city as arbiter of cultural meaning and investment, but also as a postcolonial territory subject to reinterpretation by its Latina/o majority. The nearness of its postcolonial past thus presents certain risks to elite efforts to incorporate, reconfigure, and commodify the city's multicultural landscapes. This nearness of the past is not uncommon to postcolonial situations like those that are more or less evident across the cultural spectrum in Los Angeles. "The colonial aftermath" says Leela Gandhi, "is marked by the range of ambivalent cultural moods and formations which accompany periods of transition and translation" (5). These periods are ongoing and never finally resolved. So, it can be expected that in Los Angeles's elite and elite-striving culture industries will continue to create narratives and images that seem to render harmless whatever oppositional tendencies its inhabitants preserve in their memories: the elites know they cannot fully control and exploit the landscapes of the present without also patrolling the landscapes of the past. The creative destruction of landscape formation is more than a material process; it is the language of power, the means by which elites include and exclude symbols to construct and communicate the urban images, narratives, and visions they hope to make appear real. To Zukin, for instance, the symbolic economy speaks especially clearly in restaurants.

One cannot expect the ambitious attempts of urban elites to make transparent and accessible the cultural and historical world of the Other to go uncontested. "Despite appearances" argues Bhabha, "the text of transparency inscribes a double vision: the field of the 'true' emerges as a visible sign of authority only after the regulatory and displacing division of the true and the false" (110). So, although urban elites use the critical infrastructure to attempt to dominate the means of symbolic production and distribution, there are reasons they do not control this absolutely. To begin with, the huge costs of constructing their grand narratives depend upon the consent of the culture-consuming, taxpaying, and voting public. Moreover, their texts are continually contested and thus subject to the give-and-take, to the inherent ambivalence, of a cultural dialectic. We learn from Jameson that self-consciousness is the driving force behind dialectical thought, that it is "thought about thought, thought to the second power which at the same time remains aware of its own intellectual operations in the very act of thinking" (Jameson 1971, 53). Effective, dialectical thought includes consciousness of one's complicity. After a while, exposure to the symbolic economy of multiculturalism, whether one is of the elite class or otherwise, is likely to yield private and public considerations of not only what the associated signs of culture mean, but the very conditions of their meaning, as well.

Mediating the Public Sphere in Latina/o Detroit
Heart and Margin of an Embattled Metropolis

CATHERINE L. BENAMOU

Apart from the fact that, for nearly a century, Detroit has served as the hub of a sprawling corporate automobile industry with assembly plants and markets across the globe, it has rarely been considered a global city. Even less likely has been its identification as a "Latino metropolis," attracting migration from Latin America and the Caribbean, and projecting and nurturing a Latina/o cultural presence in multisensorial forms along public thoroughfares, over the airwaves, and in private-public places of commerce and leisure. Yet Detroit's global status, to the extent that it still exists, is inextricably—if imperfectly—tied to its ability to harbor a Latina/o public sphere, alongside other spaces for transsocial and multiethnic interaction. Key to this ability is the role of communications media and citywide events in bridging sociocultural spheres within the multicounty metropolitan area and in articulating the local urban with the national and international spheres of visibility and activity. To what extent do uses of urban public space, including the multilingual airwaves, provide the opportunity for collective identification and a sense of belonging in a shifting, globalized socioeconomy? And why do Latinas/os figure so prominently in Detroit's local/global equation?

Although these questions could (and should) be posed of the mediated public sphere in any major port city in the United States, they are particularly pressing in the case of Detroit, given the steady shrinkage of its economy and population overall, its legacy of residential and employment segregation (see

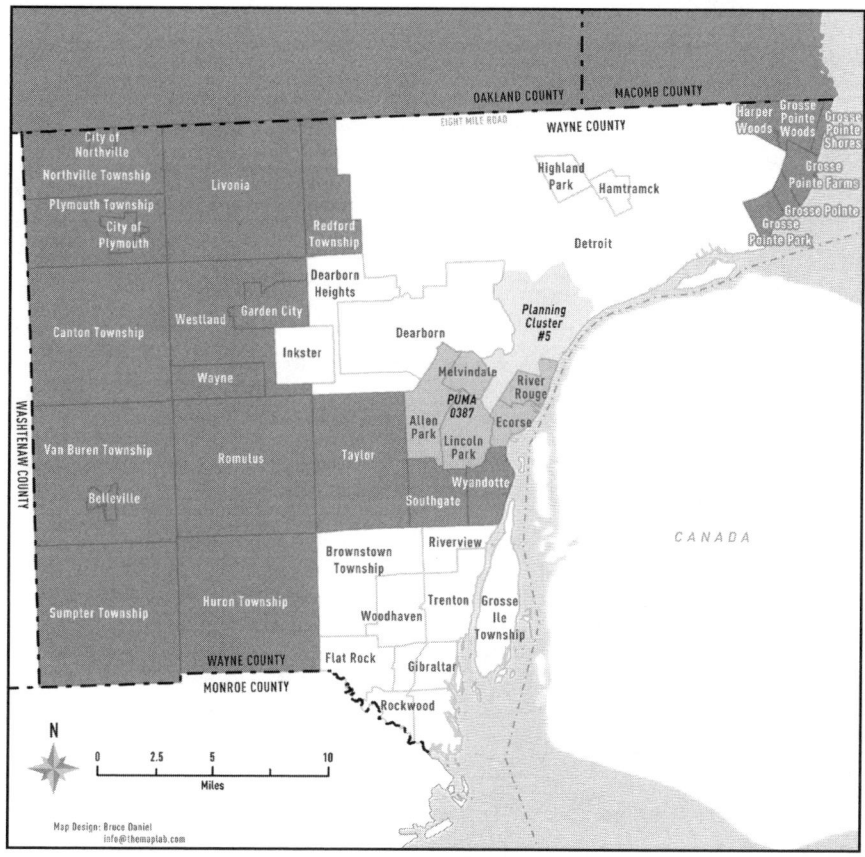

FIGURE 4. Detroit metropolitan area (design by Bruce Daniel, 2010)

Farley 2003) and interracial conflict (both lived and intensely mediated), the city's proximity to the U.S.-Canadian border, and the relative and absolute increase in its Latina/o population over the past decade. Corrected census figures for Detroit indicate a continued decline in the overall population, from 951,270 in 2000 to 868,822 in 2006. Yet during roughly the same period (2000–2005), the self-identified "Hispanic or Latino" population decreased by only 0.4 percent (indicating an increase relative to the whole), and actually grew by 7.3 percent in Planning Cluster 5, near the city center (see figure 4).[1] This Latino/a-sparked revitalization of the inner city—which in any other U.S. metropolis would be seized as a marketing opportunity—has barely been acknowledged outside inner government circles, and it has yet to exert a noticeable impact on Detroit's predominantly anglophone, biracially oriented mediascape.[2]

A more complex intercultural dynamic is suggested by the uses of Detroit's public space on the ground. Since the 1980s, Detroit's global self-image has, save the nostalgic mining of the city's more prosperous mid-twentieth-century past in repeat performances of Motown hits and the annual Dream Cruise of automobiles down Woodward Avenue (itself fortified by Latina/o participation from Pontiac and Southwest Detroit), revolved around the city's high-profile sports arenas (such as Ford Field for the 2006 Super Bowl), postmodern architectural attractions (such as Renaissance Center), casinos, and top-tier entertainment venues. When, on rare occasions, Latina/o talent has been featured at these venues, the events have been promoted so as to appeal first to a mass suburban audience, with pricing and advertisement tailored to the nearby Latina/o and other core city communities only as an afterthought. The notable exceptions to this rule have been the Detroit Institute of the Arts, which since 1933 has housed the frescoes of Diego Rivera as one of its international treasures, and which currently opens the gallery space to free concerts featuring local musicians; and the Detroit Tigers baseball team, which, with eleven players from Colombia, Dominican Republic, Latino Southern California, Puerto Rico, and Venezuela in key positions on its active roster, offers special opportunities for Latina/o families to attend games and for local youth to be coached by the players. As suburban interests (stemming from a population which, mostly "white" and Anglo-identified, continues to flow to the north and west) have steadily placed economic and cultural claims on the corporate-driven path followed by globalization at the city center, an inversion in the valuation and definition of periphery and center has occurred.

What follows is based mainly on multimethod field research conducted in Detroit since 2005 and shows the paradoxical process whereby, just as Latina/o Detroit was beginning to recapture and revitalize its own public sphere and to make new inroads in terms of enfranchisement and visibility (both local and beyond), its very livelihood and collective claim to place within the unevenly globalized and developed urban matrix became imperiled. This peril arose from stepped-up immigration enforcement, disregard by state and local agencies of local community needs and initiatives, downsizing of the regional economy (Western Ontario, Canada, Northern Ohio, and Southeastern Michigan) owing to the U.S. automobile industry cutbacks and plant closures, and the subprime mortgage crisis, which has hit Latina/o as well as black homeowners in Detroit particularly hard.[3] Throughout this process of enfranchisement, retrenchment, and readjustment, new interethnic alliances and media players, including Univisión network's recently owned and operated station WUDT, have played a crucial role.

FIGURE 5. Inscribing the Latina/o presence in Detroit history. T-Shirt at Cinco de Mayo, 2007 (photo by Catherine Benamou)

By *enfranchisement*, I refer to the interdependent factors of political recognition and empowerment—access to mechanisms that provide an effective say in the articulation of local-global initiatives and uses of urban space—and cultural enfranchisement—the degree to which the language(s) and expressive culture(s) of a community figure in the public image of the city at large and also continue to be enjoyed by that community in a manner reflecting its self-defined modes of public engagement.[4] As a working concept, *public sphere,* as the key theater within which to observe and evaluate processes of enfranchisement, has been extended and adapted here from its Habermasian formulation, in which the stress is on bourgeois social institutions forming a third, or intermediate, realm between private interests and the state (see Habermas 1991 and Edgar 2006, 124–25), to denote the ensemble of open civic spaces and channels of sociopolitical discourse and cultural expression accessible, without undue impediment, to residents as well as interlopers. These spaces, often stratified in a multiethnic city, may take on virtual (constructed through media and communications networks) or actual form at specific urban locations. One's ease of movement between socioculturally distinct spheres, however inhabitual, together with a sense of enfranchisement, however modest, is essential to one's attainment of a sense of "place" in a city as well as with respect to the global processes of trade, communications, and policymaking in which denizen and city are ensconced.[5] Whether or not the prospects for enfranchisement or for achieving a sense of place are different for Latinas/os, in comparison to those for other groups in Detroit, or for Latinas/os in other cities, can only be grasped by describing the community and its public sphere from the inside out.

LATINA/O DETROIT—PALIMPSEST

Unlike emergent destinations for Latinas/os, such as Atlanta or Kansas City, Detroit has a history of Latina/o settlement that stretches back to the early twentieth century. Five waves of migration can be identified, each of which has inflected the composite, pan-Latina/o contours of the inner public sphere. Mexicans and Mexican-Americans first arrived to the area as the result of mobility facilitated by railway employment in the southwestern United States, followed by agricultural employment under contract to sugar beet growers (after an 1897 tariff on foreign sugar increased production in the Midwest dramatically), and the attraction of the local automobile assembly lines from the early 1910s through the 1920s (Balderrama and Rodríguez 1995, 16–17, 21–25; see also Hoffnung-Garskof 2008, 407–8). The flow from Mexico was disrupted and reversed shortly thereafter, when worsening economic conditions in the United States fed the flames of racism and xenophobia, leading to the dominant view among Anglo-American authorities that too many people of Mexican origin were either occupying precious jobs or burdening the public assistance coffers and therefore should be expulsed. After a series of snap immigration raids at public locations in California and the Southwest, beginning in 1928, mass deportations of Latinas/os (regardless of citizenship status) followed in areas of Mexican employment in the Midwest. The faces of some of those who became subject to deportation in the 1930s remain immortalized in the figurative depictions by Diego Rivera of the Ford Motor Company assembly lines, which are on view at the Detroit Institute of Arts,[6] and detailed accounts of this exodus have been gathered as part of an ongoing oral history project led by Elena Herrada at the Detroit Center for Workers, based in Southwest Detroit. Only some of those who were repatriated in the 1930s returned to Detroit during the Bracero Program (temporary worker program) in the 1940s and 1950s.

The availability of industrial employment, especially in the Detroit automobile plants, also attracted a Puerto Rican migrant population, which streamed into the eastern United States when economic pressures led to an official policy after World War II of exporting the island's unemployed. Subsequent waves

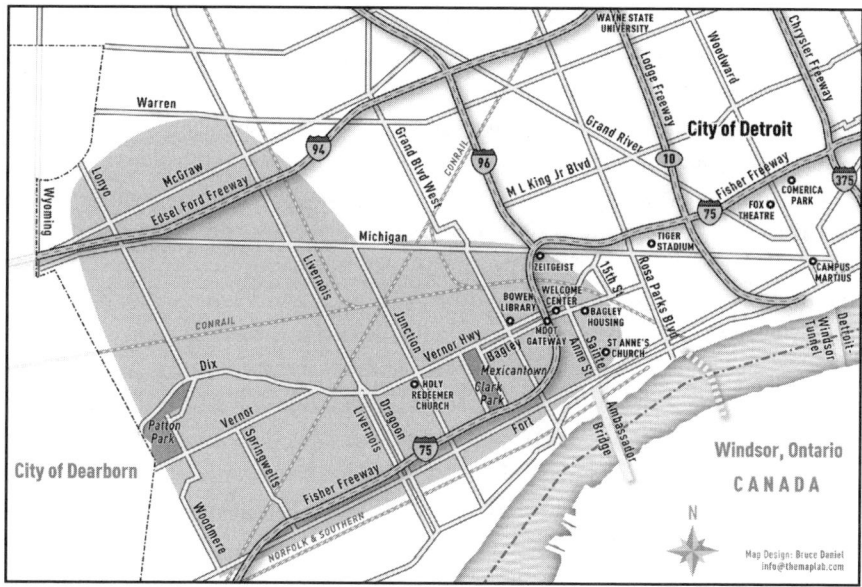

FIGURE 6. Southwest Detroit and environs (design by Bruce Daniel, 2010)

of settlement have included Cubans who left after the 1959 revolution (some of whom still participate in a local Liceo Cubano that meets in Detroit's Mexicantown), Central Americans fleeing from repressive governments in Nicaragua, El Salvador, and Guatemala, and, more recently, from the devastation of Hurricane Mitch; and Dominicans making their way to Michigan from Florida and New York.[7] The settlement of postwar migrant waves, coupled with freeway construction (M-10 and I-75) and urban renewal projects, caused the Latina/o community to drift westward, away from the corridor along Michigan Avenue that connected Mexicantown to Corktown and major downtown venues, such as Tiger Baseball Stadium, into areas that were previously inhabited by peoples of Eastern European, German, Irish, African American, and Middle Eastern origin (see figure 6).

Not surprisingly, the more longstanding Latina/o groups enjoy a greater degree of political clout in relation to the non-Latina/o city and state government; partly as a result, they have set the tone for the public cultural profile of the district. The century-old Mexican core is reflected not only in the name Mexicantown but also on the shelves of groceries, clothing, and crafts stores and in yearly celebrations, such as the Day of the Dead and the Fiestas Patrias (Patriotic Holidays). Yet layers of international migration and cross-sector residency have produced a palimpsest weaving a more pan-Latino texture into the local eth-noscape. The longstanding presence of Puerto Ricans in Southwest Detroit has translated into Cinco de Mayo being celebrated as though it were also Puerto Rican Day (officially, June 12), with Puerto Rican flags and paraphernalia dis-played in abundance during the parade to Clark Park. The benevolent hegemony of Puerto Rico alongside Mexico as geosocially (and politically) viable channels of cultural identification has prompted residents of other Latino/a American nationalities to enthusiastically wave either or both national flags (occasionally in combination with their own) while cruising down Vernor Highway in the Motor City-style celebration. At the center of Cinco de Mayo is a lowrider cul-ture, which, in 2007, having won the admiration of mixed ethnic crowds in at-tendance, made a closing performance at the annual Motor City Dream Cruise (an amateur display of vintage and souped-up cars that crawls down the full length of Woodward Avenue to Campus Martius Park downtown). In addition to designating tourist-friendly sites of celebration to attract Anglo Detroiters and Canadians, community leaders have made efforts to promote generational crossover, by including rock and hip-hop bands in the parade and staging a Fi-esta Marathon de Reggaeton Hip-Hop at the Mexicantown Fiesta Hall on West Vernor Highway.

Paradoxically, the sustenance of the founding cultural nationalisms of Southwest Detroit has thus depended on the "people power" furnished by more recent waves of immigrants to boost these celebrations and the community's ability to attract nonresidents from the metropolitan area who come in search of the folkloric. Importantly, these recent arrivals have opened avenues for en-franchisement by stimulating the proliferation of Spanish-language media in the area, even though residents who made up its immigration waves have been progressively stripped of their civil rights, mobility, and consuming power. Al-though most of these media (especially, in Detroit, AM radio) reflect the cul-tural biases of the founding communities, their immigrant orientation and tapping of the national and global media spheres have skewed them towards a pan-Latino/a perspective. Most of the on-camera journalists working until recently at WUDT were of Central and South American descent, and newspa-pers such as *Latino Press, La Jornada Latina,* and *Nuestro Detroit.com* regularly feature coverage of the Hispanic Caribbean and its U.S. diasporas.

LATINA/O DETROIT'S URBAN HEART

Most of Detroit's Latina/o population is clustered in a heart-shaped area gen-erally referred to as Southwest Detroit, which extends West of Mexicantown near the location of the earliest Mexican American settlement on Michigan Avenue (a few blocks West of Rosa Parks Boulevard) to Michigan and McGraw Avenues, and southwestward along Vernor Highway to Patton Memorial Park at Dix Road and Woodmere Street (see figure 6). Although for decades, the parameters of Latina/o Detroit have been associated, in the minds of urban planners, with those of Planning Cluster 5 (see figure 4), a new influx of population in the past few years, mostly from Central America and the Dominican Republic, has pushed the western boundary of the "right ventricle" of this neighborhood's heart across Michigan Avenue, settling in what was previously a predominantly African American neighborhood. Additional clusters have recently been identified in the nearby cities forming PUMA (Public Use MicroArea) 03807 (see figure 4), and in the city of Pontiac in Oakland County, which, despite its suburban positioning north of Eight-Mile Road has been identified as having one of the fastest growing Latina/o populations in the United States.

Thus the estimated Hispanic or Latino population in the city of Detroit has gone from around 15,000 in the late 1920s (see Hoffnung-Garskof 2008, 409) to just under 47,000 in 2005 (against a total city population of 836,056,[8] or around 5 percent), while the Latina/o population in the metropolitan area as a whole (extending westward to Washtenaw County, and southward toward Ohio) has, according to guesstimates by Spanish-language media, including the Toledo-based *La Prensa* and WUDT-CA-Univisión, topped 250,000.[9] Until the recent crisis, this surge led to a noticeable boom in retail business, especially in Southwest Detroit, with small enterprises doubling in number between 1990 and 2000,[10] adding impetus to the growth of community-oriented media and cultural activity. A significant portion of this growth in retail occurred thanks to the entrepreneurship of Arab Americans and Chaldeans from Dearborn and other suburbs, many of whom sell Mexican products and have coexisted peacefully with the predominantly immigrant Catholic community.

The public sphere inside the area is supported by a sort of Noah's Ark of two community-oriented theatrical venues (Holy Redeemer Church on West Vernor and the Matrix Theater on Bagley Avenue at the edge of the district), two public library branches, two art galleries, one well-stocked music store (La Rancherita, on Springwells Street), two soccer-friendly public parks and several pocket parks, along with a panoply of cantinas, regional taquerías, Salvadoran *pupuserías*, barbershops and beauty parlors, specialty supermarkets, a handful of flea markets, a legalized graffiti yard (at the Detroit Hispanic Development Corporation), a shopping plaza (at the busy intersection of Livernois and Vernor), and two night clubs. Periodically, the community marks the breadth of its territory by staging commemorative parades and protest marches that flow from west to east along West Vernor (from Patton to Clark Parks). Whether geared toward political action (in support of immigration reform) or cultural or spiritual affirmation such as December 12, the day of Nuestra Señora de Guadalupe, Mexico's patron saint, these collective actions have attracted a broad cross section of participants and onlookers, including Latina/o members of the fire department and ambulance fleet (who parade with their trucks on Cinco de Mayo), Windsorites (who have experienced their own surge in Latina/o population), and former Latina/o Detroiters who periodically make the pilgrimage from nearby suburbs and other counties in Michigan and Ohio.

Just as meaningfully, many events staged in the heart are supported by neighboring communities: local African American residents bring their own classic cars for display in Clark Park on Cinco de Mayo, and many Arab American and Chaldean shop owners proudly display iconic images of the Virgen de Guadalupe and several demonstrated support for the immigration reform marches, beginning in March 2006, by closing their businesses or posting "Sí se puede" ("Yes, we can") or other pro-immigration reform slogans in their shop windows. The "we" in this slogan is a poignant sign of how Southwest Detroit has resolutely resisted ghettoizing itself. Local efforts to build bridges across ethnic sectors have run the gamut from the forging of political alliances in the New Detroit project, to public education and collaborative initiatives by local Latina/o artists, to aggressive attempts by the Latina/o business community to attract clientele outside the district and win the recognition of city planning and infrastructure authorities. Since 2002, the Hispanic Business Alliance has hosted an annual "economic summit" at prominent urban locations. After working closely with city council president Kenneth V. Cockrel Jr. (who replaced Kwame Kilpatrick as city mayor in 2008), the late Mary Barela, president of the Southwest Detroit Improvement Association, was able to bring about a change in city policy regarding immigration interrogation and detentions: as of July 7, 2007, city employees, including Detroit police officers, were prohibited from inquiring into immigration status or initiating the detention of anyone within city limits. Working on another front, Maria Elena Rodríguez, former president of the Mexicantown Community Development Corporation, who was appointed by Governor Granholm in May 2007 to serve on the state's Commission on Spanish Speaking Affairs (see Governor Granholm Statement 2007), was able to convince the Michigan Department of Transportation (MDOT) to include the community in its plans to revamp the exit to the Ambassador

Bridge so as to facilitate access to Mexicantown for travelers along I-75. Thus the two halves of Mexicantown, severed by the broadening of I-75 in the early 1980s, will eventually be rejoined with the construction of a pedestrian bridge over the highway.

SPANISH-LANGUAGE MEDIATIONS

In today's shapeshifting and multilayered urban universe (made more opaque and segmented in Detroit by the center-periphery inversions already noted), media texts, from human interest stories to live news and targeted advertisements, can affect individuals' and communities' sense of enfranchisement and place by furnishing a means of public recognition (as when, on the radio, references are made to listeners' places of origin); facilitating dialogue among the denizens of various sub-spheres and between those spheres and the loci of political power and policymaking (as when a reporter confronts political representatives with issues that concern the community); and reigniting collective urban memory (usually via audiovisual flashbacks from radio and newspaper archives and in documentaries on public television). Beaming into and out of the urban heart, and radiating out to spectators and listeners in the metropolitan area, a host of Spanish-language media providers strive to perform many of these functions, and, in doing so, have earned the support of a community chronically underserved by local and national anglophone media. In addition to WUDT-CA, the local Univisión television station launched in 2005, residents in the area can tune in to two daily Spanish-language radio broadcasts: 1440 AM leased out of a station in Romulus that boasts "100 percent Mexican" programming (live talk and music); and 1480 AM "La Explosiva" (WSDS), broadcast during daytime hours out of Canton and Plymouth, Michigan, which features a more pan-Latino musical selection, along with hourly broadcasts of news direct from Mexico on the Notimex news service.

However, as in many Latina/o communities, in Detroit the most stable source of information for Latinos/as over the past several decades has been the weekly and biweekly newspapers such as the bilingual *El Central*, the Spanish-language *Latino Press*, which features a special monthly women's health insert and a section "Desde tu Tierra" ("From Your Country") for Mexicans, *Nuestro_Detroit.com*, *Vida Latina en Detroit* (since 2006), *La Jornada Latina* (launched in April 2007) and the magazine *Nuestro Medio* (also launched in 2007), as well as the seasonal and bilingual *Southwest Detroit Newswire*, published by the Southwest Detroit Business Association. Although several of these papers circulate outside Detroit in Western Michigan and northern Ohio, few of them—given the limitations posed by language, advertising sources, and distribution—have succeeded in building a representational bridge for Detroit Latinas/os into the urban mainstream. Nor (inexplicably) have they managed to trip the radar of national surveys of Hispanic media.[11] By far the most impressive effort at connectivity and access is the website Detroit en Español (http://www.detroitenespanol.com), with links to both local and international news in Spanish from various sources, including several of the newspapers mentioned.

Over three-quarters of the 105 people randomly surveyed for my study of Southwest Detroit between March and August 2005 said they watched television in Spanish, as contrasted with under one-third (33) who said they watched English-language networks. Of the latter, roughly half (16) watched both Spanish- and English-language networks in a multilingual pattern that reflects generational differences within households and increasing self-identification with Latina/o languages and cultures. A similar pattern held true for newspaper consumption; most respondents said they relied on multiple media for their informational and entertainment needs, but less than a third used the Internet, and, of these, only five used it as their medium of choice.[12] Thus, it is mainly through active, selective consumption, cobbling together a range of analog sources, rather than by surfing the Web, that Detroit Latinas/os are able to tap into mediated information, balancing electronic sources that privilege transnational flows reaching mass and niche markets via satellite, with paper sources more focused on the local.

Although the survey results indicate that these Detroiters are not averse to, or unaware of, the range of anglophone media options, they also show a general hesitancy to rely on any of these as a main or sole source; except a few who could afford only a television set, most preferred to subscribe to services that would grant them access to transnational television in Spanish. Many felt the portrayal of Latinas/os on anglophone television was uneven at best, in both quantitative and qualitative terms: "There are channels that support us and others don't," "They don't have any idea of what we are and what we can achieve," "It's offensive and prejudiced," "They need more Spanish subtitles." Among the local English-language network stations mentioned in my survey, Fox was a clear favorite, quite possibly because of the community-oriented reporting by Lourdes Duarte, who has since left the station to work for WGN-TV in Chicago. Until Univisión began its local broadcasts, Duarte was the only Latina/o media professional appearing on local Detroit television, and none of the other anglophone providers contacted in 2007 said they were developing programming that targeted the local Latina/o audience.

A number of factors—including, but not limited to, the political and cultural shortcomings of the anglophone media and the language barrier for re-cent adult migrants—enhance the market edge of Spanish-language media in Southwest Detroit. In addition to helping viewers and listeners reconnect with the homeland, navigate the cityscape, and become aware of new policies and of changes in community access to public resources, local Spanish-language media have become more community-sensitive: residents are invited to assist with news gathering, call into radio programs, comment on programming on-line—all key to a sense of place and enfranchisement. Jorge Avellán, a reporter for WUDT-CA-Univisión since its inception, took care to include images of lo-cal residents and settings within the frame during each report on location; he consistently interviewed local Latina/o experts and sought the opinion of com-munity members regarding problems close to home, such as the fire risk posed by using gas ovens to heat homes or the rising cost of applying for citizenship papers. In a special December 2007 report on the Hispanic vote, Avellán inter-viewed local youth about their expected role in, and opinions regarding, the 2008 presidential election.

Since Detroit has yet to be recognized as a Latina/o city in the national imaginary, representation of this locale within U.S. Spanish-language network coverage is less frequent than for other local Univisión affiliates, and nonexis-tent in the case of national radio; however, the potential exists for a boomer-ang effect of local to national (and even transnational) transmission, thereby assisting with the task of deghettoization. When, after the March 27, 2006, im-migration protest in the Southwest, eleven workers were dismissed at a local meat packing plant in retaliation for their failure to appear at work that day, despite prior permission to take the day off, and WUDT's coverage of the in-cident made the national Noticiero Univisión evening broadcast, the company was forced to reconsider its actions. Alternatively, by interviewing represen-tatives from local and state government, the weekly WUDT news talk show, *¡Informando!,* probed issues and policies of vital interest to many Latina/o com-munities elsewhere in the state and in the tri-state area; among the show's 2008 guests was Marta González Cortes, director of the Migrant Workers Office in Lansing, who alerted migrant workers to their labor rights in Michigan, and to the rights of their children to receive public services.[13] Finally, in a bold move that demonstrated recognition of the regional demand for Spanish-language coverage of sports in the United States, the Detroit Fox Sports Network (FSN), which reaches viewers as far away as Northeastern Wisconsin, launched the first Spanish-language telecast of a baseball game with its coverage of a special, Latina/o-friendly Tigers home game, *¡Fiesta Tigres!,* in August 2008.[14]

LATINA/O DETROIT ON THE URBAN/NATIONAL MARGIN

Sadly these community-generated initiatives, which de facto have been a central force in urban and regional revitalization, have been relegated to a barely discernible periphery in mediated representations of the city and in the organization and delivery of most public services. As anyone who has watched local network news knows, it is not just public visibility, but a particular *kind* of visibility in mediated representations, that stimulates and reinforces the sense of place and enfranchisement for members of a given community. In stark contrast with the Spanish-language news sources, local anglophone television news reports, with rare exceptions, show Southwest Detroit (when they do show it) as the locus for criminal activity and lethal accidents (such as a fire or a gas line leak), in a frame filled by barren streets, often without signage indicating precise location. With no other human figures to gravitate toward, our attention begins and stops with the English-speaking reporter in the foreground, who tends to be suburban and phenotypically white. Urban citizenship and subjectivity are confined to privatized and suburban zones; the visible public space is divorced in the camera from a surrounding context that could furnish local residents with the data needed to make a meaningful linkage between news event and place. Although this scenario of EuroAmerican-biased visibility and sociocultural excision might be unthinkable today in local English-language newscasts of Boyle Heights (Los Angeles), Washington Heights (Upper West Side, New York City), or even Pilsen (Lower West Side Chicago), its frequency in the Detroit mediascape is not entirely a function of deliberate exclusionary policies within media-producing organizations (although a grain of knee-jerk ethnocentrism should not be discounted). Exclusion stems instead from the continual underestimation of the Hispanic/Latina/o demographic in metropolitan Detroit; disregard for the level of civic engagement and modes of media consumption within that demographic; and the folding of Southwest Detroit (in the aggregate) into the black-white binary "donut" logic that has haunted media portrayals and scholarly studies of Detroit since the early 1970s.

Although various media portrayals to date have distinct historical roots and approaches to the figuration of urban space, the post-1960s popularization in documentary and fictional media of inner Detroit as an urban battleground very much resembles the zero-sum game described by Valle and Torres in relation to the balkanized and racialized representations of post-1992 Los Angeles, a predominantly Latina/o city where media industries are headquartered.[15] According to the mass-mediated discourse, racial identities are essentialized and foregrounded, and social groups are portrayed as "at odds with each other, each group 'naturally' apart from others and antagonistic toward members of other groups" (Valle and Torres 2000, 11). The immediate effect of this game in the Detroit media- and political power-scapes has been the exclusion from representation of residents who, owing to their ethnic background or recency of arrival, find themselves ambiguously positioned in relation to U.S. racial categories, yet who, given their urban location and daily labor, have contributed long enough to the local economy and civic life to have a substantial claim to enfranchisement: Arab Americans and Latinas/os, along with other emergent groups, such as Asian Americans, Canadians, and non-Hispanic Afro-Caribbeans. Encompassing up to eight city wards, Southwest Detroit has historically lacked Latina/o representatives on the Detroit City Council, which is elected "at large," and the mayor's office only recently engaged a Spanish-fluent liaison. There is only one Latino/a state representative in Lansing, the state capital. This sparse representation of Latinas/os contrasts sharply with the national trend: according to the National Association of Latino Elected or Appointed Officials (NALEO), as of November 2006, Hispanic candidates were listed on the ballot for national, state, and local positions in thirty-eight out of fifty states, a 46 percent increase over the candidacy rate in 1998 (*El Central* 2006, 4).

Remarkably, and despite national trends to capture the Hispanic market (which in Detroit has been estimated as having an annual purchasing power of around $2 billion [Bodipo-Memba 2005]), the Latina/o community in Southwest Detroit has suffered as well from corporate neglect, as evidenced in the billboards along I-75 and Livernois Avenue, the two main corridors leading into the community, which cater overwhelmingly to an Anglo-oriented population, barring the occasional alcoholic beverage advertisement featuring slogans in Anglicized or noncolloquial Spanish. On the one hand, this semiotic rebuff of local Latina/o consumers has allowed nearby ethnically owned businesses to enjoy unimpeded access to the multiethnic Detroiters and Windsorites curious enough to venture beyond the billboard façade; on the other, it signals the insensitivity of Anglo Detroit and Windsor (half the billboards tend to plug the Windsor casino) toward a community that has resided for decades on both sides of these thoroughfares. It also signals the relative disarticulation of local, small businesses from the citywide market. The deflection of drivers' gazes from the surrounding cityscape onto the billboards has the same effect of ghettoizing this community, positioned neither to consume nor to be consumed, as the administrative neglect of the abandoned buildings near the northeastern entrance to the district.

The indelible blight/flight trope in news reports, which builds on the public and commercial media's timeworn susceptibility to a binaristic national racial imaginary—with palpable consequences for local patterns of urban development and enfranchisement—has found reinforcement in the 1990 and 2000 U.S. censuses, which singled out Detroit as the "blackest" city in the United States (81.6 percent of total population in 2000) and the suburban city of Livonia, also in Wayne County, Michigan, as the "whitest" (95.5 percent in 2000).[16] It is difficult to subscribe to this logic, however, upon the realization that the data has been discursively inflected to the disadvantage of a significant number of respondents. When one takes into account the conflationary nomenclature of the census (whereby all peoples of North African and Middle Eastern origin are to list themselves as white), the relative growth (prior to the recent immigration crackdown) in the number of undocumented, and therefore underreported, residents, and the diverse daily commuter flow from Ontario, Canada, the racialized dichotomy between donut center and ring loses its solidity.[17] When considered on the ground rather than at the margins of the news frame, the burgeoning in the city center and suburbs of a multiracial, multinational Latina/o population further disrupts the binary donut model.[18]

Positioned near the heaviest point of trade between the United States and Canada, Southwest Detroit has also played a vital role in the articulation of U.S.-Canadian relations. Visitors from Windsor and other parts of Ontario provide the clientele for many of the restaurants, shops, and nightclubs in Mexicantown. Mexican cultural centers in Detroit and Windsor are in active dialogue with one another, and for decades, church parishes, such as St. Anne's in Detroit and the Church of the Assumption in Windsor, both founded by Basilian missionaries, have shared feast days and other cultural events, such as the Day of the Dead.[19] Yet, caught, like other border towns, within the double logic of NAFTA and U.S. Homeland Security, Southwest Detroit and the bridge and tunnel crossings adjacent to it have become heavily policed, as new "Real" identification requirements, introduced post-9/11, have become a prerequisite of border passage. The transborder flow of big business cargo (and tons of refuse from Toronto) takes increasing precedence over that of cultural expression, health care, and social ties; this has hardly benefited the Detroit metropolis, and even less an ethnic district already in the throes of severe cutbacks in industrial investment and employment.

Taking its cue from recent census figures, along with the intensification of Latina/o public engagement mid-decade, WUDT-Univisión in March 2007 expanded its broadcast area through a partnership with Comcast Cable so as to cater to growing numbers of viewers in Washtenaw, as well as Wayne, Oakland, Macomb, and Monroe Counties (see figure 7). Yet in June 2008, WUDT ceased its daily Spanish-language newscast, primarily for lack of commercial sponsorship—a sponsorship already compromised at the metropolitan level by the fact that local broadcasting in Spanish had been preceded by a lengthy history of transnational transmission, meaning that a considerable portion of the station's potential client base was still subscribing to satellite dish services with marginal local programming content.[20]

On the other hand, notwithstanding the municipal ban on police inquiry into immigration status, the Wayne County Sheriff's Department and U.S. Immigration and Customs Enforcement (ICE) agents have in recent years scoured Southwest Detroit, rounding up hundreds of residents and sending thousands of others into clandestinity for fear of detention and deportation. And, as of January 2008, proof of permanent resident status is required to obtain a Michigan driver's license (see Michigan Secretary of State 2008). These developments have not only discouraged Latina/o participation in the local public sphere; they have cut into the ability of local businesses that support the inner sphere to survive, let alone thrive, under what, by all appearances, is a state of siege. A guest worker policy in Canada, along with what has reportedly been more humane treatment of newcomers by immigration authorities (new immigrants are able to stay up to one month in a YMCA facility in Windsor while waiting for their papers to be processed) have encouraged "second border" crossings from the United States into Canada, mostly by Latino/a Americans from Detroit.[21] WUDT was the first U.S.-based news organization to report on this new pattern of emigration.

The dynamics of public culture in Southwest Detroit, despite its political marginalization and undercapitalization, yield insights regarding the construction and sustenance of a viable urban public sphere in relation to a globalized national political economy. First, the bridging of gaps on the path to Latina/o enfranchisement and cultivation of place need not be restricted to the dyadic interaction between a local ethnic subsphere and a global urban public sphere, as encouraged by a "managed and corporate multiculturalism" that Victor Valle and Rodolfo Torres have noted in relation to Los Angeles (2000, 11), between ghetto and mainstream. Indeed, recent scholarship has demonstrated how, in cities such as New York and Los Angeles, where the Latina/o presence is highly mediated and widely disseminated, the concerted attention of corporate capital and of public agencies to this demographic for the sake of profit and global public relations can actually be counterproductive to Latinas' and Latinos' sense of place and enfranchisement (see Dávila 2004 and Valle and Torres 2000). By contrast, Southwest Detroit has been "context generative" (Appadurai 1997, 186): by feeding Windsorites and suburbanites in Mexicantown, servicing diasporic customers at grocery, clothing, and music stores, welcoming and frequenting

Arab American-owned stores, chronicling municipal and national policies and the community response on its airwaves and in newspapers, cheering for Detroit at hockey and baseball games, and displaying low-rider panache at the annual Woodward Dream Cruise, Latina/o Detroiters continue to demonstrate their capacity for local and global citizenship. Through its historical adaptiveness and open door policy, Southwest Detroit has demonstrated that the substantive quality and stability of the broader urban sphere can be enhanced, for the wider public good, by the formation of tryadic and even quadratic bridges, in this case, among the predominantly Latina/o population within the neighborhood's parameters, the Arab American community just north of it, and the multiethnic communities of Windsor, Canada, and the African American stronghold at city center. Meanwhile, Spanish-language media and a handful of anglophone reporters and editors have succeeded insofar as they have identified the idiosyncratic, palimpsest nature of the Latina/o regional demographic rather than having targeted Latinas/os as a "one size fits all" niche market. At the same time, as my survey revealed, transnational media, although they may provide instantaneous access to global events, a cultural comfort zone, and a break from daily hardship, are limited in their ability to open possibilities for local engagement and enfranchisement. The future of Detroit's public spheres, both citywide and district-bound, remains in the hands of enlightened public servants, community leaders, cultural entrepreneurs, and proud and vocal residents. To those who will listen, Latina/o media consumers send these anonymous messages: "We need more programs for youth, so they don't get involved in drugs and gangs, and go to school," "Keep struggling for improved city services," "Give us more information about the community and the state of the city," "Stop the gossip and broadcast more educational programming," "Provide more Spanish-language channels because the Hispanic population is growing," "You won't be in power forever."[22]

Textual Revisions of Identity   Nostalgia and Modernity in Asunción

AMANDA HOLMES

a ciudad en que vivimos (2004) by Juan Manuel Prieto and *Postales de Asunción de antaño* (1999–2002) by Jorge Rubiani are illustrated collections
of articles published recently to celebrate the often neglected capital of
Paraguay. Promoting local interest in Asunción, above all, these works
seek to reevaluate the image of the contemporary capital and recognize
its distinctiveness. Both representations fluctuate between a nostalgic
perspective of the city and the expression of a desire for its modernization, a dualistic approach that parallels, more generally, a series of juxtapositions inherent in urban Latin American lifestyles and attitudes—the
modern and the traditional, the rural and the urban, the local and
the global—as well as contrasts in economic conditions. Although, as Vivian
Schelling has shown, urban cultural projects in Latin America often confront
the challenges of resolving such complex dichotomies (26),[1] the means pursued
by the two Paraguayan chroniclers analyzed in this chapter derive from a narrow perspective on the city. The authors' emphasis on nostalgia and modernity,
described in the first half of this chapter, reveals their aim to develop a meaningful position from which to construct a positive identity for the city; however,
the remoteness of their work from contemporary Latin American thought and
writing on the city, discussed in the second half, confirms that, by disregarding
critical realities, Prieto and Rubiani fail to participate in essential debates that
are leading toward a more comprehensive representation of urban experience.

Nostalgia for the Asunción of a former time is common enough, and the
two eras that, in hindsight, paint the capital most successfully are often evoked
in representations of the contemporary city. As a new Spanish colony, founded

in 1536 or 1537, Asunción replaced the abandoned River Plate settlement in the area of modern Buenos Aires and enjoyed its status as a principal trading center until Buenos Aires was firmly established as a port. Similarly, the postindependence rule by the "Supreme Dictator of the Republic," José Gaspar Rodríguez de Francia (1814–1840), stands out in the history of Paraguay and Asunción. Although, during this era, the country was isolated, its borders closed both to Paraguayans and foreigners, this policy allowed it to develop independently without the incursion of outside interests; even though Paraguayans remained largely uneducated and secluded from external influences, the fact that under Francia the country prospered economically, and was known for its peace and order, still resonates positively for some.

Coupled with a yearning for the past is Asunción's ambiguous entry into modernity. Its reputation as an economic backwater and center for smuggling and drug trafficking developed in part from its historical position in relation to Europe and the rest of the Americas, but Alfredo Stroessner's regime (1954–1989) also sanctioned smuggling and other illegal activities to maintain favor among military officers (Miranda 114). Although infrastructures improved during Stroessner's thirty-five-year rule,[2] the distribution of land and wealth remained the most uneven in Latin America, and violence and intimidation eliminated political dissent, leading many Paraguayans into exile. As in other Latin American urban centers, infrastructural and technological changes have been implemented in Asunción in a simultaneous rather than sequential manner, leading to a situation in which traditional and modern lifestyles coexist.[3] A typical Asunción neighborhood such as Villa Aurelia, Villa Morra, or Sajonia includes a combination of ostentatious houses of the very rich, surrounded by six- or seven-foot walls topped with barbed wire or broken glass (along with a night-time security guard and guard dog), next to squalid one- or two-room shacks housing large families. Some of the city's roads are paved, but a large number are rough cobblestone and even more are dirt. Asunción's sewers, mostly open, overflow and flood the streets during the annual rainfalls, although this infrastructural problem has been largely repaired in the downtown center. Donkeys pull wagons from the country with wares to sell in the central *asunceno* market, even while SUVs with tinted windows skirt around them. In the mid-1990s, four U.S.-style shopping malls with boutiques and food courts selling imported goods were built to cater to the upper and middle classes, in dramatic contrast with the outdoor markets serving the lower classes. This eclectic and conflictive urban environment that highlights economic, social, and racial inequalities, contrasts starkly with the historical and Europeanized image of Asunción advanced by Prieto and Rubiani.

Indeed, for these two authors, the creation of a modern urban lifestyle refers almost exclusively to the development of a more livable and convenient environment comparable to Western European and North American cities through controlled urban development and infrastructural changes such as paved streets, covered sewers, garbage collection, access to electricity, and phone service. For the most part, neither author tackles questions of political, social, and economic modernization regarding democratization in governmental and professional opportunities together with industrialization and mass access to education. Nor does either conceive of modernity as accelerated and dynamic change as theorized by Marshall Berman (1982) and others reading through Marx. Instead, their version of the concept revives the Eurocentric definition, in which what is modern is considered superior. Their limited understanding of the modern reflects the expectations of the intended audience of their texts—middle- and upper-class educated Paraguayans, who remain intimately connected to European family origins. It also underscores a perspective that develops from their professional interests and backgrounds as an adviser for the Paraguayan government's tourism department, in the case of Prieto, and as an architect, in the case of Rubiani.

For educated Paraguayans, Prieto and Rubiani bring a new attention to the city and reflect the desire to construct, restore, and exhibit a unique and positive identity for the Paraguayan capital. Their perspectives on Asunción find resonance in Svetlana Boym's nostalgia types: a restorative nostalgia that seeks the recuperation of the lost home; and a reflective nostalgia that interprets the past as lost, but does not attempt its reproduction (41). Inherent in the term *nostalgia,* coined in 1688 to mean the pain of missing one's homeland,[4] Boym's categories are based on the interaction of space and time: "If restorative nostalgia ends up reconstructing emblems and rituals of home and homeland in an attempt to conquer and spatialize time, reflective nostalgia cherishes shattered fragments of memory and temporalizes space" (Boym 49). Along with the desire to recuperate a historical object, perhaps a monument or a church, restoration always implies a modification of the original. In Boym's example, the restored Sistine Chapel is an attempt to replicate the chapel's original "aura," following Benjamin's definition. However, in its restored form, the chapel incorporates new technology, such as lighting and cameras. This ironic and inevitable result demonstrates that, although it is possible to replicate the past, reinventing a historic object involves the loss of essential elements. Because complete recuperation of the past is impossible, the nostalgic is forced to meet modernity head on.

Influenced by this inevitable tension, Prieto and Rubiani seek balance between nostalgic attitudes and the modernizing drive. Prieto calls for the embrace of urban planning and modernization to complement the preservation of elements of the historical city, drawing on the spatial dimensions of identity, and on comparisons with other urban centers. By contrast, Rubiani emphasizes the legacy of the past as the primary constructor of Asunción's identity through feelings of nostalgia that highlight the relationship of the contemporary city to its own history. From the perspective of both authors, an approach balanced between respect for Asunción's history and the city's participation in contemporary economic and infrastructural possibilities will allow it to flourish.

Prieto's articles, each characterizing a different barrio of Asunción, began as a guide for visitors, as a series of notes and photographs published during the 1980s in the Paraguayan journal *Contacto Turístico* as well as in the Asunción newspaper *Última Hora*. Beyond this collection of articles, Prieto has contributed regularly to Paraguayan newspapers and magazines, and has worked to promote tourism in Paraguay through the country's national tourism department, Secretaría Nacional de Turismo (SENATUR). In one recent project, he is serving as adviser for the revival of the "Guaraní route," a network of paths used by the Guaraní Indians in their search for the "land of no evil" (Sciscioli). On the surface a conventional touristic celebration of the city, Prieto's texts list traits that make each neighborhood unique, whether landmarks, urban myths, historical events, or important residents. However, *La ciudad en que vivimos* is intended not only for tourists, but also for Asunción's inhabitants, who can nostalgically recall the detailed events Prieto recounts, or become incensed at recent political decisions affecting the city he describes.

As a member of the educated class, Prieto has a perspective on Asunción that emphasizes aspects that allow its comparison to a European city, an argumentative approach that undercuts the value he wants to attribute to this lesser-known urban center. Parallels between the strengths of the global city and those of the peripheral city implicitly dominate Prieto's descriptions. He focuses on society's awareness of cultural continuity, propagation, and heritage, insisting repeatedly on the existence of a rich artistic community in Asunción. Almost every neighborhood description ends with a list of cultural contributions by these areas in the arts.

Prieto favors the modernization of Asunción to make its cityscape and infrastructure more similar to contemporary capitals elsewhere, with planned infrastructural developments perceived as beneficial for Asunción's image. He idealistically calls for the introduction of positive elements in contemporary urban construction—new roads, apartment buildings, well-designed urban plans—while also combatting the spread of the unsavory aspects of urban development, such as pollution, corruption, and kitsch. He decries modernization and consumerism in the case of the park, surrounding the Seminario Metro-politano, that would have been "sacrificed" (36) in 1994 for the construction of a shopping center; however, he approves of the transformation of Sajonia from a quiet neighborhood to an area known for an active nightlife, with res-taurants, *parrilladas*, hamburger stands, pool parlors, and the famous *lomito árabe*. Similarly, he praises Asunción's mayor of the late 1990s, Martin Burt, for the beneficial construction of new roads, but notes the problems of rapid development in the barrio Republicano, not the least of which is environmental degradation. These examples demonstrate a desire not only to define a positive identity for Asunción, but also to encourage urban projects that would improve the city's image: Prieto recognizes the importance of a well-organized arterial infrastructure, but not at the expense of a cohesive neighborhood and a clean environment.

At the same time, Prieto promotes local respect for the city's heritage to im-prove the urban image. His texts reveal a longing for the recuperation of Asun-ción's past, through projects such as the restoration of the Teatro Municipal, and betray reservations about new urban development. In one case, Prieto ex-claims, "It would be a mistake if in the name of progress an entire historical process were eliminated irreversibly!" (140). Indeed, he recites a litany of these sorts of lamentations: the closing of cinemas for lack of sufficient audiences in Sajonia and in Las Mercedes; the quiet of the tourist shops in the old port area, the Recova, now that tourism has subsided; the demolition of buildings in an Italian architectural style in downtown Asunción; the razing of the Plaza de los Héroes; the decrepit state of the Hotel Guaraní.

The chronicler betrays an uneasy relationship to new development. He considers it possible and appropriate, in part because of the perceived loss of historic connection with European architecture and the arts, to revive some as-pects of the historic city yet also laments the permanent loss of others. Prieto's conservative approach to urban image construction reveals a sense of despera-tion to repair Asunción's negative reputation and its infrastructural problems. Although he provides a vision of Asunción intended to launch the development of civic pride, he does not comment meaningfully on the city's deep economic inequalities, the difficulties of its racial hybridity, and the essential influence of its indigenous population on the social fabric.

The second of the two collections of articles, Jorge Rubiani's *Postales de la Asunción de antaño*, approaches the capital from a historical perspective that represents and interprets the legacy of its colonial life. A professional architect, Rubiani has developed his career through positions as a professor of architec-tural theory, design, and Paraguayan cultural history at universities in Asunción, and as a correspondent on urban matters for local newspapers. He has also served on municipal and national committees including, in separate years, as general director of the Dirección de Cultura and of the Dirección General de Planeamiento Urbano. The articles compiled in his book appeared in *Última Hora* from April 12, 1997, to September 9, 2000, mostly in the Saturday edition. The volume is organized around themes such as "Habits and Customs," "People," "Streets," "Villas and Buildings," and "Trees," each topic including a series of two-page articles complemented by a photograph or postcard. An attempt to restore traits of colonial times into the collective memory of Asunción, the volume portrays the city as an "urban palimpsest," a notion developed by Andreas Huyssen, in which the idea of memory "extending both in time and space" (101) is embedded in the city. More specifically, Huyssen explores the urban palimpsest with regard to the memory of trauma that some cities evoke. It is striking that, though Asunción suffers the impact of the recent dictatorship, both Prieto and Rubiani ignore this chapter of the city's history, choosing rather to emphasize the prominence of earlier eras for the construction of Asunción's identity.

Although limited by Asunción's deeply peripheral status, Rubiani seeks to create a rich image of the city both by recounting its past and by emphasizing its contact with Europe.[5] As is clear in his introduction to the city's barrios, Rubiani evokes nostalgia to inspire a consciousness of a consolidated urban identity, which for him develops from the city's history. The first chapter, "Reason for Memory," introduces a conceptual framework that explicitly addresses his purpose to construct or reveal Asunción's identity. In this chapter, Rubiani rejects the possibility of a unique identity for Asunción, since it has not conserved its colonial past as have other Latin American centers such as Lima, Valparaíso, Cuzco, and La Habana. Indeed, according to Rubiani, the corrosion of its inhabitants' behavior and manners has led to the deterioration of Asunción's reputation, since the 1930s or 1940s, over the second half of the twentieth century. Even though Asunción in the 1930s and 1940s "manifested itself in decipherable and recognizable codes" and "the citizens had a clear idea of the 'place' they inhabited" (17), the chronicler claims that "a visible reduction in environmental quality" went hand in hand with "the deterioration of social conduct" (17). He argues that for the capital to reflect the Paraguayan character, clarity of place must be restored verbally and visually to reveal and construct an urban identity.

Like Prieto, Rubiani seeks to add depth to the perception of the city, to elicit the pride of its inhabitants. A palimpsest that includes the written and photographic representation of the colonial city serves to recreate Asunción's collective memory, barely perceptible in Asunción's streets. By reviving historical anecdotes related to the urban experience of Asunción, he emphasizes the city's fictionalized image that appeals to the tendency to romanticize the past; to this end, he traces the trajectory of the outsider's perception of the city. Spanish colonists assigned Asunción the nickname of "Mohammed's paradise" (36) because it was said that they could enjoy many Guaraní women without marrying them. American indigenous populations perceived Paraguay as "a mythic, idyllic place, a prize for those who would get to know it" (122). In contrast, Rubiani notes, Domingo Faustino Sarmiento made scathing comments about the people of Paraguay; in a description of his entrance to Asunción in 1869, the Argentine intellectual and politician critiqued the character of both the ruling dictator and the people: "Thousands of animals who obey him and die of fear accompany the phrenetic, idiotic, brutish and fierce drunk Solano López. . . . It was necessary to purge the earth of all of the human excrement: a lost race from whose contagion we must liberate ourselves" (quoted in Rubiani 2002, 102). Foreign perceptions, both utopian and dystopian, exoticize the country; in this way, Rubiani underscores how Paraguay and Asunción were thought about and imagined by outsiders, resurrecting their exaggerated, romanticized views.

An analysis of two images, a postcard and a photograph, from Rubiani's volume exemplifies his approach toward the reconstruction of Asunción through its past. These pieces are two of over two hundred postcards, photographs, portraits, sketches, and collages that illustrate the articles. Although most show buildings, landscapes, cityscapes, or political figures from the nineteenth and twentieth centuries, there are also twelve photographs of the Guaraní engaged in their traditional lifestyle. Included are images of indigenous families, with men, women, and children all topless, posing for the camera; the back of a naked man holding arrows in one hand and a large fish in the other; and a shaman treating a man who is lying on the ground among some reeds. These photographs elicit a contrast with the European lifestyle, and their inclusion as reflection of the "exotic" indigenous lifestyle underscores Rubiani's Europeanized perspective.

Along with the few reproductions of sketches and paintings that illustrate aspects of the colonial era, the photographs of rural Paraguayan life in the twentieth century are used to evoke the country's pre-independence history. Accompanying the section "The Beginnings," which recounts the founding of Asunción, a postcard (figure 7) depicts men, women and children of various ages involved in processing corn for starch, the group posed beneath a thatched roof completely open to the elements on three sides. Two of the seated women are wearing cloths as head covers, and the third sports a hat with a design that recalls the colors of indigenous handicrafts. The one wall at the back of the structure is a series of vertical wooden boards loosely pulled together. Accord-

FIGURE 7. Milling corn at a farm in the interior of Paraguay (Charles Muller Collection; courtesy of Jorge Rubiani)

ing to Rubiani's caption, both rural and urban homes consisted of this modest form of dwelling that had not, until recently, changed in style since the first colonial constructions over 450 years before; Rubiani also includes the image of a school class inside a similar structure.

In itself, the format of a postcard that involves the photographing of a so-called typical scene (obviously by someone not a member of the social group being photographed) for the purpose of advertising the country to the outside world develops the romanticization of place with which Rubiani engages his reader. The postage stamp, dated 1904, and the somewhat legible handwriting that has bled through from the other side of the card both contribute further to this process. The postcard of the corn workers underscores the country's poverty and the perpetuation of poor labor conditions and wages. Of course, because of the vast differences in quality of life in the Paraguayan capital, the members of the educated class there (as in other urban centers in Latin America) relate more to Europeanized perceptions and worldviews, an attitude apparent in Rubiani's presentation of this historic image. By imagining the simplicity of life in the earlier era and connecting its traditional lifestyle with that of twentieth-century Asunción, the educated Rubiani, personally protected from these conditions, is detached from his subject and afforded a distanced perspective that equates his view with that of an outsider.

FIGURE 8. Calle Palma, Asunción (Charles Muller Collection; courtesy of Jorge Rubiani)

In another image (figure 8), this time a photograph, Rubiani encourages pride in Asunción's European heritage. Here, the heart of a Europeanized downtown is depicted at the turn of the twentieth century: the words *gran* and *francesa* can be made out on the side of a large building; Rubiani points out in the caption that the Societá Italiana is portrayed in the photograph and that the Centro Español was located on the next block. A scene of a modernized city, this photograph depicts people dressed in European attire, the men in suits and the women in full-length dresses, hurrying on their business along the sidewalk next to a cobblestoned street.

The two contrasting views of Asunción lifestyle in these images provide a conflicting but enticing vision of the Paraguayan capital. By offering anecdotal snapshots of the past, Rubiani surrounds Asunción in an appealing aura that contrasts with the modernizing drive adopted from Europeanized conceptions that equate modernity with progress. Nelly Richard describes the Europeanized perception of modernity as a "metropolitan fantasy" that "rendered absolute the value of the New" (260). Current discussions of modernity regard the Latin American version as a cultural heterogeneity, which Richard defines succinctly as "a heterodox modernity that juxtaposes dissimilar fragments of social temporality in a 'collage' of memories and experiences that shatter the uniform-standardization of programmed consumption by the North American hegemony" (261). Although Rubiani's collection of historical descriptions and anecdotes begins to reconceive Asunción's identity in light of this more complete contemporary understanding of Latin American modernity, he falls short, given his recurring reliance on nostalgia, of constructing an image of this city to replace the initial Europeanized understanding.

The conventional Westernized notion of modernity as progress is portrayed by Rubiani as counterproductive for the reconstruction of Asunción's identity. However, the chronicler's perspective remains so defined by historical occurrences that the past overshadows attempts at a contemporary intellectual reconception of the Paraguayan city. Most strikingly, Rubiani reveals his consternation at Francia's urban reforms of 1821, almost two centuries earlier. As if it were possible and desirable to return to the colonial era, he repeatedly argues for the "natural" city rather than the ordered one designed by Francia. In Rubiani's perspective, before Francia's changes, Asunción was "a faithful reflection of itself. The city in its state of natural grace. 'Orderedly' anarchical" (286), whereas Francia's reforms caused Asunción to lose "all of its most genuine delights" (61). Instead of approaching the past as part of the urban palimpsest, Rubiani remains so connected to it that he argues against the dictator's decision. Although not falling into the same argumentation as Prieto, who clearly equates modernity with the Europeanized concept of progress, Rubiani also does not move toward the representation of cultural heterogeneity that defines more current conceptualizations of Latin American modernity. Rather, the author remains intellectually, and even emotionally, linked to past episodes that no longer centrally define the Paraguayan capital, and which survive best as textures of the palimpsest.

In this sense, Rubiani does not temper nostalgia, as does Prieto, by endorsing urban reforms of the contemporary city. Instead, he claims that a successful urban center is constructed through spontaneous, organic growth, rather than through planned development. Although Rubiani seeks to modify the image of the past, apparently to rectify common assumptions about the utopian nature of the city's beginning, or about the supposed lack of racial discrimination in colonial Asunción, he remains nostalgically attached to the romanticized anecdotes and reproaches the limited vision of the people in power in both the colonial and the contemporary city alike. Rubiani finds egregious the lack of restoration work performed currently, blaming it on the "governments and businesses" who have been "voracious in their mediocrity and without the historical consciousness to invest in even one restoration project" (221). His blatant attack on the condition of today's cityscape as a result of historical apathy appropriates the nostalgic impressions to foment changes in current attitudes.

Although both Prieto and Rubiani attempt to endear their readers to Asunción through some combination of the romanticization of the past with the hope for an auspicious future, their representations ignore the recent violent chapter of the city's history, the oppression associated in particular with the Stroessner dictatorship. This politically uncompromised approach conforms to the norm in contemporary Paraguayan literature, although there are some authors whose work is deeply political. Francisco Corral, in *Los años robados a Emilio Barreto* (2003), for example, creates disturbing associations between the prison and the city during the Stroessner era through the story of Emilio Barreto, a contemporary asunceno artist who was twice wrongfully imprisoned. Similarly, although dealing with political unrest after the dictatorship, in *El país en una plaza* (2004), Andrés Colmán Gutiérrez entwines political meaning with personal and national identity in his interpretation of the March uprising on the downtown governmental plaza in 1999.[6]

Although the reasons for Prieto and Rubiani's silence regarding the emotional impact of twentieth-century political history are not addressed, their reticence is most likely unrelated to attitudes, such as those of post-Holocaust writers, that consider the possibility for any form of artistic representation of trauma extremely problematic. Emblemized by Theodor T. Adorno's oft-quoted statement in 1949 that to write poetry after Auschwitz was barbaric, the German postwar literary movement became distinctly experimental in its incessant search for a new language that would not bear the mark of the past. During and after dictatorships in Latin America, experimental art and writing were taken up also as a means to avoid censorship, most prominently in recent times during Augusto Pinochet's regime in Chile.[7] The memory of military rule has also had a residual effect on urban landscapes, in which edifices and memorials remind residents of the recent violent past. In Buenos Aires, numerous current cultural projects purposefully weave the memory of the dictatorship into urban architecture; poignant examples of these endeavors include the Memory Park erected on a location by the Río de la Plata where many of the disappeared were drowned during the Dirty War; the Madres de Plaza de Mayo's conversion of the notorious center for detention and torture, the Escuela Superior de Mecánica de la Armada (the ESMA), into a cultural center that opened its doors in June 2008; and the *baldosas* project, which commemorates the disappeared with the placement of engraved sidewalk tiles in front of their former homes.

Unlike its southern neighbor, Paraguay has not yet engaged, on a significant scale, in the essential cultural projects that help redefine meaning for the urban landscape; the work of writers such as Corral and Colmán Gutiérrez and the earlier work of Roa Bastos serve only as a beginning for this necessary and momentous undertaking that allows a nation to cope with the memory of mass-scale oppression. No significant public memorials have been erected in Paraguay to commemorate the victims of the regime, likely in part because the democratic era only opened definitively with the election of Fernando Lugo, the first non-Colorado president in sixty-one years, in April 2008.

Indeed, most literary treatments of Asunción in the late twentieth century follow the same uncompromised approach as that of Prieto and Rubiani, reflecting rather an interest in the country's increasing urbanization. The works of Mario Halley Mora are cited most frequently as asunceno novels. Although there were a few isolated examples of novels set in Asunción during the first half of the twentieth century,[8] his *La quema de Judas* (1965) is considered the first of this genre. Since then, all his works give special prominence to Asunción. *Los hombres de Celina* (1981), for example, uses the formal structure of a Bildungsroman to tell the story of a young boy who moves from his rural home to mature and seek success in the city. In the detective novel *Memoria adentro* (1989), Halley Mora recounts the history of Asunción from the 1930s alongside the plot of a murder case. This time Asunción emerges as a degrading site, rife with criminal activity spawned by events such as the revolution of 1947. Another example of asunceno literature is Margot Ayala de Michelagnoli's novel *Ramona Quebranto* (1992), distinct for its reproduction of the colloquial language of *jopará*, a mixture of Guaraní and Spanish, to represent one of the poorest neighborhoods of Asunción, the barrio of Chacarita (Peiró Barco 1466).[9] Although Ayala de Michelagnoli reflects on the poverty of the neighborhood through the voice of the protagonist, Ramona, the novel does not go so far as to present an alternative to social inequality. Even the technical innovation of writing in jopará recalls European works written in local dialect, such as Galician or Basque, Bavarian or Viennese German, to reflect the identity of people and place.

Notwithstanding these few examples, significant literary production dealing with the city in Paraguay is scarce. As Néstor García Canclini has remarked in *Hybrid Cultures*, other Latin American cities have enjoyed an "exuberance" of modernity with respect to cultural production in relation to politics and the economics of daily life. Modernity in this context becomes a simulacrum enjoyed by the elite who cultivate artistic production, but do not share the same reality experienced by the majority of citizens (García Canclini 1995, 7). Paraguay has had to struggle to develop even in this one significant, albeit elitist, area. There are, of course, several outstanding Paraguayan artists: the novelist Roa Bastos and the composer and guitarist Agustín Barrios-Mangoré perhaps being the most well known. But among Paraguayans there has developed a need to underscore the importance of their country's contributions to Western-style arts, a need that leads frequently to reproduction of textual forms imitative of

Euroamerican expressions from previous eras rather than to innovation particular to the region and time.

Temporal and spatial comparisons with historical or foreign models continue to guide asunceno perspectives to the detriment of other possible, more complex representations. Although Paraguayan authors proudly represent Asunción, they also find their most appropriate forms of expression in Euroamerican designs, demonstrating a blinkered vision of their surroundings that encompasses both the desire to return to their colonial past and the drive toward modernization. Ana M. López has defined this complexity as characteristic of Latin American modernity, "a global, intertextual experience, addressing impulses and models from abroad, in which every nation and region created, and creates, its own ways of playing with and at modernity" (49). In Paraguay, authors have embedded local themes into Euroamerican genres and styles, evident in Halley Mora's Bildungsroman and detective fiction, Ayala de Michelagnoli's colloquial novel, and Prieto's and Rubiani's chronicles.

Among these examples of contemporary Paraguayan literary forms, the urban chronicle has the greatest potential for thematic renewal and innovation with respect to the representation of the city, given the liberating nature of its formal structure. With a stylistic and expressive freedom unavailable in other genres, the chronicle accepts not only the mixture of fiction with the so-called objective approach of newspaper reportage, but also the combination of social analysis and literary creativity. Although the genre has flourished recently in various forms in Latin America, it has its origins in colonial descriptions of the New World as an exotic space as well as in the *costumbrista* sketches characteristic of Romanticism.[10] Hispanic *modernista* authors such as José Martí, Manuel Gutiérrez Nájera, and Rubén Darío famously initiated the use of this genre for the depiction of the city,[11] using chronicles, according to Aníbal González, as "literary laboratories" for experimentation in expression and ideas (1993, 84).

Contemporary Latin American chroniclers have exploited the genre's versatility to the full. This is perhaps nowhere more evident than in the work of Mexican chronicler Carlos Monsiváis, who insists on the literary aspect of the genre in his definition of chronicle as a "*literary* reconstruction of events and figures, a genre in which the formal effort dominates the informative urgencies" (13; original emphasis).[12] His witty and erudite sketches of contemporary life in Mexico, particularly Mexico City, move freely among anecdote, philosophical prose, journalistic commentary, fiction, and poetry; his readable writing style incorporates an intellectual rigor through which he brings to the fore the experience of the subaltern and marginalized and provides incisive analyses of population explosion, the overwhelming influence of television and film on society, the politics of globalization, religiosity, and the obsession with football and wrestling, among other topics.

Although Monsiváis has exploited the genre further than other contemporary authors, the chronicle has thrived in Latin America since the turn of this century. Mexican writers Juan Villoro, Elena Poniatowska, and José Joaquín Blanco have written often humorous chronicles that nevertheless describe Mexico City as an apocalyptic space.[13] The Chilean chronicler Pedro Lemebel critiques the privileged classes of Santiago for their oppression of the marginalized, and also represents the contemporary city as a violent site that reflects Pinochet's dictatorship. Urban violence is also underscored by José Roberto Duque and Fabricio Ojeda in their accounts of late-twentieth-century Caracas. From Puerto Rico, Edgardo Rodríguez-Juliá's chronicles in *San Juan, ciudad soñada* (2005) combine poetic representations with personal memories.

The Paraguayan author José María Rivarola Matto uses the chronicle form to parody nostalgic asunceno attitudes in *La Belle Epoque y otras hodas* (1980). He adopts the genre to underscore the truth in his critiques, while also treating his subjects playfully. In this collection of anecdotes, Rivarola Matto ironically calls attention to the glorious exaggerations of hindsight, commenting that, in the early twentieth century, Asunción's unevenly paved roads allowed for animated games of marbles. Clothing styles, he notes, especially the type of hat and the use of shoes, defined the social classes; courting involved chaperones, and a huge effort on the part of the gentleman caller. The author satirizes, too, provincial reactions to technological developments in Paraguay. In one anecdote, a man panics when the first truck in Paraguay has a minor explosion and advances unexpectedly; when he fails to detain it by shooting at the motor, he screams to the crowd for help to tie down the wild creature with lassos. These texts not only poke fun at unsophisticated modalities, but also critique contemporary nostalgic attitudes.

It becomes evident, in this broader context of the Latin American chronicle, that Prieto and Rubiani fail to make full use of the genre's openness to experimentation in style and content. More daring incursions into social memory that would also probe the impact of violence, social and economic inequality and political oppression on the population remain unexplored in their works, leading the reader to query the authors' reticence. More than all else, after all, the liberty of the chronicle allows for the interrogation of difficult topics through the incorporation of personal perspective into a journalistic style. As Susana Rotker argues, the chronicle is particularly suited for a discussion of these types of subjects: "Its hybrid form permits it a (potentially rebellious) value of autonomization in the system of representation while simultaneously allowing it to enjoy the prestige of the space in which it is published: the press as vehicle for exchange and identification, constructor and diffuser of discourses and symbols" (10). In this sense, Prieto's and Rubiani's choices to engage in less heated and more distant debates, such as on nineteenth-century decisions regarding urban design or on contemporary development projects, weakens the impact of their works.

Although both chroniclers advance efforts to build local pride for Asunción, their works do not fully nuance the profundity of the historical and contemporary conflicts faced by the city, nor do they provide innovation on a formal or literary level. The nearness of Asunción's most recent dictatorship excuses them, in part, for their inattention with respect to this violent chapter of their nation's history, forcing them instead to rescue earlier aspects of Asunción's history that risk being relegated to insignificant elements of a peripheral Latin American city. However, far from salvaging the city's deeply peripheral reputation, not just in comparison to global centers (as Buenos Aires is famously characterized by Beatriz Sarlo) but also with regard to cities in neighboring countries, these chroniclers, in their failure to enter into consequential dialogue with contemporary debates on Latin American urban representation, achieve only a further validation of the continued distance between Asunción and other Latin American centers. A revival of the city's historical significance stimulated by current interpretations of urban representation would lead to a more comprehensive and meaningful response to Asunción, one that would include sociopolitical realities essential to any contemporary account of a Latin American city.

Northeastern Images
Recife and Salvador in Contemporary Brazilian Cinema

ANGELA PRYSTHON

When one thinks of cinematographic images of urban Brazil, Rio de Janeiro or São Paulo come to mind almost immediately. One rarely remembers that the most important filmmaker in Brazilian history, Glauber Rocha, was from Salvador, the third most populous city in the country and the capital of the state of Bahia, or that Recife, the fifth largest metropolitan area and the capital of the state of Pernambuco, had an important film industry in the 1920s. Moreover, Recife, Salvador, and the other northeastern cities are not usually conjured up when it comes to notions of the urban, cosmopolitanism, or the city imaginary. Generally, the *sertão* (the hinterland, the dry land) and representations of drought serve as the most powerful metonyms for the Northeast, not only in cinema, but also in other fields of culture. Yet Recife and Salvador certainly have a place in the national imaginary that transcends their association with the *seca* (drought). Both cities have vied in several ways with other northeastern capitals to become the main source of cultural and urban reference for the region. Recife and Salvador have a positive image in Brazil for their tourist attractions, for their sandy and warm-water beaches, for their exotic gastronomy and their popular music. In a more negative vein, both cities are cited for their poverty, violence, and underdevelopment.

During the last two decades, however, perceptions of them have been sharply modified and widened at the same rate as their tourist industry has boomed. Their economies have improved relatively, their popular culture industry has occupied a pivotal role on the national scene, and their rates of violence and crime have risen. But there is another source for a more complex and nuanced understanding of these urban centers: the cinematographic representations spread by the growing film industry in the region, mainly in the state of Pernambuco but also in Bahia and Ceará.

The second half of the 1990s saw a sort of renaissance in the audiovisual arts in Brazil. The film industry boomed, while in the cultural press and academic circles critics began to speak of a Retomada (retaking) in Brazilian Cinema, a very heterogeneous movement that had many critics drawing parallels with Cinema Novo in the 1950s and 1960s. One of its principal characteristics is the emergence of peripheral focuses, not only in terms of content and narrative (which may be considered a kind of extension of the Cinema Novo project), but also with respect to less centralization of production. Not that Rio de Janeiro or São Paulo have ceased to be the main axes of production and distribution for the industry, but that other regions and, more fundamentally, other Brazilian cities (eminently Recife, Porto Alegre, Salvador, and Belo Horizonte) have come to figure more prominently.

This situation was not strictly foreign to Brazilian cultural history of the twentieth century. Recife had already been a very important center for film production in the 1920s and early 1930s with the Ciclo do Recife (Recife Cycle), a movement that resulted in thirteen feature films and some documentaries, or *filmes naturais* (natural films), as they were called at the time. The influence of the cultural environment of Salvador (and of northeastern culture) for the intellectual and artistic formation of many of those involved in the Cinema Novo movement, including its leading figure, the Bahian Glauber Rocha, is also worth mentioning. But it is equally relevant that the roles played by Recife and Salvador in Brazilian culture since the late 1990s are much more decisive and prominent than in previous times, not just in film, obviously, but in popular music (perhaps in a more incisive fashion) and in other arts.

Using contemporary filmic representations of these two cities of northeastern Brazil as the main points of reference, our gaze falls on the movement toward a hybrid, peripheral, and particular cosmopolitanism in the cinema:[1] "It is as the representation of living representation that cinema invites us to reflect upon the imaginary of reality as well as the reality of the imaginary" (Morin 1997, 16). It is in this sense that we affirm the need to analyze cinema through its materiality, above all through the interpretations it offers of reality and the impact it has on the real. The emergence of cinema as one of the most relevant cultural forms since the early twentieth century, and its connections with the development of the metropolises, are the core of a significant portion of cultural studies concerned with the audiovisual arts (Shiel and Fitzmaurice 2001; Barber 2002; Vitali and Willemen 2006), and the present chapter is inscribed in that tradition. It will therefore explore the connections between the urban fabric, that fabric's cinematographic representation, and the forms in which cinema transforms and is transformed by life in the city. Thus the text falls into three sections: discussion of the real and the forms of representation of cities in film; consideration of the mediatic discourse of the cities as a strategy of memory; and, lastly, a direct engagement with the problem of the periphery, both in its more immediate and geographic meaning and in a more expanded sense.

EFFECTS OF THE (UN)REAL

Our first hypothesis is that the *visible cities* in cinema are not necessarily a reflection of the real; they do not correspond to exact simulacra of the real, but very often transform or modify the real. In view of the relationship between the city and cultural media, urban representations in cinema are generally considered superfluous details in comparison with the narrative and structure of the film, in the same sense that Roland Barthes (1984) considers minute realistic descriptions as literary "filler" with respect to the literary text. The inclusion of urban details with no apparent meaning within the plot appears an attempt to obtain a pure and simple representation of the real—in Barthes's terms, the effect of the real: "In other words, the very lack of meaning, for the exclusive sake of reference, becomes the very meaning of realism: it produces an *effect of the real*" (136; original italics).

The urgency to expand the modes of representation of Brazilian reality in the 1990s has led to the multiplication of urban focal points in film. As if demonstrating that the classic trio of sertão/favela/metropolis of Brazilian cinema (epitomized almost exclusively by Rio de Janeiro and São Paulo) were insufficient for the aesthetic and social demands of contemporary cultural paradigms, filmmakers of the Retomada gradually invested in regions of the country other than the ubiquitous Southeast or the ever visible hinterland. In this respect, *Baile perfumado* (Perfumed Ball; 1996), by Paulo Caldas and Lírio Ferreira, was very significant, as it was one of the first films produced in the state of Pernambuco after the long hiatus that followed the Ciclo do Recife and the experimental Super-8 boom of the 1970s, winning several national prizes and critical recognition in the Brazilian press. The film concerns the story of the Lebanese Benjamin Abrahão, the only person who in the 1930s succeeded in filming the notorious bandit Lampião and his gang.[2] The film combines scenes from the cinema of the 1920s, including some from one of the best-known Ciclo do Recife movies, Jota Soares's *A filha do advogado* (The Lawyer's Daughter; 1924), with sequences filmed in colorful Bom Jesus Street in Recife. At the time that *Baile perfumado* was shot, the street had been recently renovated in the style of the Pelourinho, the historic center of Salvador, and of European trends in urban gentrification. Its historic buildings had been painted in extravagant colors, its former brothels transformed into restaurants or tourist shops, and some of its undesirable inhabitants (prostitutes and beggars, mostly) evicted. These images of Recife represent an intention to give moviegoers not only the sensation that the film reveals the life of the people who came to Recife at the beginning of the twentieth century, but the certainty that modernity (with its movie theaters, tramways, cafés, and nightclubs) had arrived at the periphery of capitalism.[3] The images of cities in the cinema have, above all, the primary function of leading to the acceptance of the fictional as real (or at least as an approximation of the real), of promoting a certain appearance of reality, especially when they are documentary and historical images, as in the case of *Baile perfumado.*

Since Bahia provides much of the scenery in television soaps, music videos, and films, its capital, Salvador, is naturally more present in popular culture than Recife. Salvador is also generally taken as a strong symbol of Brazilian identity, especially for its particular context as a kind of black capital for the country. We could refer to Anselmo Duarte's *O pagador de promessas* (Payer of Promises; 1962), for example, to see the city's churches and spaces, the fat black women, and the buildings of the Pelourinho functioning as an index of everyday life in syncretic Brazil. But it is in a film like Monique Gardeberg's *Ó pai, ó!* (Look at This! 2007) that the possibilities of Salvador as a metonym for urban hybridity appear at its most exotic, musical, and colorful. *Ó pai, ó!* is set in Bahia on the first day of Carnival, and we watch the inhabitants (an aspiring singer, a taxi driver, a transvestite, a disillusioned migrant, a fanatical protestant woman and her two young boys, among others) of a lively tenement house located in the Barroquinha Quarter, just below the Pelourinho. Just as *Ó pai, ó!* indeed means "Look at this!" in Bahian dialect, the film turns its lenses toward this private space, a tenement house, to comment on the urban reorganization of the public spaces of Salvador.

Sérgio Machado's *Cidade Baixa* (Lower City; 2005) also displays some of Salvador's better-known landmarks, evidently choosing those related to the area referred to in its title. The film revolves around two childhood friends who own a small steamboat in Bahia. They both fall in love with a young prostitute named Karina, who performs striptease in a seedy nightclub in Salvador. The two friends, Deco and Naldinho, end up fighting in the streets of the lower part of the city while residents open the windows of their dilapidated two-story homes to watch the scuffle. In a similar vein, the final credits of the film show men, women, children, buildings, and symbols of a city that do not usually appear in travel brochures. Apart from being extremely photogenic, Salvador serves in *Ó paí, ó!* and *Cidade Baixa* as a much more emphatic sketch of national identity than does Recife, and as a panoramic sample of lower-class reality.

But how can we speak of the "effect of the real" if, in general, the cities in the cinema are often marked with an aura of unreality? These images, even when captured directly from the real (from actual, existing cities), even when they preserve the exactness of precise references, transmit a fantasy of a city. Very often it is a stereotype, a cliché: it is not Salvador or Recife that is *really* at play in these representations, but images of these cities that suit the average expectations of an urban idealization (in senses both positive and negative). The mediatic urban representation is very often the result of an expected mosaic of postcards or documentary newsreel images (especially Salvador, with its prominent touristic avocation, or the favelas in general as an index of Brazilian urban violence).

From this mosaic, it is even possible to delimit some frontiers between cities in one film or another. Take, for instance, the Recife of Cláudio Assis's *Amarelo manga* (Mango Yellow; 2003), a film that addresses the miserable lives of various inhabitants of the impoverished city center, especially the residents of the Texas Hotel, a filthy, rundown building. Here, the city is markedly decadent, polluted, rotten. It is obviously very different from the sunny bohemian and affluent Recife of Lírio Ferreira's *Árido movie* (2006),[4] a story about a TV weatherman who returns to his hometown in the interior of Pernambuco for the funeral of his father. This, in turn, is of course quite different from the civilized, modern, cosmopolitan Recife in *Baile perfumado*, or the broken, violent, and impoverished city in Paulo Caldas and Marcelo Luna's *O rap do pequeno príncipe contra as almas sebosas* (The Little Prince's Rap against the Wicked Souls; 2001), a documentary showing the parallel paths of two young men, a vigilante and a rap musician from Camaragibe, a destitute suburb of metropolitan Recife. There are similarities, recurring elements, and continuities between the different Recifes, and these films possibly even converge into a sole narrative of the Northeast, but the filmmakers assert their desire to transcend the commonplace of northeastern representation and undoubtedly succeed in magnifying the effects of the real intended in their sequences focused on Recife.

Cinematographic cities at times appear a response to some kind of dissatisfaction with the real city. They insist on an image of urban tranquillity, although this is more common in certaub films that refer to Rio de Janeiro and are concerned with showing a wealthy, modern, hybrid Brazil.[5] Thus it is important to stress the kind of encapsulation performed by this type of city in the cinema, an encapsulation that seeks to substitute for experience through mediation, as a kind of consolation or even utopian projection in contrast with the harsh day-to-day reality of the actual cities. On the other hand, there are also some films intent on "denouncing" cities, where the urban representation seeks to reveal a city closer to the real, and more faithful to daily experience. These cities are akin to those of the newspapers and television news; they are the opposite of the expected postcard images. In them, we almost step outside the territory of the "effect of the real" toward an explicit attempt at a transposition of the real, an endeavoring to enter the realm of a perfect simulacrum. This is evident in parts of the films already mentioned, as in the scenes depicting Salvador's carnival, the images of the pursuit and killing of two street boys in *Ó pai, ó!*, in some documentary segments in the middle of *Amarelo manga,* and in the final credits of *Cidade Baixa*, which are run against a kind of nonfictional account of the district referenced in the title. In these sequences, the city comes across as an open wound, simultaneously symptom and consequence of the decline of urban life in contemporary Brazil.

URBAN MEMORIES

Another relevant aspect of the cinematographic cities is their function as a source of memory. The visible cities of the cinema provide a good sample of the almost invariably paradoxical relationship between media and memory and, to some extent, between the real and the mythic. As noted already, in the mediated narrative of the cities a relationship of absolute proximity to the real prevails at times. Experience is overlapped by mediation, so that *what* is being represented no longer matters: the city—the banal or bizarre, quotidian or extraordinary, insipid or rare urban experience—is no longer the referent; it loses its referential function and what matters is the very act of representation, the *moment* of representation. At other times, the cities are a mere artifice of approximation to the real, signs of a referent that does not always exist. In one form or another, such representations end up determining a kind of urban mediatic museum with the most diverse matrices: "These are the memories necessary in order to construct differentiated future locales in a global world. There is no doubt that in the long term all these memories will be modelled to a large extent by digital technologies and their effects, but they will not be reducible to such technologies. Insisting on a radical separation between 'real' and virtual memory shocks me as much as any Quixotism, because anything remembered—by the experienced or imagined memory—is virtual in its very nature" (Huyssen 2000, 37).

The real urban configurations of documentaries and their fictional counterparts demonstrate this museum-like inclination. Again, contemporary cities (and not just those of the cinema) are oriented toward a very strong appeal to images, to stereotypes. Through a Disneyfied conception of history, these cities need to seduce through artifices and highlight their attributes: the louder and gaudier the better, for the perpetuation of this urban memory.

Thus, cities can no longer be sober or discreet on either the real or the representational plane. From the standpoint of urban planning and material configurations, the contemporary city seems to have two options: become a caricature of itself (with excesses of make-up and a certain false nostalgia—the bizarre idea of revitalization); or invest in the poorly made parody of an archetypical Los Angeles (a succession of an ever greater number of post-metropolises scattered and fragmented throughout the world). In general, we live on the border between these two options, but it is not a peaceful border, nor are its lines very clear. There is not even a very clear internal prescription for the two conceptions: the caricature constantly rebels against its "historical" referent, imposing new uses, involuntarily betraying its own normative tackiness, while the parody of Los Angeles is invariably invaded by shantytowns.

From the standpoint of representation, this image excess is quite evident in the cinema. The idea of urban caricatures may be related to many films in recent Brazilian cinema, including those from the Northeast already mentioned. In Ó pai, ó! the intention to compose a regional, attractive, and multifaceted portrait of contemporary Brazil for global audiences led to a somewhat clichéd, touristic, and, in the end, empty attempt. Most of the scenes have the manifest goal of cataloguing the vibrant gallery of urban specimens of the Pelourinho, and some sequences could be mistaken for music videos by the celebrated Bahian bands Olodum and Araketu; there is an exuberance of local color, an almost redundant emphasis on the vernacular, especially in the carnival scenes and in the composition of some characters' accents, hairstyles, and costumes.

Amarelo manga also presents these caricatured exaggerations, particularly in the journeys of the necrophiliac Isaac through the city center in his stylish vintage car. But, in fact, the other characters and their life stories are all haunted by a decadent imaginary. The film constructs its short and intermingled narratives on the basis of a very resolute notion of a collective space—namely, Recife, or more precisely its central streets, the Avenida Bar, the slaughterhouse, and, most prominently, the Texas Hotel—establishing an almost naturalistic determinism. Further, in an urgency to show the cruder aspects of underworld life and decadent conducts, the alleys, markets, bars, and bridges of Recife are photographed in a highly baroque mode—set in the most immoderate tone possible, with all their color, noise, putrefaction, and filth. One can almost smell some of the scenes.

Although it concentrates more on a very small village in the interior of Pernambuco, *Árido movie* still emphasizes the modernity symbolized by Recife. As if to register the contrast between the brutality and barrenness of the hinterland and the (underdeveloped) modernity of the city, the cameras, whenever there are shots of Recife, invest primarily in the wealthy residential buildings of the Boa Viagem district and the bars downtown frequented by the protagonist's young hippie friends. These sequences imply that it was necessary for the protagonist, a television weather announcer named Jonas, to return to Recife, not only the nucleus of his formation but the inescapable place of passage for his journey to the interior. Although he no longer much identifies with his almost permanently drugged *recifense* friends, and is so distant from his upper-middle-class mother that he calls her by her first name, the camera decidedly chronicles this Recife as a pivotal vestige of Jonas's past.

ON THE OUTSKIRTS OF THE PERIPHERY

Finally, it is important to consider how the modes of urban representation reflect the gaps in contemporary urban Brazil, the permanent tension between the center and the periphery of Brazilian society, the immense space that separates classes, ethnicities, and cultural origins. This is also to highlight, to some extent, certain singularities in the contemporary conception of the periphery (in its varied senses), particularly as seen in the Recife of *O rap do pequeno príncipe contra as almas sebosas* and *Amarelo manga* and in the Salvador of *Cidade Baixa*. Insofar as we sound the depths of the concept of periphery, we may conclude that the Brazilian Northeast could be very properly defined as the periphery of the periphery, as a place in the national imaginary that is at the margins of the margins, in relation to Brazil and to the world.

The films previously mentioned address diverse orders of marginality and subalternity suggested by their characters and situations: poverty, black awareness, homosexuality, prostitution, urban decadence, and public disorder. They align with a form of representation that features a cosmopolitan reconfiguration based on the periphery, or as Silviano Santiago puts it, a "cosmopolitanism of the poor" (2004), what I have called "peripheral cosmopolitanism" (Prysthon 2002a). The images presented in these films are closer to the most current mode of multiculturalism, in counterpoint to an archaic and condescending praise of the melting pot. In a rather eloquent manner, they seek to distance themselves from the official image of national identity, to detach themselves from the bureaucratic record of history, and (to some extent uselessly) to delineate a point of view of the subaltern—an instance of a more direct representation of the peripheral layers of Brazilian society.

The growing profusion of images of periphery, subalternity, and excluded individuals in the Brazilian media is irrefutable (Prysthon 2003, 2005), especially since the 1990s, after the cosmopolitan enthusiasm over postmodern culture had subsided (Prysthon 2002b). The representation of issues, characters, styles, places, and situations regarding local identities, peripheries, and differences of one or several "Brazilian essences" seems to be the emphasis of most national cultural production. As the defining trait of recent decades in all spheres of culture in the audiovisual realm, such Brazilian essence is configured as virtually an absolute norm, a recipe for success: somewhat ironically, audiovisual culture in Brazil seems to be contributing energetically (even if the process is not always conscious and systematic) toward the constitution of a canon of the periphery.

In the developing cinematographic production of the Brazilian Northeast, there is a patent adhesion to this canon. The purpose of *O rap do pequeno príncipe contra as almas sebosas* (hereafter, *O rap*) seems to be to demonstrate that the excluded have two distinct paths stemming from their condition. In an attempt to overcome an inherent Manichaeism, the film seeks to excavate and intensify the implications entrenched in these choices: "The documentary shows that, amid the socio-urban chaos, there are two possibilities: the first is presented by Garnizé, who becomes involved in music and social projects in an attempt to overcome adversity. On the other hand, Helinho becomes a vigilante in order to "cure" the problem of violence in Camaragibe, which yields a positive image for him in the eyes of the community. By making statements that praise Helinho's activities, we see that the notions of 'evil' and 'good' are both mutable and relative" (Souza 2006, 56). However, what is of most interest is the way in which some scenes of *O rap* objectify the peripheral subject. Shohat and Stam (2002, 190–91) speak of a "burden of representation" that carries with it an entrenched series of stereotypes as well as aesthetic, religious, political, and semiotic connotations. Of all recent films, *O rap* is the most thus "burdened," perhaps by being a documentary and therefore supposedly representing the real in a relatively direct fashion. Nonetheless, its process of objectification of the periphery does not differ all that much from that of fictional cinema.

Some of the more revealing scenes in *O rap* are those in which the vigilante's mother appears. A series of extreme close-ups focusing on parts of her face alternate on the screen, with a strong emphasis less on what the woman is saying and more on the numbing aesthetic effects that the proximity to her mouth, cheeks, eyes, and nose provoke. At another point in the film, Helinho (who would be killed by prison inmates some time after the filming) appears in a cell (or room) of the Aníbal Bruno Penitentiary in a sequence that features nearly the same resources of camera moves and framing as used in the scene with his mother. His face is contrasted with a colorful background of printed cotton fabric—a contrast consistent with the taste of the *mangue* aesthetic,[6] with which, admittedly, Pernambuco filmmakers, including Caldas and Luna, dialogued. The appearance of one of the more caricatural figures in the documentary (the suburban police chief in charge of Helinho's case) embodies the mechanism of stylization of subalternity undertaken by this type of cinema, in the most elucidative way. With his fake Ray-Bans, 1970s sense of fashion and boorish posturing, the police chief serves as much the purpose of comic relief (the directors having wanted, perhaps, to relieve some of the heavy context of violence in the film) as the affirmation that the subaltern is, above all, stylish. The subaltern, the peripheral, the excluded, the marginal: this subject/object of contemporary culture is elevated not only as a theoretical category, but also as an aesthetic element, a stylistic resource.

In comparison with *O rap*, the film *Amarelo manga* perhaps presents a peripheral urban world in living flesh in an excessive but not caricatural fashion by pushing the limits of the grotesque (as if losing control over its characters and plots, as if the grotesque were spilling over) while, at the same time, avoiding any type of paternalism or sentimentalism in relation to urban degradation, poverty, and misery in its portrait of contemporary Recife. The film accentuates a certain aesthetization of the subaltern (apparently one of the more evident marks of contemporary Brazilian cinema) and of the city, foregrounding the characterization of eccentric pariahs and the attractive ugliness of objects, costumes, and locations in a most acerbic manner. Several parallel stories are told, from that of the necrophiliac Isaac to those of the adulterous butcher, the modest churchgoer, the camp homosexual, the asthmatic fat woman, and the exasperated bar owner. These constitute a mosaic of undeniably unique images, giving a view of the periphery as an aberration. Paradoxically, scenes from everyday life and figures representing ordinary people also appear, creating a documentary counterpoint to the overwhelming fiction of some of the main and secondary characters: "Other contradictions: the characters of this hellish sitcom are at times ludicrous to the point of appearing to be stars of a freak show that, once in a while, sends someone bleeding to the hospital. On the other hand, the characters also resemble people (on the street, in the bar, at the barbershop) that you know, to whom you talk or simply say hello. Is this film real, theatrical or a shock performance in the style of Grand Guignol? The confusion is healthy and notable" (Mendonça Filho 2003).

The confusion of which the critic speaks, besides being an interesting aesthetic element, perhaps increases *Amarelo manga*'s density with regard to the representation of the subaltern. By alternating between freak hyperbole and ethnographic naturalism, confronting likely characters (the true-believer, the tough homosexual, the bar owner, the hotel owner, the butcher) and unlikely characters (the necrophiliac, the fat woman, the priest, the indigenous family in the lobby of the Texas Hotel), the film simultaneously points to both the impossibility and the urgency of the appropriate representation of subalternity, and to a discussion of the peripheries of Brazilian cities, particularly Recife. In a certain manner, the film annuls the possibilities of sensationalism, in part by being *excessively* grotesque and sensationalist, in part by extreme naturalism.

Amarelo manga effectively distances itself from a possible official interpretation of Brazil, for its carnality, its excesses, and its boorishness construct a mosaic of cultural differences that are not easily appeased, homogenized, or classified. It is not an NGO cinema, to paraphrase the apt expression of Ismail Xavier (in Leite Neto 2003), referring to productions such as *City of God* (2002) or *Carandiru* (2003). Nor does *Amarelo manga* have the symptoms of a full-blown "cosmetics of hunger," to employ the term used by Ivana Bentes (2001) to compare contemporary Brazilian cinema to the Cinema Novo. By not being an authorized variant, an established transcription within the mainstream, or perhaps by not opting for either the exaggeration of the grotesque or a description of the typical, *Amarelo manga* possibly manages to represent the subaltern in a direction less marked by (positive and negative) preconceived notions. It offers characters more autonomous in relation to either a condescending version or a disdainful translation of the inhabitants living on the outskirts of the periphery.

The trio of drifters in *Cidade Baixa*, a kind of *Jules et Jim* from the state of Bahia, brings to the screen a more delicate manner of presenting the image of the subaltern and urban decay in the Brazilian Northeast. The excluded individuals of a love triangle (the prostitute Karina and two handymen, Deco and Naldinho, owners of a small steamboat) wander through the backstreets, alleys, and two-story homes of the neighborhood known as Cidade Baixa in Salvador, revealing a city quite different from the expected clichés of *axé* music and Bahia culture for export. The Salvador of *Cidade Baixa* is not the sun-drenched parade of partying black figures, in the fashion of *Ó pai, ó*, or the carnival of second-rate celebrities seen on Brazilian television. It is rather a meeting place for the most varied pariahs: stevedores, street vendors, prostitutes, sailors, street-fair merchants, small-time mobsters. The most unique characteristic of this ensemble, however, is the discretion with which it is presented. In an almost contradictory manner, *Cidade Baixa* maintains some ties with *Amarelo manga*, especially in a comparison of the minidocumentaries of the former to the final credits in the latter, the images of houses in ruins, the Modelo market, its characters, and even its utensils and trinkets. But, distanced from *Amarelo manga*'s hyperbolic urgency or from the touristic exoticism of *Ó paí, ó*, the images of the periphery in *Cidade Baixa* do not seek style so eagerly and are not presented as a travel brochure.

Nonetheless, identifying the discretion with which the periphery is presented in Machado's film is not the same as saying that stereotypes are entirely absent. It is more appropriate to say that there is an attenuation of the typical, but this attenuation still occurs within the film's parameters; the peripheral subjects are discreet; they are "mild," while still embodying the expectations of the canon of the periphery, as the documentary sequence accompanying the final credits demonstrates in a manner even more emblematic. The documentary character of this sequence seems to state that the filmmakers want to show the Cidade Baixa that exists in real life; it stresses, decidedly, that their film is also an account of the *bairro* from which they took their title. Filming these anonymous individuals, showing average people walking through the streets of Salvador (reinstating a degree of normality to the trio of protagonists through the normality of the commonplace), is also to seek a synchronization with the spirit of the times, with "this new, indispensable manner of conceiving politics in the realm of culture on a global level" (Shohat and Stam 2002, 329).

To consider the role of the city in culture necessarily involves a reading of urban cinematographic representations as fundamental parts of a communications and cultural system, but, more than that, demands an understanding of how a city is both transformed and transforms itself via its mediatic representations. Recife and Salvador are not suddenly being reinvented through the motifs presented in the films and all the visibility accomplished by the growing film industry in the Northeast in recent years, but they are unequivocally more present and more perceived in the Brazilian contemporary culture industry, and in more unexpected ways, than ever before. Even a superficial analysis of recent developments in films focused on the urban environments of northeast Brazil, especially with respect to the outskirts of the periphery (which accounts for most of the characters in all films discussed here and, for that matter, for most of the inhabitants of the region), highlights uncommon, if not completely new, perceptions of Brazilian urban life. Such an analysis reveals, undeniably, a facet of a country that is not much heard from or even thought of in mainstream media.

Even if the incipient northeastern film industry is still at a precarious stage of its development and irrelevant in international terms, it has had a tremendous impact in the everyday lives of many people in Recife and Salvador and in other parts of the region. The Ministério da Cultura and its local agencies are investing significantly in the audiovisual arts in the Northeast, through specific and general measures and partnerships with the private sector. Several local video and film festivals have been established in the region and are financing the first works of young filmmakers. Major television networks and small production companies have been promoting and/or funding a movement in documentary production. Recife has had one of the most popular film festivals in Brazil, since 1997. A significant number of film courses and workshops have taken place in the two principal cities and in several smaller ones in the region. And two northeastern federal universities, the Universidade Federal da Bahia in Salvador and the Universidade Federal de Pernambuco in Recife, have both introduced graduate programs in Cinema Studies. These ways in which society is affected by the products of the cinema industry are all evidence, at the most basic levels, of the economic relationship between the city and the cinema. However, as the preceding commentary on several films has shown, the conjunction of the two has also had an aesthetic and cultural impact. The expansion of the cinema industry has opened up a vein of images and alternative stories suggested by the urban contexts of Recife and Salvador that have begun to significantly impact perceptions of Brazil itself.

PERFORMANCE AND THE RITUALIZATION OF URBAN IDENTITIES

Performing Citizenship
Migration, Andean Festivals, and Public Spaces in Lima

GISELA CÁNEPA

n the 1990s, political demonstrations were no longer held in downtown Lima, especially at the Plaza Mayor, which was not reclaimed by civil society until 2000 during the movement to bring down Alberto Fujimori. The absence of demonstrations reflected the control over the internal war achieved by Fujimori's civil dictatorship, as well as a process of "depoliticization of politics" (Comaroff and Comaroff 2001) promoted by his government. Fujimori's 1990 campaign slogan was "Honesty, Technology, and Work," which he dramatically applied in 1992 when he shut down the congress on the grounds that the political class had proven itself inefficient and ought to be replaced by the regime's new generation of technocrats.

Work on the restoration of Lima's Historic Center (Centro Histórico), begun during this period, also contributed to the depoliticization of public space. The restoration was part of a project by the city government undertaken in the context of UNESCO's declaration of Lima as a Cultural Heritage Site in 1991. The heritage designation of the city center also brought developments in public policy intended to solve the problems of urban decay, overcrowding, crime, and pollution, and to create a modern infrastructure to administer, sustain, and protect the center. Moreover, the project was conceived in the context of economic policies promoting tourism as a way out of underdevelopment. It was not, however, part of a process of deindustrialization such as often figures prominently in studies, in urban anthropology, on the social and economic life of the city in the context of globalization (Low 1999, 12–14). Since Lima never was an industrial city (see Golte and Adams 1987), it is difficult to argue that it has undergone a process of deindustrialization, even if there are clear signs that its recent cultural and economic development correspond to late capitalism. Having become itself an object of consumption, Lima is above all a city oriented to a consumer economy. This process implies its objectification as "scenographic sites" (Boyer, quoted in Low 1999, 16) and its conversion into heritage as an identifiable public property. In the terms of cultural capitalism, the city has been turned into an object over which players such as the state, the church, private enterprise, and cultural organizations claim symbolic or economic rights or the right to protect and oversee.

Formulated in the discourses of hygiene, public safety, and cultural authenticity, the restoration project ran the gamut from the elimination of itinerant vendors to the renovation of colonial and republican buildings and the resurrection and promotion of criollo cultural traditions and festivities. The language of restoration appealed to the feelings of nostalgia among the traditional Lima elite, who had watched *their* city transformed by the presence of migrants, mainly from the Andean provinces, who had been arriving for the past half century. As a heritage and consumer asset, the Historic Center became a field of discourse and action through which a traditional criollo population expressed the desire both to recover the criollo or limeño character of a city overrun and transformed by migrant masses, and to guarantee their own status as original inhabitants. As part of the recovery, the square hitherto known as the Plaza de Armas was renamed the Plaza Mayor on the grounds that this was its original name. At the same time, some of the design of the plaza was restored and many streets regained their colonial names. By laying claim to a past written in the walls and streets of the center, the criollo segment of the population sought to represent itself as the native population of Lima and as the legitimate depository and custodian of the city's heritage. However, these objectives overlooked the exclusion and marginalization of a broad migrant population that also aspired to make the city its legitimate place of residence. In this respect, the restoration project resorted to technical means to deal with what in reality was a political problem: the struggle of groups of differing origins to legitimately occupy, manage, and serve as the custodians of public space in the city.

During the same period that political demonstrations were banned from the center of Lima, the Plaza Mayor and the streets surrounding it were periodically occupied, although not without first overcoming certain difficulties, by processions and parades of dancers put on by Andean migrants to honor the patron saints of their hometowns. The cultural expressions through which migrant groups have participated in the public culture of Lima are varied and sometimes affect business activities, traffic, and mass consumption (Alfaro 2005); indeed, the recontextualization and proliferation of Andean festivals in the Peruvian capital, brought about through migration, have made Lima a so-called sacred city (Low 1999, 20) with a landscape of sites of worship for groups and individuals to configure their identities and moral subjectivities as well as locate themselves in a social geography. Although the religious festivals celebrated throughout the year do not have the same appeal as other mass events in Lima's emerging public culture, they are widespread, with the periodic attendance, according to one questionnaire, of 69.5 percent of those surveyed, in preference to other kinds of cultural events (Ávila 2002, 221).[1] Significant social and economic resources are mobilized to undertake the festivals, and their staging entails considerable displacement of people, objects, and religious artifacts between hometowns and Lima. In its current form, the festival in Peru is largely a product of the migration of the last fifty years. Its development is a response to, and a consequence of, migration as both a social and cultural process through which social actors are engaged in making and remaking the geographies of identity (see Cánepa 2007).[2]

Like the choreographic repertoire fundamental to it, religious/festive worship has a localizing and essentializing effect for the community it unites (see Marzal 1983 and Sallnow 1987). In this sense, the recontextualization of worship (in another place, on other dates, and for new groups) challenges the links among identity, place, and culture. For the same reason, and also because the festive ritual is placed in the framework of a structure consisting of calendars and places of worship, the staging of Andean religious practices in Lima is central to the configuration of new regional landscapes and to how Lima and the provinces are relocated in a geography of identity hitherto centralist and fragmentary. More precisely, the politics of identity implied by the recontextualization of Andean religious festivals in Lima, may be defined in terms of a geopoetics and a geopolitics of identity.

Although countless Andean religious festivals are celebrated in different locations of the city during a crowded religious calendar, those held in the Historic Center are of particular interest because the activities associated with the celebrations imply access to and use of spaces of worship (churches and altars), as well as of public spaces (the streets and squares in the center) that symbolize Lima's criollo tradition. For the statue of a patron saint to be housed in a church, its devotees must have engaged in complex negotiations with the religious authorities of the parish. The authorities must have provided a chapel in which to place the statue and have also ensured the participation of a significant number of parishioners in the annual liturgical and social activities of the church. For its part, the *comunidad de devotos* remains responsible for the care of its patron's image, including cleaning, maintenance, and restoration, and the church becomes the center for monthly masses or for the main festival with its masses, processions, and dance performances.

Negotiations with the city and with the Instituto Nacional de Cultura (INC) are also required for a festival to be held, and these negotiations have become contentious as a result of both the declaration of Lima as a heritage site and the project for the restoration of the Historic Center. A municipal ordinance (No. 062-1994) , put in place after the heritage declaration, allows only traditional religious and civic celebrations to be held in the center of Lima, celebrations such as Corpus Christi, the anniversary of the founding of the city, or the feast days of the Virgen del Carmen de Barrios Altos and El Señor de los Milagros. At the same time, the architectural restoration phase of the urban recovery project is under the supervision of the INC, which ensures that renovations are carried out according to architectural, historical, and aesthetic criteria that respect the colonial and republican character of buildings and plazas. Access to and use of public spaces, as well as the restoration and adornment of churches involved in Andean religious festivals, are consequently forms of strategic action through which different groups of migrants interact with church and state. Their participation in the project of recovery of the Historic Center and their acceptance and inclusion as legitimate residents of the city are therefore at stake. Such outcomes require the transformation of the festive calendar and places of worship, acceptance of dance as a legitimate religious expression, and the valorization of sculptural and architectural aesthetics of Andean and recent derivation. In other words, at stake is the possibility of founding tradition anew and transforming the Historic Center, thereby disputing the status of the criollo class as the legitimate inhabitants of Lima. The process is not separable from the transformation of the Historic Center as a space: it translates politically into the possibility of the comunidades de devotos of migrant origin acquiring cultural agency and becoming the legitimate interpreters and custodians of the traditions and monuments of the Historic Center as a heritage asset. In short, the celebration of Andean festivals in Lima entails the repoliticization of public space through the performance of specific cultural repertoires.

At the same time as the Andean festivals were established, the municipal government promoted other festivals recognized as belonging to a criollo religious/festive tradition. During the term of office of Alberto Andrade as mayor (1995–2002) the city began its patronage of the feast of the Virgen del Carmen of Barrios Altos, a neighborhood on the edge of the Historic Center considered the cradle of criollo culture, an initiative launched as part of the activities intended to revitalize this identity. The city promoted and supported the participation of criollo music groups and publicized the celebrations through radio announcements in which the mayor invited the population of Lima to attend. The organization of the procession of the Virgin del Carmen from Barrios Altos to the Plaza Mayor could be read as a reply to the strategy of the immigrant comunidades de devotos of appropriating the streets and the Plaza Mayor through their processional routes and the choreographed displays with which they were establishing a public presence.

In a context similar to that of the celebration of the Virgen del Carmen de Barrios Altos, the feast of El Señor de los Milagros, patron saint of the city, has conquered the media to become the most significant event in October and the most important religious celebration of the year. The daily masses and processions are broadcast, and politicians, state institutions, and private businesses include activities associated with the festival on their October calendars. Politicians and other public figures attend the celebrations; public institutions with offices in the center make ready to receive the processional float bearing the statue of the patron along its processional route. The image of El Señor de los Milagros is reproduced on the labels of numerous products, on the billboards of supermarket and pharmacy chains, and on the altars erected in city stores. El Señor de los Milagros becomes, in effect, a necessary source of reference and interpretation for any event occurring in October.[3]

Nevertheless, the religious festivals held in celebration of Lima's patron saints are predominantly liturgical events, different from the Andean religious celebrations characterized by more openly festive elements, among which the performance of dance repertoires stands out. The transformation of Lima into a city associated with those public performance repertoires was therefore a bold stroke, an act of contestation against a geography of identity that had displaced the indigenous population toward the Andes mountains and excluded them from the national project.

THE GEOGRAPHY OF MIGRATION, CITIZENSHIP, AND IDENTITY

The inscription of ethnic and racial classifications on the Peruvian landscape, so that identities are conceived as essentially tied to geographic location (Poole 1988; Orlove 1993), has led to a localized and territorialized geography of identity that has been instrumental in a political and cultural order, making Lima the center of the nation-state and leaving the rest of the country a fragmented landscape, a distant, internally disconnected territory. As Sarah Radcliffe and Sallie Westwood have remarked: "The geographical imagination of Peruvian citizens and the state in the post-colonial period has associated the indigenous population with the Andean mountains, and has seen 'development' as a task to overcome the physical and social 'obstacle' represented by this racialized geography" (1996, 27). Configured through various discourses and centralist politics, this vision has naturalized the relation between identity and geography, shaping the spatial and social meanings of place and regulating the movements of ethnic groups, individuals, and cultural objects and repertoires within national boundaries. When identity is expressed in geographic terms, migration to the cities by those who venture to leave places that are "natural" and "proper" to them is seen as an invasion and an act of audacity. To the extent that geographic location determines access to education and health services, not to mention the presence of the state, the condition of citizenship itself acquires a geographic correlative. The higher in the Andes that people are geographically located, the more Indian they become and the less of a citizen they are seen to be.

As Radcliffe and Westwood have also noted, these phenomena have counterparts throughout Latin America. Not only is the centrality of capital cities a dominant force, as in Mexico City and Buenos Aires, but the regionalization of identities is commonplace, as in countries such as Colombia, Venezuela, and Ecuador, where it is also fostered by stark differences in geography between coastal regions and the interior. In light of this geography of identity, migratory processes throughout the twentieth century have become a central mechanism for the cultural and political transformation of groups and individuals, and have acquired meaning with respect to democratization. In this context, insertion into urban space and the city of Lima has acquired epic proportions in the construction of citizenship (Degegori 1994; Degregori, Blondet, and Lynch 1986), and the concept of itinerancy has become the basic rhetorical figure in representation of this situation. Itinerancy not only reflects the spatial movement of a community but, according to the theory of metaphor, also indicates the movements it desires to make in the culture it occupies (see Fernández 1986, 24). The topographic model proposed by James Fernández to understand "what metaphoric predication does"—namely, to achieve movement in quality space—has a material and existential correlative in the geography of identity in Peru because quality space is inscribed in geography and is lived *in* and *from* geographic location: thus the rhetorical figure of itinerancy translates both into real movements (migrations) and dramatic activities (the transplantation of festive and choreographic events). In other words, itinerancy "act[s] as a plan of ritual behavior" (Fernández 1986, 42). Thus, the *geopoetics of identity* contained in the metaphor of movement operates in two senses: it offers the image through which the migrants configure their identity from different localities, by giving meaning both to the history of their migration and their condition as migrants; and it gives structure to the staging of the resultant itinerant identity.

Concerning the second point, I propose that the metaphor of itinerancy is activated by what Edward Casey (1996) calls events of emplacement; in the case we are considering, these are obtained through mechanisms related to the calendar and urban monuments implied by the celebration of a festival, the organization of processions through the streets, the enthronement of religious statues in the churches, and the performance of choreographic repertoires. To the extent that these activities create places, and form a relation between them and social subjects, the place (in this case, Lima) is reconfigured each time a festival occurs. Thus the ritualization of the rhetorical figure *itinerancy* engages a geopolitics of identity, and the cultural practices involved in the events of emplacement are forms of cultural representation that objectivize public space and heritage assets, making these into objects of reflection, engagement, and contestation. In effect, the religious festival and the production of particular choreographic repertoires are what have shaped the cultural arena in which the predominant geography of identity has been historically configured. As performative practices, they are instrumental to a geopoetics and geopolitics that define a significant part of the cultural dynamic and the construction of citizenship in Peru.

CITIZENSHIP AND CULTURE

The social sciences have approached the problem of migration, the constitution of political subjects, and citizenship by emphasizing processes such as land seizure and the struggle for basic urban services that made possible the rise of base community organizations as mediators between the state and the new urban settlements. This emphasis is understandable given the involvement of popular neighborhood organizations as a key factor not just in determining agendas and the means of political action but also in the fight to obtain recognition for the full and complete status of citizenship (Degregori, Blondet, and Lynch 1986).

Citizenship is also configured and realized, however, through cultural arguments, practices, and agencies. Efforts to obtain it do not stop at the seizure of land as a place to live, nor at participation in base organizations, but also include the practice of effective and creative forms of public intervention in the field of culture, such as the recontextualization and reinvention of Andean cultural expressions. More precisely, following the distinction established by Partha Chatterjee (2004) between civil society and political society, actions directed at obtaining recognition of citizenship and social inclusion undertaken in the field of politics (in the form of popular organizations) or in the field of economics (the financing of a small-business sector and a middle class with consumer capacity) are no guarantee of the incorporation of migrant sectors as civil society. The movement of collective action to the field of culture, however, constitutes precisely a possibility of changing the "terms of recognition" (Appadurai 2006) to gain access to the moral status required to obtain a more complete and real citizenship.

Actions undertaken in the cultural realm, such as the celebration of Andean religious festivals in the city, are indicative of the configuration of cultural citizenships expressed in the situation of the resident, and may be understood in two senses: first, as a citizenship with identity, whereby the cultural is defined as difference (see Turner 1991) and, in the case at hand, is specifically concerned with the configuration of citizens who self-identify as limeños but also differentiate themselves by a geographic criterion, their common place of origin; second, as a performative citizenship constituted through repetition of a tradition whereby a religious festival and devotion are staged and brought into play as a cultural resource. As George Yúdice has argued (2003), the use of culture to achieve ends belonging to other fields has gained legitimacy in the context of globalization characterized by the culturalization of the economy and the politicization of culture: in other words, where culture has been rediscovered by entrepreneurs, policy makers, and social movements as an important means to achieve development, strengthen collective identities, assure governance, and serve as an argument for cultural recognition and self-determination. Such is the context in Lima, where the celebration of religious festivals has, indeed, become a strategic mechanism in the creation of cultural agents and where the center has been transformed into a heritage asset.

THE RESIDENTE AND CULTURAL CITIZENSHIP AS DIFFERENCE

Compatriotship (*paisanazgo*) functions as an important agglutinant and basis of classification among limeños of migrant origin or descent (Golte 2001, Altamirano 1984). The members of migrant associations, fraternities, or sporting clubs refer to themselves as *residentes*, a term not used alone but in combination with the name of a place, district, province, or department of origin, so that in Lima we find "residentes de Pomacanchis," "residentes de Paucartambo," or "residentes del Cuzco," for example. The attribute *residente* makes it possible to locate a person both within and beyond the city because the person is both a resident of Lima and a native of another place. Moreover, the term also introduces a geopoetics to mark cultural differences and hierarchies while alluding to the nature of an identity defined as itinerant and establishing a capacity

FIGURE 9. Qhapaq Qolla dancers during the procession of the Virgen del Carmen de Paucartambo. Downtown Lima, July 1998 (photo by Gisela Cánepa)

for movement as its most important resource. In this sense, *displacement* and *emplacement* are two significant axes providing a perspective from which to understand the process by which Lima is constituted as a multicultural city and through which to observe the character of cultural citizenships.

Embodied in the person of the residente from one place or another, cultural citizenship repeats and contests geographically codified ethnic differences and hierarchies because it distinguishes a common origin according to locality, district, province, or department. Yet, the geopoetics and geopolitics implied in the notion of residente raises the possibility of imagining different ethnic groups within the city while also imagining the new resident of Lima as connected to other places, and thereby configuring a geography of identity in which the relation between the capital and the provinces may be redefined.[4]

In the festivals celebrated in the city center, the residentes, as both limeño and provincial, along with their itinerant character, are configured by various performative mechanisms, three of which are: the manner in which processional routes are determined; the creation of festival calendars on which some dates are established for the exclusive celebrations of a particular community of devotees and other dates are commemorated through coordination by several communities; and the existence of differing choreographic repertoires.

The processional routes followed by floats bearing religious statues such as those of the Virgen del Carmen de Paucartambo, El Señor de Qoyllur Riti, or others from Cuzco (all located in churches spread throughout central Lima) have changed over time. The processions not only cover the streets surrounding the churches that house the patron saints, but now include routes extending as far as Lima Cathedral, with stops in front of the Palacio de Gobierno, the Palacio Municipal, and the Cathedral itself so that dignitaries may offer their greetings at each stop. Between 1998 and 2004, the confraternities of El Señor de Qoyllur Riti and the Virgen del Carmen de Paucartambo were even able to have the main masses of their festivals celebrated in the cathedral itself.

However, neither the municipality nor the church has remained impassive to these initiatives. Although the ecclesiastical authorities remain open to housing the statues of patron saints of migrant origin in the churches in the center of Lima, they have limited access to the Cathedral in recent years, to the extent that, since 2004, the possibility of celebrating the festival mass there has been rejected completely, even if this right had hitherto been habitually granted. Nevertheless, a geography of identity is reproduced through the creation of places of devotion within the area of the Historic Center, dispersed in relation to the Cathedral as a central place but interconnected by processional routes so that the spatial dimensions of the procession appear as a staging of the process of migration between the places of "otherness" and the center. Thus, at a representational level, the processional journey implies putting itinerancy as a right of citizenship into practice at the same time as it manifests a *limeño* identity that is both shared and different.

The festival calendars developed by the comunidades de devotos allude to a cultural citizenship that, through connections to a distant place of origin, is claimed as both equal and different. The confraternity of El Señor de Qoyllur Riti, for example, has added the celebration of the anniversary of the founding of Lima (in February) to its festive calendar. Similarly, the calendar of the confraternity of the Virgen del Carmen de Paucartambo not only includes the feast of El Señor de Qoyllur Riti in Lima (in June), but also the anniversary (in February) of the coronation of the Virgen del Carmen de Paucartambo by Pope John Paul II, and the feast of the Virgin of the Rosary (in October), both belonging to the festive calendar of the town of Paucartambo, where the community originated.

Finally, the choreographic repertoires of devotional dances from Cuzco are a traditional heritage in the sense that different versions of the same dances are arranged and staged as belonging to different ethnic, district, or provincial groups. Thus, not only can the devotees of the Virgen del Carmen de Paucartambo mark their difference in relation to, for example, those who celebrate the

FIGURE 10. El Señor de Qoyllur Riti receives greetings from church authorities at Lima Cathedral, June 2006 (photo by Gisela Cánepa)

Virgen del Carmen de Barrios Altos, which is part of the pantheon of criollo and limeño saints and virgins, but also in relation to other comunidades de devotos from Cuzco who celebrate the same virgin or another patron saint from their own place of origin. Indeed, the difference established by devotees of the Virgen del Carmen de Paucartambo with respect to groups from other localities or districts who celebrate their festival in the center of Lima reproduces a geopolitically codified classificatory and hierarchical system. In other words, citizenship with identity does not necessarily guarantee equality in relation to difference.

THE NUEVO LIMEÑO AND CULTURAL CITIZENSHIP AS PERFORMANCE

When the social sciences drew attention during the 1990s to the rise of a new middle class in Peru, they did so on the basis of economic activity (see Portocarrero 1998). Emerging sectors were identified with the figure of the small business operator, and the question of integration of the citizen was looked at in economic terms, specifically through the transition from the informal to the formal economy (De Soto 1987). It was barely noticed, however—although the media, business people, and marketing professionals were more perceptive than social scientists in this respect (see Arellano and Burgos, 2004)—that, alongside the quest for economic power, the practices of broad sectors of Andean origin were also directed at cultural presence and agency, as reflected in such practices as food, music, radio, and visual design. This process, beginning in the 1970s with the spread of *huayno* through recordings and radio and then in the rise of *chicha* in the 1980s (see Romero 2002), has subsequently attained a significant dimension. Not only have a variety of forms of cultural expression been produced (from music to the plastic arts and cinema), but they have been generated and promoted thanks to specific public sectors and circuits of mass coverage and circulation, which, in some cases, have sustained the development of an entire culture industry.

The importance of these developments lies in the fact that it is precisely in the field of public culture (see Appadurai, Arjun, and Breckenridge 1995), in a context in which politics acquires a performative character, that migration and the status of the residente in Lima are represented thematically, and that urban space is configured. At the same time, both in public debate and in the shape of some public policies, the concept of cultural diversity as a national asset and an economic resource is beginning to be felt, so that cultural action becomes relevant in the public agenda of some groups and in the economic projects of others. In such a context, much of the struggle for civic rights, not only in Peru but in the world at large, takes the forms of a politics of identity and of cultural revitalization (see Álvarez et al. 1998; Yúdice 2003; Turner 1991). This is exactly the context in which the Andean religious festivals celebrated in the center of Lima since the 1980s have developed and become so prominent. The declaration of the Historic Center as a cultural heritage site, along with the implementation of policies intended to promote it as such, favored its strengthening as an effective cultural resource for public intervention, which both supported citizen recognition and led to a rethinking of the relation between citizenship and culture. The staging of festivals thereby became a mechanism through which to refound the festive tradition and, more specifically, transform the Historic Center into more of a cultural heritage site, to such degree that new groups could become its legitimate interpreters and custodians.

As mentioned already, the confraternities having statues of their patron saint located in the churches in the center of Lima have produced increasingly fuller calendars; their activities and public presence emerge for more than one occasion during the year. By including the celebration of the founding of Lima, the confraternities not only add a civic festival to what was initially an exclusively religious calendar, but also endeavor to ensure their involvement in a festival legitimately recognized as part of the living heritage of the Historic Center. Thus every staging of a festival implies a continuing negotiation between authentic reproduction, or fidelity to the tradition of a place of origin, and adaptation to the conditions and agendas pertaining to the city. At the same time, the celebrations include elements alien to Lima's traditions (among which elements the devotional dances stand out), so that an eventual transformation in the traditions of the city is also provoked.

A similar phenomenon occurs in connection with celebrations of the Virgen del Carmen de Paucartambo and of El Señor de Qoyllur Riti, which, in contrast to the festivals for the Virgen del Carmen de Barrios Altos and Corpus Christi, include dances. Traditional religious festivals in Lima do not include dances, but are entirely liturgical and processional in character. Dancing in the streets and plazas, unlike what is seen in the cities and regions of the interior, is not considered appropriate either as public behavior or as a way to express and experience religious fervor. The body of the procession for the feast of El Señor de Qoyllur Riti, bringing together images of virgins and saints from different districts and provinces of Cuzco, has lost its character as a pilgrimage festival and taken on the appearance of a Cuzco Corpus Christi procession. Its coincidence on the calendar with Lima's Corpus (promoted as one of the city's traditional festivals) has allowed it to become a kind of alternative Corpus distinguished by the celebration of mass in Quechua and, above all, by the presence of devotional dancing, not part of the limeño tradition. Moreover, all these innovations suggest a transformation of heritage itself with respect both to cultural life and to the monuments of the city, given that stylistic changes to church altars have been introduced, renovations to the atria and façades of churches have been undertaken, and the enthronement of new devotional images in the churches of the Historic Center has changed the city's religious pantheon. Further, an interesting dynamic has arisen in some cases between heritage monuments and living expressions of heritage: the devotees of the Virgen del Carmen de Paucartambo have had the main entrance of the Church of the Sacred Heart rebuilt so that its great doors can be used; the deterioration of the church had meant that only the small doors could previously be opened, making it impossible for the float carrying the statue of the Virgin to be borne facing forward into the church, as tradition dictates. In other words, the material monuments are being reshaped to suit the requirements of the staging of living culture.

Although the changes introduced into the material and nonmaterial heritage of central Lima have met with resistance from the municipality and the church, some of the most elaborate and popular of the Andean festivals have begun to catch the attention of tourist agencies, who take advantage of festival dates so that visits to the Plaza Mayor are enhanced by the presence of processions and groups of dancers. In the context of discourses and policies promoting the concept of Peru as a brand name, whereby any cultural manifestation is a potential economic resource, possession of a distinctive cultural repertoire and the capacity to perform it are enough to turn the owners into potential agents in the development of the city and the nation. Within this logic, cultural citizenship and the right to exercise it are understood as a strategic capacity to perform that citizenship effectively and efficiently for the benefit of the marketplace and in the name of development. In other words, cultural diversity is a guarantee of citizenship whenever it contributes to development. This neoliberal conceptualization of cultural citizenship opens a possibility, not always without contradictions, for the legitimization of culturally diverse manifestations that, like the festival, may even contest established social and cultural orders.

As a strategy for participation in a cultural project such as the restoration of the Historic Center, which has been promoted by state and private institutions like the Fundación Pro Lima, and which brings together artists, intellectuals, and the traditional limeño business elite, the Andean festival is instrumental in the generation of a discursive and performative framework through which migrant groups may contest the public image of the *nuevo limeño* as an economic subject. At stake is the possibility of obtaining recognition in a cultural, political, and moral sense as a legitimate actor in the construction of the nation. The mechanism brought into play for the purposes of citizenship recognition consists precisely in implementing the performative principle of "showing doing" (Schechner 2000, 22). Control of the competencies required for "showing doing" is, according to Jon McKenzie (2001, 4–5), not only essential in the realm of contemporary knowledge and power but also the condition of *being* in the world today. That is, the possibility of recognition relies on the display of appropriate competencies in order for citizens to present themselves as citizens in action. Indeed, in arguing that one of the aspects of cultural citizenship should be understood as performative citizenship, I was referring to citizenship through competency (a participatory citizenship hailed today as the basis for democratic governability). Control over and competence in a cultural repertoire, such as that involved in staging the Andean festivals, is certainly a valued and relevant resource for performing citizenship.

In the person of the nuevo limeño or *emergente* (emerging citizen), the Andean migrant has been invoked in the academy and the media as an emerging small business operator and new economic agent in a national project. Yet, even as the economic capacity of such figures is granted, their condition as a cultural subject and political activist in the development of the city and the country is denied. In other words, the relative economic success of certain sectors has redeemed the image of the migrant, but at the cost of a subordinate classification in the social hierarchy, where the migrant is relegated to the informal sector as an economic agent and is deprived of moral authority. In the festival, however, public cultural action is engaged and there is space to challenge this classification. The quest for recognition as a cultural actor and moral subject by performing a festive-religious repertoire and engaging in the restoration of church buildings is precisely an indicator of "showing doing," a "doing" that consists of participation in the process of development of the city and emphasizes, of course, that "showing doing" does not have to do with the economy, but with culture.

On the other hand, efforts by migrant sectors of the population to obtain recognition as citizens have not been without contradiction, because the performance of cultural difference is only acceptable to the extent that it serves the marketplace. Yet when this performance effectively redefines public spaces and their uses as well as the city's heritage—that is, when it entails a redefinition of the city and of limeño identity—it is delegitimized in the name of authenticity, in two ways: the Andean festival is unacceptable as an authentic expression of the historical and cultural heritage of Lima and it is unacceptable as an authentic expression of Andean traditions because it is not performed in its place of origin.

The attempt to become a cultural agent presents a paradox in that, from a hegemonic perspective, as Renato Rosaldo (1991) points out, culture, understood as difference, is what defines the *other*. Hence the equation: "The greater the culture, the less the citizenship." In this sense, the challenge facing the construction of cultural citizenship lies in the possibility of redefining the cultural and of relocating difference in the dominant geography of identity. The challenge amounts, in effect, to configuring society in inclusive terms so that it is possible to be equal by being different. This requires rethinking culture in terms of capacities or, more precisely, in terms of the capacity to aspire (Appadurai 2004, 69), and less as set of features or repertoires bound by tradition.

The challenge is undoubtedly a difficult one, in that the academy, tourism, and the media have contributed to essentializing cultural difference and locating cultural authenticity in specific geographic locations. Authentic Andean culture is thus only to be visited in places where pre-Hispanic and colonial architecture exist, or where traditional technologies and forms of social organization continue to function or are preserved for tourist purposes. By contrast, local initiatives in modernization in terms of urban architecture, art, and expressive culture are not made available by tourist agencies. Nor are they taken into account as part of Peru's multicultural character. Cultural innovation is only accepted as part of a legitimate cultural creativity and pluralism when it is performed by hegemonic urban sectors—for instance, fusions performed by musicians like Manongo Mujica or Tito la Rosa, or nouvelle Andean cuisine produced by the chefs best known to the media and even promoted through television programs. When, however, innovation and creativity, or the daring of crossing cultural frontiers, are pursued by marginalized groups, they are rejected in the name of authenticity. By contrast, the success of participation in the project of restoration of the Historic Center as a strategy for acquiring cultural agency, of configuring cultural citizenships and obtaining political and moral recognition, depends not only on the possibilities of effectively instrumentalizing cultural resources but, to a large extent, on the possibility of redefining the field of *the cultural.*

The TransMilenio Experience
Mass Transit in Bogotá and National Urban Identity

HÉCTOR FERNÁNDEZ L'HOESTE

> Hegemony is not an external relationship between pre-established social
> subjects, but the very process of construction of these subjects.
> —Ernesto Laclau and Chantal Mouffe

his chapter analyzes the case of TransMilenio, the new mass transit system in Bogotá, and argues that, through the speedy application of its formula to other corners of the country, it is being developed as a mechanism of national hegemony to support a particular version of Colombian identity in accordance with the government's ideology and understanding of the role of public space within an organized society. In a country like Colombia, as in other Latin American states such as Argentina, Brazil, and Mexico, ridden with inner conflict and lacking a strong project of nationhood, Bogotá's bus rapid transit (BRT) design serves as an ideal means for the enforcement of a new, cohesive idea of nationhood. That is, amid the eagerness of regional administrations to address transportation predicaments, generally viewed as demanding costly solutions and substantial political commitment, the central government has discovered an opportunity to transform the way many Colombian cities are experienced and imagined by daily users of public transportation. Through the emulation of the TransMilenio experience and the subsequent reproduction of a determined sociospatial profile, the government's objective is to empower a new regulatory spirit for the idea of a nation, ratifying the validity of a specific version of the urban setting as a sociocultural ideal. In this context, TransMilenio is employed to legitimate the superiority of a precise model of the Colombian city, that of the capital district, home to the national government and not yet confident center of the nation. The mass transit system thus becomes an instrument of central authority, sustaining a distinct idea of *colombianidad* in the city.

Within this framework, the success in the application of this project is irrelevant, since failure of implementation at the regional level also would corroborate the superiority of a center anxious to consolidate its position of power. In the eyes of the central administration, if the provincial capitals take advantage of this opportunity, they will gain a more dignified mode of transportation, albeit at the expense of aspects of local identity, since they will end up imitating the capital and sacrificing some distinctiveness. On the other hand, if they fail to complete their corresponding projects according to designated deadlines, they will merely ratify their inferiority in comparison with the spirit of progress and modernity emanating from Bogotá. In this sense, lack of adequate completion would authenticate the allegations of a long-standing matrix in Colombian historiography, within which Bogotá has been portrayed since the nineteenth century as socially, culturally, and politically superior to the provincial capitals. Whatever the case, either alternative would legitimate the central administration's position in the nation, an outcome that, in the midst of negotiations with paramilitary and subversive groups, would be particularly useful in authenticating its standing.

In matters of national identity, there is no doubt that Colombia bears a lengthy, deeply rooted tradition of violence. After all, Colombian violence is a well-documented matter, evinced by the many actions of subversive groups, paramilitary organizations, and drug-trafficking cartels, as well as by certain government agencies. Although the violence is usually interpreted as the product of widespread social inequality, the situation is radically altered when a substantial part of the violence emerges from the articulation of government policy in terms of urban planning. According to Walter Benjamin, the consolidation of power through institutional and juridical forms implies an act of violence (see Benjamin 1991). For Benjamin, "all violence as a means is either law-making or law-preserving" (1966, 243). Violence distinguishes between foundational forms (law-making) apparent at the birth of an institution, and forms pertaining to the right to power (law-preserving) linked to the sustainability of the institution's position of power on a long-term basis; the tension between these two sets of forms largely defines the viability of a rightful state or government. Yet, to Benjamin, "all law-preserving violence weakens its corresponding law-making form, by repressing hostile and opposing forms of violence" (1991, 44;

my translation). In other words, once an order is established, the inner dynamics of a political system operate in such way as to inhibit the possibility of violent and disruptive inner change so that new forms of power cannot contest the established order. It is clear to Benjamin that if new expressions of violence (or previously repressed ones) come to predominate over the previously established foundational violence, the possibility for a new rightful state arises, engendering change in the social order. Much of the argument in this chapter with respect to the impact of TransMilenio on national identity is concerned with this latter form of violence. The consolidation of government power implies the establishment and recognition of a dominant, hegemonic form of violence supported by coercion and the will to impose an order; for, if the awareness of a latent presence of violence diminishes, substantial weakening of institutional power follows immediately. In other words, a government must portray itself as capable of violent action; otherwise, its inactivity might be interpreted as weakness by the parties contesting its right to power. Thus, the TransMilenio, given its material dimension and the fact that its implementation involves an alteration of the cultural and social fabric of the urban environment, provides a face for the efforts of the central government to effectively assert its presence throughout the nation.

This assertion is consistent with the dictates of *seguridad democrática* (democratic security), the name for a key policy of the Colombian administration to which many supposed achievements pertaining to public safety during the years 2002–2007 are attributed, and which is ingenuously portrayed as the basis for a return, in many parts of the country, to a lawful state of affaris. Despite its Orwellian connotation (or perhaps precisely because of it) democratic security has become a household term in Colombia. It describes the many efforts by President Álvaro Uribe—military, economic, political—to reassert the central government's primacy over sizeable segments of national territory, lost as a result of the shortcomings and ambivalence of previous administrations. After decades of social instability, primarily from the actions of armed organizations, Colombia's population seems decided to support political platforms that, unlike what is happening in the rest of Latin America, endorse a pragmatic rhetoric firmly anchored on the right of the political spectrum.

Like other Latin Americans, Colombians are also embracing cynicism and willingly placing their trust in forceful agendas that promise to rescue a few basic civil liberties at the expense of greater ones; nevertheless, the recent voting record of Colombians differs diametrically from those of neighboring Latin American countries, where left-leaning agendas seem to have gained the public's favor. Amid a subcontinent quickly embracing multiple varieties of social democracy and populism, Colombia stands out as a rightward-moving exception. Democratic security, or its many façades, has much to do with this difference. It is therefore imperative to recognize a connection between policies implemented at the national level, such as mass transportation, and the ideological content of certain political platforms.

In recent years, Uribe gained wide popularity by promoting a heavy-handed approach in matters involving national security, relying mostly on the righteous ring of catchphrases like "democratic security." In brief, this policy results from a package of measures that have visibly served to recover the population's ability to travel through a national highway network besieged by armed groups. Never mind the fact that travel in Colombian highways is an activity favored eminently by middle- and upper-class sectors, proud owners of the largest proportion of automobiles in the country, and that, generally traveling in buses, working-class sectors are a less likely target in the government's effort for the recovery of sovereignty on the national roads: the strategies pursued by the government seek to put an end to violence in the countryside, where the presence of officialdom is noticeably rare, to stabilize the situation at a time when the rapid circulation of goods is of utmost importance in anticipation of the probable implementation of a free-trade agreement with the United States. Thus, from a sociogeographic point of view, a substantial part of *seguridad democrática* is interpreted as the restoration of the rule of law in rural space.

There are urban equivalents for these strategies, brought about mostly by the general improvement of conditions in Bogotá in terms of the recovery and reorganization of public space since the late 1990s. One of the main accomplishments of Antanas Mockus (1995–1998, 2001–2004), a son of Lithuanian immigrants and former president of the National University, and Enrique Peñalosa (1998–2001), a Duke alumnus with graduate degrees in management and public administration from France, both progressive mayors of Bogotá, was the successful promotion of the importance of public space. Their governments succeeded in convincing many that public space, previously understood as belonging to no one, was in fact the property of all, a veritable redefinition of the urban social paradigm. Thanks to these two mayors, *bogotanos* learned to see the issue of public space as directly related to their quality of life. Both administrations brought forward a large number of concrete and general public initiatives that impacted favorably on the standard of living in the city.

Mockus's forte was his pedagogical bent, reflected in a new view of city life and a conciliatory mindset. His writings, which emphasize the importance of the role of the *other* in the development of citizenship (1996), contrast deeply with Uribe's policies, which embrace the *other* as an instrument of fear. In fact, in an article for the newspaper of the National University, Mockus wrote, "We become citizens when we refuse to answer violence with violence, when we accept a constitutional order that prohibits taking justice into your own hands" (Mockus 2003).

Peñalosa's strength was his managerial skill, which brought many concrete, tangible proposals to fruition. In a few years, the city saw its crime rate drop drastically. Projects included the construction of over 100 nurseries for preschool children, major improvements to over 150 school buildings, 50 new public schools, a large network of bike paths (over 300 kilometers), a state-of-the-art network for all public schools (with 14,000 computers), a new public library system with three main, large facilities and many smaller ones, and numerous projects for the rejuvenation of city squares and the recovery of public space.

The implementation of the new mass transit system for Bogotá was a remarkable source of support for this reorganization of city life. The expansion of this system at a national level, however, with the intention to replicate the capital's experience and obtain corresponding improvements in the levels of urban safety at the provincial level, suggests the need for deeper examination of the role of public transportation as a tool of social engineering and instrument of peace (La onda Trans 2005).

According to Catalonian expert Jordi Borja, greater access to public space, in terms of mobility or in terms of landscape, promotes greater social tolerance and a more effective redistribution of economic resources (Es cuestión 2006). There are few things as effective for addressing general violence in a country as a heightened presence of the state in the urban setting—personified primarily, in this case, by the greater visibility of the transportation infrastructure. Such a presence implies the patent consolidation of central power in smaller cities. In other words, to counteract violence (the presence of extraneous forces, such as subversive or criminal groups), it is imperative to resort to more violence (the presence, according to Benjamin, of the state as the legitimate champion of an order, notwithstanding its indifference toward widespread social injustice). Following Benjamin's arguments, violence is inherent in the actual constitution of the state and its theoretical articulation of an order. This is a "socializing" violence, which represses in order to regulate, to create a certain notion of organization in society. In a place like Colombia, in which a weak governmental apparatus desperately tries to recover the viability of its executive capability, this form of violence may attain multiple faces—chief among them, a brand new mass transit system, celebrated as a grand expression of autochthonous modernity.

Twenty years ago, if anyone had asked what particular aspects of a city made it Colombian (which elements empowered its *colombianidad*), the assortment of answers would have been remarkable, bearing in mind that most responses to the question would have been essentialist. On account of a long historiographic and political tradition, regional identities in Colombia are interpreted in a quasi-deterministic fashion. Geography and the government's unwillingness to tackle its constraints certainly contribute to the fragmentation of Colombian identity, and are reflected in the dismal coverage by the country's national highway network, requiring considerable upgrading to maximize the impact of the much-awaited trade agreement.

Usually, Caribbean cities like Barranquilla or Cartagena have little in common with the metro areas of the mountainous region, like Cali, Medellín, or the capital, which are marked by territorial insularity and characterized by local versions of Andean culture. Until the 1940s, before national air travel matured, Andean cities lagged behind ports like Barranquilla, which did not require substantial road connections to trade successfully, given its location at the mouth of the Magdalena River. Later, with the advent of modern airports and reliable airline service (as well as substantial government investment), both Medellín and Cali surpassed Barranquilla economically, yet maintained their inward-looking identities. Air travel stimulated economic growth, but Cali and Medellín never really embraced cosmopolitanism, open to migration from other parts of the country or the world. In particular, Medellín is a place where economic penetration by foreign companies presents challenges unless local connections exist. As a result, the culture of these cities in the heart of the country is distinctive: food, music, business activity, and language vary widely from one place to another; despite the demographic changes of the past twenty years, regional differences in Colombia have been exacerbated to incredible extremes, primarily through the absence of a strong project of *nation*. Colombian nationalism is, on the whole, the result of private efforts, with the government, until now, playing a distant second in the celebration of a national character. The fact that Uribe comes from Antioquia, a region renowned for its fierce defense of local traditions, is particularly relevant to his efforts to heighten the profile of the state as an architect of identity.

Things began to change radically on December 18, 2000. On that date, Bogotá inaugurated its new BRT system, culminating the unprecedented period of urban development sponsored by the duo of progressive administrations. The system was called TransMilenio, with capital letters both at the beginning and in the middle of the name, a relatively unusual phenomenon in Spanish and more in keeping with the liberties commonly taken in English. The onomastic license, initially perceived as something fashionable, denoting the influence of the language of technology, might have had more to do with the hope of selling a modern image to the public. Bogotá's system is celebrated as an improved version of the transportation infrastructure in Curitiba, capital of the Brazilian state of Paraná, Brazil, with a network based on the extensive application of busways: that is, lanes for the exclusive use of long, articulated buses, each with a capacity of up to two hundred and seventy passengers. As in the Brazilian case, Bogotá's network of red articulated buses is supported by a feeder system, composed of local bus routes bringing passengers to transfer points for an articulated bus to their destination. In Bogotá, these feeder buses are bright green, whereas Curitiba's feeder lines are orange, with green reserved for inter-neighborhood buses. However, the Colombian BRT is larger, given Bogotá's overall population of eight million (more than twice the nearly three-and-a-half millions of Curitiba. When it comes to size, the Colombian version is a major innovation, extending the busway model appreciably. Indeed, the size of the system asserts the viability of busways as solutions for large metro areas. Within weeks of its inauguration, the network gained considerable popularity and appreciation—sustained principally by the lack of dignified alternatives—establishing itself as the favorite form of public transportation in the metro area. Within months, small, bright red replicas of the network's buses, manufactured in China, were available in the street stalls. For a Latin American capital such as Bogotá, with a penchant for things British, this development highlighted a parallel with the double-decker Routemaster buses associated with London. Clearly, a sentimental bond had been established between the system and the population, signifying an important shift in the way users viewed themselves and their life in the urban environment (Sandoval 2001, 34; Sobre ruedas 2001).

The rapid success of the Colombian experience did not go unnoticed. The main reason for local, regional, and even national pride was the realization that the system embodied a domestic version of modernity, that is, a home-grown alternative to large, heavy, and expensive networks, such as the Metro in Medellín, which emulate the means of transportation in more industrialized nations and usually spark ample controversy as a result of their impact on national budgets. In fact, during the late 1980s and early 1990s, amid the planning and construction of the Metro system in Medellín, there was great controversy about the costs of the project and its impact on national debt for two significant reasons: first, the system was being built in a city that, though important, wasn't the capital, giving grounds for questioning the investment on the basis of its relevance to national government; and second, the involvement of an expenditure so large it was generally viewed as a cost shared by the entire national population. Medellín's Metro was eventually completed in 1996, despite the long debate surrounding its cost of construction and operation. In the process, Colombia became a Latin American anomaly, with better transportation infrastructure in one of its provincial centers than in the much larger national capital. Five years later, TransMilenio demonstrated that it was not necessary to spend billions of dollars, as engineering consortia had argued, or drastically alter the fabric of a metropolitan center to provide dignified and efficient transportation to the citizens of poverty-stricken Latin American nations (or, for that matter, many other growing countries).

Curitiba's model was a renowned success, but the implementation of the busway on a larger scale had generated considerable skepticism. To many, it was a relief to see that an expanded version of the network actually worked. The travel time across a wide metro area was reduced and the emission of pollutants was decreased thanks to streamlining the circulation of vehicles, and, quite literally, giving the city a fresher, more modern face. In a matter of years, as the city embarked on the subsequent phases of development, the Colombian version of the busway became established as one of the main alternatives for remedying the transportation headaches of insolvent municipal administrations, many of which hesitated before the prospect of large international credits and prohibitively expensive modes of public transport. Transportation experts and urban development committees from cities throughout the world traveled to Colombia to observe and study the busway. In fact, before long, the company in charge of TransMilenio—a mix of private and public enterprises—was advising other Latin American capitals in matters of transportation (Volver 2004). Given the system's popularity and size, the Colombian BRT model inspired other Latin American countries contemplating pragmatic solutions for their transportation problems: Argentina (Posadas), Brazil (Rio de Janeiro, which was also influenced by Curitiba's Metrobus, São Paulo's Interligado, and Porto Alegre's EPTC), Costa Rica (San José), Ecuador (Quito's Ecovía and Guayaquil's Metrobus), Guatemala (Guatemala City), Nicaragua (Managua), Puerto Rico (San Juan), and Venezuela (Mérida and Barquisimeto); it was also an inspiration to expanding Asian urban centers: Jakarta, Delhi, and Beijing. And, in effect, the Colombian experience paved the way for new systems in Latin American capitals like Santiago (Transantiago) and Mexico City (Metrobús, which worked with the assistance of Colombian advisers) (La troncal 2005). With Santiago, the relationship is characterized by exchange, since Bogotá is considering the adoption of some features of the Chilean capital, chiefly, the privately contracted initiatives that transformed the urban landscape with toll-supported modern highways in the matter of a decade. In Mexico, given the highway and heavy-rail tradition, inhabitants were initially hesitant to accept the busway formula, although they eventually warmed to the new system.

In the years since its inception, the Colombian network has witnessed steady progress, part of a collective effort to bring order to improvised, accelerated urban growth. In a way, BRT tames the city, suggesting new directions for urban growth and generating public space at improbable locations while discouraging car use. A decline in the number of cars was a key consideration in the design for Bogotá, since the objective from the outset was to encourage alternative urban transportation. For Peñalosa, who oversaw its creation, TransMilenio was a key piece in a personal quest against car-oriented urban environments, part of a greater package of measures. In fact, according to a referendum held during his tenure, bogotanos agreed to ban all cars from the city during peak hours by the year 2015. Other programs included the placement of bollards throughout the town (to discourage parking on sidewalks) and banning the use of cars for an entire day. Since 2000, every first Thursday of February, Bogotá celebrates *el día sin carro* (car-free day), during which only taxis and buses (TransMilenio's as well as independently managed ones) may operate, fostering an increased reliance on the massive network of bike lanes (*ciclorrutas*, as the locals call them) in the metro area; TransMilenio has become a cornerstone of the celebration of this event, and is relied on by a growing portion of the public. By late 2005, the first segments of the second stage of the network, completed by late April 2006, came into service, suggesting an even greater face-lift for the city. Once fully implemented, the master plan for the network envisages eight stages, covering the entire metro area (Infraestructura vial 2003). Current estimates suggest that the system transports close to a million users per day, a figure that by 2030, the projected date of completion of the final stage, is expected to grow to three million, covering 80 percent of the city's transportation demands (Vía al desarrollo 2004; Primera estación 2004).

Given the system's reputation and its impact on the population's sense of worth, the national government, concentrated in Bogotá and always eager to capture national attention, has decided to embark on an ambitious plan of BRT systems, modeled on TransMilenio and geared toward smaller cities. In Colombia, a country with the second largest Spanish-speaking population in the world, this decision was not taken lightly. The number of smaller cities is, within a Latin American context, rather significant. According to the plan, the busway model will be duplicated in six of Colombia's main cities in ten years. In an unexpected move, the current national administration, normally given to financial austerity and synergies in the context of public services, has committed to financing a sizeable portion of the project, up to 1.8 trillion pesos (approximately 800 billion dollars), comprising 60 to 70 percent of the funds for each location (A toda máquina 2004). In other words, the megaproject responds to the transportation needs of diverse municipalities, and will be the product of a coordinated effort between central and local administrations, yet represents, for the most part, an initiative of the national government. The list of favored cities includes Barranquilla (Transmetro), Cali (Metrocali), Cartagena de Indias (TRANSCaribe), Medellín (Metroplús, where BRT will operate as a feeder of the Metro system), Bucaramanga (Metrolínea), and Pereira (Megabús). The government has argued that these cities (and smaller ones, such as Soacha, a suburb of Bogotá) will benefit from the lessons learned in TransMilenio and share in the improvement of quality of life. On a practical level, the designs and specifications of the new systems will be almost identical to TransMilenio, with minimal changes to address each setting's particular demands.

In the case of Cartagena, with its Caribbean location, six boats are included in the master plan, ferrying passengers from one to another end of the city's bay. This measure grants a distinct quality to the Cartagena system, though the elements replicating TransMilenio are plainly evident. Yet, even in Cartagena or Barranquilla, the most distinctive cities within the group, the resemblance to TransMilenio will be remarkable (Les llegó 2005); to the eyes of the occasional visitor, a common characteristic of most Colombian cities will be their reliance on a BRT system, very alike in operation and design.

The practical implications of this transportation policy are very significant. In few places in the world has there been an initiative advocating such homogeneity in public transit, giving more than twenty million people, close to half the national population, a similar design for public transportation within a short time frame. Within Latin America, this is a remarkable novelty. Mexico has a similar approach, but its systems, planned for Chihuahua, Monterrey, Querétaro, Torreón, and Aguascalientes (together with the BRTs in Mexico City and León, already in service), have an impact on a smaller percentage of the national public. As the product of an experience leading to a distinct urban identity, public transportation usually displays a great variety of alternatives, given the need to attend to the specific demands of each urban environment to guarantee network effectiveness. Take, for example, Medellín, where the local network of elevated cable cars (Metrocable), a system relatively rare in Latin America, figures as an effective transportation solution for neighborhoods surrounding the valley. It operates in close conjunction with the Metro's railway network, which, in turn, is supported by Metroplús, the local version of the busway. In all, Medellín's mass transit involves three systems operating in close coordination. By contrast, except in regard to Cartagena, the master plan promoted by the Colombian government pays little attention to specific local conditions.

It is also important to consider the implications of this measure in terms of individuality. Although urban distribution serves as a spatial paradigm, echoing Borja's arguments, citizen mobility contributes substantially to the interpretation of identity, given its effect on how people perceive and construe a personal experience of modernity as they travel. How one travels through a place says much about how one internalizes aspects of one's surroundings to construct an identity. This is evident from research conducted by Néstor García Canclini chronicling the impact of public transportation on the development of urban identity in a rapidly changing Mexico City. In *La ciudad de los viajeros* (1996), Canclini signals how urban travel plays a significant role in the reproduction of the labor force's social structure and in the appropriation of living and working space. In the latter part of his text, in particular, he examines the relation between urban displacement and the development of narratives of identity, evincing the bond between modes of public transportation and the citizenry's conception and imagination of its place of dwelling. He highlights, within this context, the significance of urban traveling, taking the nineteenth-century flâneur as its predecessor.[1]

Should the TransMilenio experience be regulated by a narrower definition of mobility, dictated by unyielding issues of nationality, the consequences of the homogeneity resulting from the practice of imposing the same system of transportation on different cities would not be hard to guess. Even if Colombian cities remain as different as they are today, given their differences in geography, the circulation of its populations will be similar in the future, validating a common way of moving around and making sense of urban space. Thus, a national notion of sociospatial identity—a standardized way of understanding the city from moving through it—will be legitimized, inspired by Bogotá's experience at the beginning of the twenty-first century. If busways are built according to initial specifications, which virtually replicate the design for the capital, Colombians will learn to interact and make sense of the experience of urban life in very similar ways; to live in a Colombian city will become an experience shared by millions in a homogenizing, flattening manner that fails to take individual dissimilarity into consideration. When these seven BRTs (as well as others that may follow) are successfully completed, a good part of Colombia's population will share a mode of transportation that, although having a favorable impact on standards of living, will also standardize urban experience throughout the national territory.

Social space embodies power. Moreover, social space is shaped by the cultural practices that usually regulate our daily life. Taken together, these practices, reflecting how we live, move, and work within society, result from relations of power between individual interests and collective priorities, which in turn address issues of identity. Thus, the construction of BRTs can be interpreted as the central government's way of enacting its power over the populations of more distant urban centers, determining how many city dwellers will generate social space in the future and, consequently, favoring particular forms of urban identity. On the one hand, the disbursement of funds gives the government a tool for the negotiation of concessions from municipal offices, in the context of a genuine struggle for resources. On the other, it sanctions the idea that the models developed, explored, and experienced at the heart of the nation are suitable for the resolution of conflicts in more distant corners, a concept with a vast potential for application in other aspects of Colombian affairs. Given how it is envisaged, BRT endorses a hierarchical relation between the national center and the periphery, and suggests that automotive diversity, best exemplified in multiple modes of public transportation, is of negligible significance when it comes to mass transit solutions. In an analogous fashion, one could conclude that political and cultural diversity, although nominally appreciated—of all places, in the Colombian constitution, one of the most progressive in Latin America—is, in practice, a non-issue. Thanks to this limited mindset, provincial populations appear eager to join in these developments and have their cities share some of the capital's modernity.

In view of the preceding, clearly not everything is a matter for celebration. Viewed as a communicative process, responses to TransMilenio evince other shortcomings, which have made Bogotá's network the object of such increased criticism. Among the network's flaws are constant congestion in many stations, resulting from the relatively small capacity of its vehicles—150 passengers per unit, as opposed to the 270 of the Brazilian buses; the adoption of diesel instead of environmentally friendlier natural-gas-powered units, thereby missing an opportunity to reduce contamination in Bogotá (the third most polluted capital in Latin America); and, as a consequence of the delay in the disposal of obsolete vehicles, a displacement of the uneeded buses to other independently owned routes, with increased traffic congestion in other parts of the metro area (Mucho caos 2005). Moreover, just a few years after the inauguration of Trans-Milenio, many roadways needed roadbed repairs. Although the matter was resolved swiftly, it affected the scheduling of service routes and generated dissatisfaction among customers.

In addition to these problems, there are the habitual charges of social engineering. Most routes built thus far do not go through—in some cases, even seem to avoid—well-off neighborhoods. Moreover, BRT is being increasingly portrayed in terms of social class: its main function is seen as the displacement of the workforce from the less affluent areas of the city to support the lifestyle of the rich, mainly through the service sector (Gané 2006). Future routes allegedly include Seventh Avenue, one of Bogotá's most fashionable thoroughfares, hinting at some level of social integration in the system, but recent performance evaluations and impact studies have carefully avoided mentioning this road. At the same time, disputes among members of the city council substantiate the growing awareness of a need for additional modes of transportation: Seventh Avenue—as well as Tenth Avenue and Twenty-Sixth Street, all parts of the programmed third phase—has been suggested as the ideal site for a light-rail or streetcar network to complement TransMilenio and be more in touch with historical tradition (Volver al tranvía 2004). After all, while providing an alternative, light-rail or streetcar transportation would not be so costly as a full-blown heavy-rail system; further, until the popular revolt following the assassination of political leader Jorge Eliécer Gaitán on April 9, 1948, during which Bogotá's downtown was virtually razed, streetcars were the main mode of mass transit, and, until the 1970s, there was a marginally operational network of trolleybuses. Hence, increased reliance on a single mode of transit is viewed suspiciously.

There have been other setbacks. In late April 2006, when TransMilenio's second stage came into service, a transportation strike organized by independent contractors virtually paralyzed Bogotá. Although the strike gave some leverage to the city administration, TransMilenio was unable to keep up with demand. Its feeder network, though extensive, was (and is) still poor in comparison to the tentacular reach of the many independent bus routes operating throughout Bogotá. To make things worse, the effect of the strike was compounded by changes effected as the second stage of BRT went into service. The introduction of new color coding for all lines and the division of the network's grid into zones, with barely a week's notice, contributed to much frustration in the customer base. Unlike other transit systems around the world, which assign a single color to an entire line, TransMilenio's management opted for a complicated setup by dividing the network into districts. Consequently, a single line, such as the one crossing Bogotá from north to south, bears up to three different colors (green, blue, and orange). To complicate things further, the number of trips allowed per travel card was abruptly reduced in 2006, so that users, accustomed to cards with up to fifty trips, discovered in the course of a few days that only single-trip cards could be purchased. Finally, although services operated with greater frequency, the number of transfers and the average time of travel per route did not decrease, as promised by management.

The combination of all these factors threw the system into disarray. Unlike what happened with bomb threats, in the past, when the citizenry showed its support for the network, there were massive demonstrations and users twice blocked operations; customer displeasure was evident. Nevertheless, as impediments to adequate operation gradually become apparent, management tried to address them. In the end, the situation worked to the benefit of Mayor Luis Eduardo Garzón (2004–2007), a former union leader who, ironically, had to neutralize the strike paralyzing the city. Garzón confronted the strikers tenaciously, a move that gained him substantial political support, even among upper-class sectors that do not usually endorse the Left. His position was also strengthened by full support from Uribe, head of the national government. It has, in effect, become evident that the concept underlying TransMilenio has enhanced Uribe's political capital and that his influence is not limited to the one instance of this citywide strike.

TransMilenio's third stage, well into its construction, is already a matter for controversy. Uribe has argued that the cost per kilometer of construction of future routes is $7.1 million, whereas Garzón argued that costs increased to $14 million per kilometer (Pulso de 2006). The difference lies in the national administration's offer to pay for the dedicated lanes only, whereas the municipal government included the cost of modifying surrounding areas in its estimates. In any event, between incessant strikes, the confrontation between city hall and independent bus operators, and the struggle with Uribe, Garzón's time as mayor was challenging. The most recent administration, with political scion Samuel Moreno Rojas (2008–2011) as head, has focused on the development of a metro system as well as regional commuter rail, leaving TransMilenio aside. In the meantime, the number of buses in Bogotá has skyrocketed, generating massive traffic congestion. Although many bus routes were displaced to distant neighborhoods, complementing service, a number managed to occupy main venues, avoiding the programmed recycling of old units. Thanks to loopholes in government subsidies, many of these vehicles ride almost empty and become cash cows for the many private consortia handling transportation. Recent research confirms the dissatisfaction of small public transportation subcontractors, particularly those concerned with an appropriate time frame for an eventual integration of their networks into TransMilenio—a process requiring, in many cases, up to fifteen years (Burbano Valente 2005, 323). In addition, in September 2006, there were massive protests over the poor operation of feeder routes; the case of El Tunal, in which police had to disperse a crowd of four hundred persons, was amply covered by media (El conflicto 2008).

At the national level, the obstacles evident during the initial implementation of further BRTs are even more comprehensive. The difference between carrying out contracts with the state in the capital, home of the national government, and in the provinces, where things acquire a different hue, has become evident. In the outlying areas, a decidedly oppositional perspective has influenced negotiations between parties, making it impossible to portray events as a collaborative process. In Cartagena, for example, the appointment of the management team for the project took up to eight months, when it then became necessary to replace the team on account of its differences with the project's board of directors. Subsequently, there were differences with subcontractors over the final design of facilities, which resulted in delaying the date of inauguration of the system and meant that it was not ready in time for the celebration of the Central American and Caribbean Games, hosted by Cartagena. In Cali, a city once admired for its efficiency and civic spirit, there were irregularities in the assignment of responsibilities (irregularities that suggested corruption), protests surrounding the removal of trees (despite the immediate creation of a planting program), and scandals related to changes in the guidelines for bids on some contracts. In Medellín and Bucaramanga, the monies corresponding to the project, to be approved by local municipalities as part of their agreement with the state, were processed less swiftly than initially guaranteed. In Barranquilla, there were delays in the approval of credits, arising from the city's delicate financial situation, beleaguered by a continuous stream of financial scandals. In Pereira, the city with the first completed project (August 21, 2006), the deadline for the end of the construction phase went by with many facilities still unfinished, hurting sales in the downtown district and virtually paralyzing the economy in some sectors of town. In summary, despite government diligence and the unanticipated availability of large sums of money, the original hope of having six systems operating by the end of 2006 was not realized.

These obstacles do not affect the contention that the consistency with which BRT is sponsored by the national government has serious implications for the negotiation of identity. Amid a country besieged by conflict, BRT has become an ideal mechanism for the reimplementation of the normative idea of nation and for a vision of order stubbornly fostered by Uribe. Thanks to the eagerness of some provincial administrations to solve their transportation dilemmas, the central government has identified and taken advantage of an opportunity to recreate and influence the way many Colombian cities are experienced and imagined by their inhabitants. BRT has thus become a tool of hegemony, sustained as the primary form of conceiving *colombianidad* in an urban location. Everything considered, the idea of BRT as the main means of city transportation has been co-opted. The Colombian busway may be an idea born under Peñalosa's guidance of the national capital, yet members of the existing national government, who see it as an ideal mechanism for the interpellation of the masses have appropriated it systematically. To state this point succinctly, Uribe has transformed the busway system into the urban face of the democratic security policy: in a matter of ten years, half the country will be very alike in terms of urban mobility. In the end, however, the public's reaction will be paramount—how different cultural actors respond to such an alternative—in a country where one of the most tangible forms of modernity was, until quite recently, the festive circulation through the city in a *chiva*, a multicolored bus like those of the countryside, in a repeated simulacrum of the rural exodus of previous years and the ever-present conflict between national tradition and modernity.

The Feria del Libro and the Ritualization of Cultural Belonging in Havana

ANTONI KAPCIA and PAR KUMARASWAMI

The concept of cultural revolution in Cuba since 1961, although far from uncontested or unproblematic, has been central to the post-1959 process of revolutionizing attitudes. The debates and tensions of that process have generated several outstanding episodes of apparent conflict (notably between the state and the artist) dominating external perspectives of culture and revolution in Cuba. In part, this has all been complicated by one of the Revolution's most explicit imperatives: to "democratize" culture. At one level, this meant the seminal 1961 Literacy Campaign which created a potential new readership overnight and revolutionized perspectives (Fagen 1969), but at other levels it has meant, variously, an emphasis on mass culture, attempts to bring culture to "the masses" (such as the ambitious 1960s publishing projects and the pirating of copyright of foreign classics), attempts to raise the general cultural level, and, above all, the constant campaign to stress cultural participation. The latter, passing through the 1960s program of *instructores de arte*, the 1970s *movimiento de aficionados,* and the 1980s Casas de Cultura movement,[1] has been based on a consistent belief in every Cuban's innate capacity to participate in artistic production and on an inalienable right of access to such opportunities (Kapcia 2005, 135). Inevitably, these programs, for all their ambition and virtue, continually met objections and prejudices from the cultural producers, resulting in low prestige sometimes for the activities.

Whatever the vicissitudes of the question of cultural revolution in Cuba before 1989, the 1990s brought a new set of challenges and opportunities to refocus. This was because of the unprecedented economic crisis, as the Socialist

Bloc (Cuba's main trading partners) collapsed, generating the so-called Special Period, a decade of stark austerity and strategies of survival by any means. As the economy fell by one-third in three years, as employment plummeted and as the whole infrastructure of the state deteriorated, with devastating effects on transport, energy, and daily life, all attitudes, policies, and patterns had urgently to be reassessed, a reassessment that inevitably included the world of culture, whose conditions and resources (for cultural production, participation, and practice) were affected. For example, the drastic paper shortage meant new priorities, placing education above recreation, or propaganda above art, and a shortage of materials meant a quantitative decline in performances. One notable effect was a shift of emphasis in cultural practice from the national to the local, often simply because the authorities were unable to organize events or transport, but also because everyone's daily search for resources left little time, opportunity, or inclination to seek cultural activity in the city center. Thus, the focus of cultural practice shifted to the local, with de facto cultural centers springing up; one such was the nationwide emergence of municipal-level publishing, using recycled paper, handmade materials, and basic desktop technologies, and another was a rebirth of the Casas de Cultura (Kapcia 2005, 200–6). Moreover, in this respect, "local" really did mean local—the barrio and immediate neighborhood—especially in Havana. For the capital had, over the years, seen a dual process of concentration of cultural power. The first was at a national level, concentrating power in the main, Havana-based, state-run cultural spaces (Casa de las Américas, ICAIC, UNEAC, etc.),[2] reinforcing the evolving centripetal tendency of national cultural activity vis-à-vis the provinces. The second process of concentration of local power was focused within the city itself, as transport infrastructure improved between the city center and the outlying districts, effectively centralizing Havana's cultural activity in the Vedado and Habana Vieja (Old Havana) districts.

Hence, the impact of the 1990s crisis was considerable, halting and even reversing the three-decade-long trend of concentration in the capital.

However, while these developments may have created new opportunities for local participation, they tended to further the already problematic isolation of the established cultural practitioners, now cut off in several ways: from the outside world (through reduced travel and imports); from the opportunities of production, publication, or performance; and from a real or potential public. Indeed, all the prestige-conferring elements of the established Cuban cultural framework disappeared for several years. Moreover, the incipient flourishing of a localized culture challenged a system based, since 1961, on centralization and a relative uniformity of operation; for example, the development of local municipal-level publishing outlets, while welcomed as imaginative responses to local needs, also implied greater heterogeneity.

Then, beginning about 1993, economic reforms (including the legalization of hard currency) meant a new attitude to the commercialization of culture, allowing and even encouraging the sale of cultural products on an open hard-currency market, either abroad or on the island's emerging tourist market.[3] This wave of opportunity brought a potential new prestige (and security) for some, but also a new risk of greater isolation, given the growing division between a hard-currency economy and a *peso cubano* economy; while more artists were gravitating toward the former, selling abroad or to tourists,[4] those consumers who lived in the latter economy had less access to the artists' work. Hence, cultural authorities and many cultural producers began to emphasize a new challenge for the relationship between culture and the revolution: the need to reestablish links with the Cuban public and find a new cultural space. It was precisely then, partly in response to these challenges, that the Havana Feria del Libro (Book Fair) began to develop a new profile, although, remarkably, this new venture began while the Special Period was still in operation and when resources were still scarce, a coincidence that does much to confirm the social and cultural importance that the authorities placed on the renaissance of the Feria.

THE "PROBLEM" OF HAVANA

The development of the Feria's new profile was also directly linked to another significant phenomenon, namely the new emphasis on the post-1981 reconstruction of Havana and the official drive to reverse the city's steady physical deterioration. One by-product of the revolution's policies since 1959 had been the neglect of Havana in favor of the countryside: from 1963, rural Cuba had become the focus of investment and politics, reflecting two processes. The first was a growing radicalization and agrarianization, which saw the revolution redefine itself as a peasant-based phenomenon, with an implicit moral and ideological rejection of urbanism (Gugler 1980). The second was a conscious rejection of Havana, given the underlying unease with the once cosmopolitan city's associations with Spanish colonialism (until 1898) and (from 1902) American neocolonialism, but above all with its past notoriety as a focal point for corruption, major and petty crime, prostitution, and seedy glamour. For, by the 1950s, the familiar Latin American rural-urban migration patterns had created a huge informal sector, concentrated in the city's inner slums, especially in Centro Habana and Habana Vieja and in its burgeoning peripheral shantytowns, and, with that, a growing pool of the poor and unemployed for a new "service" sector dependent on criminality; the latter, already endemic in Cuba after decades of corrupt politics and sugar-linked prosperity, was boosted by the government's willingness to link up with U.S.-based crime syndicates (Cirules 1999).

Hence, as the U.S.-imposed isolation after 1960 generated a siege mentality, a form of cultural autarchy set in that identified Cuba with the countryside.[5] Meanwhile, as a response to the need to prevent the characteristic Latin American tendency toward urban primacy, policies were designed to attract people to the interior and away from a potentially "parasitical" capital. Therefore, although much investment was directed into building new housing blocks (largely through self-help voluntary *microbrigadas* [microbrigades]), and although a rapid process of relocation was effected by simply rehousing poor families in middle-class properties vacated by their owners as they left Cuba, Havana effectively wasted away, its buildings often left unprotected against the ravages of tropical weather and age, its services lagging behind those in the countryside. To some extent, this process undermined any sense of pride in Havana as a city, both among Cubans as a whole and among *habaneros* themselves.

Even while some two million Cubans continued to live in the capital, this neglect had political effects, especially as habaneros continued to be the raw material for the repeated mobilizations of citizens for labor, protest, or support. This became evident in 1980, when street protests developed into unrest and a tolerated exodus of over 120,000 economic emigrants through the nearby port of Mariel.

Therefore, when, in 1978, Havana was declared a Monumento Nacional, the long-established Oficina del Historiador de la Ciudad de La Habana (Office of the Havana City Historian), under Eusebio Leal Spengler, was given a new responsibility for the city's restoration. In 1981, a series of articles emerged from the cultural elite, lamenting the dilapidation of a once elegant and fascinating city and calling for a national effort to save it (*Revolución y Cultura* 1981).[6] In 1981, UNESCO declared Habana Vieja a World Heritage Site, and the city that had previously been a source of shame began to be seen as a source of national pride.

The slow restoration was, however, threatened severely by the post-1990 crisis. Yet, as occurred with the Feria, it was precisely then that the revolution responded to this challenge, not by cutting restoration resources but by freeing and even increasing them. In 1993, given the wider plan to replace sugar by tourism as the economy's mainstay, the Oficina was granted special permission to reinvest tourist income to develop the city as a tourist resource. However, the "contract" with the Cuban government meant an equal commitment to a parallel process of refurbishment of residential housing in bad repair. The result was an immediate and massive regeneration campaign, eventually creating over 10,500 jobs directly (Carrión n.d.), developing new artisan activity and skills, and boosting a new civic pride. Moreover, although this process of reconstruction was concentrated in the more tourist-oriented Habana Vieja, the adjacent areas were also brought in, especially Centro Havana, the most run-down area of inner-city slums, where there had been worrying outbreaks of unrest in 1994 and an increase in low-level criminality; here, the emphasis was placed on self-help programs (largely because the state could still not cope financially, but also following ingrained principles of communal action), with trained professional architects and technicians being loaned to neighborhood *talleres de transformación integral* (social action workshops), along with necessary physical resources, to allow residents to gradually rebuild and refurbish their own housing and immediate vicinity.

The evolution of the Feria partly matched this whole phenomenon. In 1982, the first Feria had taken place, a small affair at the Habana Vieja Palacio de Bellas Artes (or art gallery); for the next eighteen years, the event continued biennially, in different locations, until it lodged in 1990 at the Pabexpo site, a vast complex located, however, some nine kilometers from the city center, in the distant western suburb of Cubanacán, well beyond Miramar. Throughout, the event's focus was as an international book fair for global publishers (much like, for example, the London and Frankfurt fairs on which, at least initially, it was partially modeled), as is evident from the records that emphasize the countries represented, 1986 seeing the most (44) but the number never dropping below 25 (*Feria* 2006, 5).

Then, in 2000, a new phase began, with three new features: a shift to an annual event, a new location (the impressive old fortress of La Cabaña, along the eastern shore of the narrow entrance to Havana Bay), and the designation of *país de honor* (country of honor), as the Feria's focal point.[7] Finally, 2003 brought the event's most significant development, with the decision to take each year's Feria to the provinces after the Havana event, 18 municipios being visited in that year, rising to 35 in 2005 and 2006, and 40 in 2007. The latter change clearly explains the increase in numbers attending the event as a whole, attendances rising from 150,000 (2000) and 300,000 (2001) to 2.2 million (2002), 4.8 million (2005), 5.4 million (2006), and 5.5 million in 2007, with book sales rising from 300,000 (2000) to 5.7 million in 2005 (Feria 2006, 6).[8]

Simultaneously, the emphasis evidently and significantly also shifted from the Feria as an international event for international publishers to a nationally focused one for Cuban writers, publishers, and public. At the 2006 event, of the 142 stalls, 63 were Cuban, and only 14 other countries were represented, Mexican publishers occupying 15 stalls; most of the non-Cuban displays came from left-wing publishers.[9]

FIGURE 11. Cabaña Fortress, site of the Havana International Book Fair (photo by Par Kumaraswami, 2009)

How can one explain this sudden and dramatic change in size, location, frequency, and focus? Most obviously, it coincided with significant political developments in Cuba. For January 1998 (the year the new Feria was decided) saw the first significant mass mobilizations since the 1980s, with the Pope's visit, which was treated by all as a national celebration of survival and of the political system's underlying strength. This was followed by the even more seminal six months of mobilization, protest, and celebration focused on Elián González, a campaign that changed Cuban politics and persuaded the Cuban leadership of the value and possibilities of mass mobilization and participation;[10] it was at this point that the political emphasis shifted from a participation that was necessarily defensive (given the scale of the crisis and perceived threat) to a positive and confident mobilization. In other words, the new Feria was part of the new emphasis on mobilization (which took shape in the post-2000 official campaign of the *Batalla de Ideas* [Battle of Ideas]) and also a reflection of the accelerated shift toward a national pride in Havana as a city.

THE 2006 FERIA DEL LIBRO

Let us consider what the new Feria looks like today.[11] It is organized by the Instituto Cubano del Libro (ICL), Cuba's national publishing authority, and constitutes the major part of the ICL's annual program. The Havana event lasts some ten days and takes place mostly in the La Cabaña fortress. Although this location seemingly presents obstacles for ordinary Havana residents (the fort is on the opposite side of Havana Bay from most of the city, accessible only via a road tunnel or a long and circuitous route around the southern shore), these difficulties are overcome by the provision of a continuous fleet of buses from various locations each day (with similar transport organized through workplaces and educational institutions). Moreover, the fort's scale indicates why that location, rather than a closer one, was chosen, for it is a village in itself, including streets, buildings, and open spaces, and thus capable of accommodating the thousands who attend daily.[12]

One interesting feature is the Feria's efficiency. In 2006, challenging Cuba's (not always deserved) reputation for inefficiency, lateness, and improvisation, all planned activities ran on time (with the exception of one delay caused by the late arrival of Abel Prieto, the poet and minister of culture, and a 30-minute power outage in one building), and all advertised activities materialized. Unless the ICL has unique levels of efficiency, this indicates the event's special political importance; with thousands attending and with much political capital invested, the system generally could not afford to allow it to fall short. Hence, no expense was spared to recruit labor, implement the program, transport the public, and provide food; then, as now, the Feria provided an unusual range of constantly replenished *peso cubano* food outlets. Further, in the run-up to the event, most of the city's state-run bookshops were (and are) closed, officially to free staff to work at the Feria but perhaps also to ensure its greater impact.

In 2006, the Feria's original opening date (Thursday, February 2) was postponed because of a visit to Cuba by Venezuelan President Hugo Chávez; however, that opening ceremony (in Habana Vieja's Plaza de San Francisco) highlighted the Feria's political importance, being addressed by both Fidel Castro and Chávez (representing the 2006 país de honor) and attended by the familiar array of cultural and political luminaries, including Prieto.

Hence, the opening day for the public was Saturday, February 4. Given Cubans' tendency to praise the Feria, one inevitably approaches the phenomenon with caution, wary of exaggeration through national pride or hyperbole arising from unfamiliarity with other book fairs. However, such caution proved unnecessary in 2006, since it became clear from the first moments that anecdotal reports did not exaggerate: with the gates due to open at 10 a.m., buses arrived from 9 a.m. on, and a 300-meter-long line (taking an hour to clear) waited to enter. Moreover, some 1,500 people per hour entered the three entrances of the Cabaña on the first morning, and a large car-park (converted from the sports field of the adjacent barracks) was already half-full by midday.

Each year, every incentive is clearly offered to attend the Feria; entrance is cheap, costing Cubans two pesos (although foreigners are charged four hard-currency *pesos convertibles*, over thirty times the Cuban price), with children under twelve entering free. The first day, a Saturday, was inevitably dominated by families in 2006, anecdotal descriptions of the Feria as a family "day out" being borne out and making the weekend's atmosphere more akin to a U.S. state fair than a conventional book fair.

The Feria actually has two separate, but surprisingly related, dimensions. Each day has a full, eight-and-a-half-hour program of cultural activities in the comfortable inner buildings, consisting of *presentaciones* (book launches), poetry readings, roundtables, and award presentations. The Feria is also a public happening, where habaneros, besides going to the literary events and the publishers' stalls, mill around in the sunshine, listen to music, watch entertainers, and eat and drink. However, perhaps surprisingly, much of this popular participation in 2006 was focused on books, with some two-thirds of the public evidently purchasing books. Moreover, during the first weekend, around five hundred people at a time waited, two hours each, in a continuous 200-meter-long line for access to the two large stores that sold Cuban books in pesos cubanos—books that included a range of titles beyond those on display at the events—while other persons waited in line for free books, donated by the país de honor. The significance is clear: ordinary habaneros not only chose to attend but made efforts to acquire books, and, in the wider context of a system of book distribution not necessarily responsive to local demand, some at the Feria did so to acquire books for friends or family.[13]

There are several reasons Cubans wait in line patiently. First, in contemporary Cuba waiting in line is a deeply ingrained habit, with a two-hour wait (for something worthwhile) being more tolerated than in the United States or Britain. Hence the question is less why they wait per se than why they wait, for example, for free books. Here, local culture is again important, for, in a society that clearly values the possession (as much as the reading) of books, to acquire one's own books is a sign of culture and a statement of belonging to a literate, cultured, and thus revolutionary community. Books confer prestige in Cuba.

Second, in Cuba, where many material goods are either expensive or unavailable, the distribution of any free good is valued, especially when it has social prestige or is a possible source of income. In 2006, the fact that the free books were Venezuelan added to their attraction, mixing a familiar desire to know about other countries (since foreign travel is limited and highly sought), the prestige conferred by possession of a non-Cuban good, and the desire to register support for the official relationship with Venezuela, a nation in which many Cubans place great hopes. Hence, such registering has personal as well as collective meaning. In 2006, Venezuela's profile (as país de honor) was ensured by the presence of the Venezuelan president and three prominent writers at the opening ceremony, the distribution of free books to book-hungry Cubans, a significant number of Venezuelan bookstalls, and a regular series of discussions about Venezuela. These last were usually well attended, not only by the hierarchy whose presence legitimized the Venezuelan element, but also by the wider public; one book launch attracted 120 people, its importance legitimized by the presence of Prieto and the ICL's director, Iroel Sánchez.

The weekday events inevitably had fewer participants, and were much more focused on the organized intellectual activities; these acquired a greater status, being marginally better attended (indicating perhaps that some writers preferred to attend outside the popular weekend) and being seen more as genuinely intellectual activities than as ceremonial events. Certainly, writers (identifiable by their "Profesional" badges) were much more evident on the weekdays. General attendance was also impressive—surprisingly so, given that few Cubans are officially unemployed; this high level of attendance is partly explained by the presence of retired Cubans (among whom there is a greater, more ingrained, and more loyal appreciation of reading and books), by organized visits from schools and workplaces, and by the participation of those who could relatively easily take time off work.

The Feria discussions are, at one level, no different from the normal ICL calendar of literary events, such as book launches and seminars. However, a Feria event clearly confers prestige and often carries an explicit political purpose (about education, the país de honor, or current campaigns, for example).

An analysis of the intellectual program of 2006 makes several points. Evidently, the Feria plays a critical and central role in the Havana cultural calendar, providing the elite with an unparalleled opportunity to gather for several days, meet personalities, be seen (by the media who cover the event extensively), and above all engage in an important ritual of belonging. Indeed, several elites seem to gather in parallel; alongside the exclusively literary events, economists, social scientists, historians, librarians, education specialists, and other professionals gather for their own launches and discussions, the latter often being the best attended (often by the authors' friends and families).[14] This aspect of the Havana fair constitutes a literary festival focused primarily on writers, mirroring other book fairs in Latin America, such as those in Buenos Aires and Cartagena.

Some literary discussions are simply large-scale reiterations of previous launches, offering a book at a subsidized price, with the opportunity of a signed copy; others present works (of political value) commissioned for the Feria. For example, in 2006 a verse version of *Don Quijote* in Cuban Spanish provided not only a subsidized "Cubanized" version of a classic text, but also a special commemorative first print run; the panel (composed of Prieto, Sánchez, and an editor from the youth-focused *Gente Nueva* publishers) underlined the edition's prestige, with the launch attended by over two hundred persons. Moreover, it was announced that, although a limited number of copies had been printed for the Feria, the entire print run, a massive forty thousand copies, was to be distributed subsequently. Rather than stress the book's obvious sales potential, Sánchez emphasized that the recovery of print culture was not a reflection of its commercialization but rather remained true to the inherently socioeducational and political values underpinning literary policy.

Other sessions of Ferias launch new editions of already published works, at a subsidized price, although this is a relatively new phenomenon and an important signal of the post–Special Period recovery of print culture. It is clear from the ICL 2005 annual report that one of the Feria's aims has been to compensate for deficient production and distribution processes during the rest of the year.

Finally, a small number of "special" sessions celebrate the work of those authors particularly recognized at each Feria (in 2006, these were the poets Nancy Morejón and Angel Augier). These launches also provide subsidized versions and new editions of these prestigious writers, but are designed predominantly to honor the writer in question.

This raises the question of how Cuban writers themselves view the Feria.[15] In general, in 2006 all writers interviewed were unreservedly positive about it, though for a range of reasons. Most saw the Feria's primary function as providing space for much-needed feedback, or at least for dialogue and interaction between writers and readers, thus bringing together "high" and "popular" cultures in an event which prioritized recreation and pleasure over solely book-oriented events. Indeed, many considered the impressive attendance figures as a clear indication of the Feria's status in the Havana cultural calendar, praising the organizers' sensitive responsiveness to the public's needs and general cultural tastes. There was some indication that writers were enjoying the renaissance of literary culture and felt that the book had once again equaled other more popular cultural forms (music, dance) in terms of profile and public recognition. This suggests that the Feria serves several functions, as both writers and organizers conceptualized the importance of the book within a wider social project incorporating instruction, self-improvement, recreation, and mass participation. However, it also hints at potential perceptions of marginalization, either of writers (who are unable to compete in terms of popularity and commercial success with other artists) or of the general public (who have been to some extent excluded from the literary landscape). Some writers stressed, therefore, that popular participation temporarily occupying a literary space was only a first step to real popular participation in literature, and that there was much room to enhance democratization.

On the other hand, and logically, there were also individual writers who saw the primary function of the Feria in terms of their own production, development, and status: some prioritized the function of feedback between writers, a chance to interact with the Havana literary community, and, referring to the post-Havana "provincialization" of the event, wished for a chance to meet and interact with non-Havana writers. Indeed, discussions with both writers and organizers indicated that there is some two-way movement between Havana and the provinces, with a large number of Havana writers traveling out to the provinces, and a more limited number of provincial writers attending the Havana event.

Some writers interviewed bemoaned the reduction of the Feria's international dimension in favor of a local presence, seeing this as limiting the possibilities for dialogue with international writers and publishing houses. Finally, while some writers praised the Feria as the most successful initiative in bringing together Havana writers and the general public in a collective ritual of belonging (thus creating new habits and practices in both communities), others indicated that the two hundred or more writers attending the Havana event with their publications did not accurately represent sales figures (and therefore popularity and the tastes of the readership), but rather fulfilled the tastes of the political and literary elites, once more keeping the two communities firmly separated. At some level, however, the expanded media coverage of the event, mostly in the national media, and primarily in regard to Havana writers, was recognized as an important step in increasing literary access and participation among habaneros.[16]

It is clear that the Feria's two dimensions are closely interlinked. On the one hand, those participating in the intellectual events also brought their families and indulged in the general festival atmosphere, queuing with the general public; on the other hand, the otherwise festive public not only evidently bought books, although not always the ones profiled, but also dropped in on the event's literary activities.

One interpretation could be that both communities (writers and readers) gain prestige and legitimacy from each other. First, the public evidently gains satisfaction from participating in a high-profile literary event, ritually registering their belonging to a society that values and privileges books, and simultaneously acquiring some of the cultural prestige by contact with writers. Further, given the evident interest in children's books, there is also the opportunity for an educational experience for children and grandchildren, continuing to inculcate Cubans' long-standing investment in education and reading. In this respect, the Feria acts like the annual May Day rally or other mass events in contemporary Cuba, where collective participation (through family, neighborhood, or workplace) confers an important badge of belonging—where the important thing is to attend, to register a nominal adherence and to demonstrate that duty has been performed. Hence, the Feria, although formally a national event over the several weeks of its capital and provincial iterations, is plainly seen by habaneros as a local event in which they, as residents of a once overlooked and neglected capital city, take some pride. Going to the Feria is as much about doing what everyone does, along with family and neighbors, as about the wider questions of belonging and literacy.

It is also clear that, for ten days, otherwise isolated writers, too, feel a belonging to this same wider range of identities, through attending throughout the event and theoretically addressing the public; certainly the writers gain legitimacy from the massive public attendance. In the same way that the public gains cultural prestige by participating with writers, the writers gain political prestige by the public's attendance, by being "stars" of a social festival; even if only briefly, the Feria means that literature enjoys a popular stage and writers can feel not only that they are at the center of the public's, and the revolution's, attention, but also that they indeed have an interested mass readership.

What this means is that the Feria experience operates on, and is effective across, several layers of identity. At the most local, the fact that the buses organized to take people to the Feria leave from particular localities in the city reinforces the neighborhood-based character of each day's attendance, families and friends from each locality attending as a group. At a slightly higher level, the Feria has emerged for habaneros as an important focus for their growing identification with their city, and therefore, as a distinctly habanero social event. However, these habaneros also take a new pride in the Feria as a national event, reflecting both an increasing national pride in the capital and an increasing habanero sense of belonging. Moreover, above that level, the Feria emphasizes Cuban national participation in new political and cultural identities being created in twenty-first-century Latin America.

This last point raises many theoretical questions, not least the extent to which Havana should be seen within wider Latin American cultural paradigms. Perhaps the most relevant is the notion, conceived in the 1960s by Angel Rama, of the *ciudad letrada* (lettered city), to describe the situation and role of Latin America's colonial and postcolonial intellectual elites, who, confident in their ivory tower existence, nonetheless effectively acted on behalf of colonialism in spreading Western civilization and European cultural norms, for good and for bad (Rama 1996). Subsequent cultural historiography and cultural studies theory have largely rejected this paradigm, given the twin processes of cultural massification and globalization, both implying a necessary and greater commercialization of culture and a commodification of the intellectual.[17] One such challenge came, for example, from Jesús Martín-Barbero, who in 2005 coined the neologism *urbanía*,[18] which he contrasted with *ciudadanía* (citizenship), a concept largely related to Rama's mythical city; Martín-Barbero's argument was that modern Latin American cities no longer create and depend on such cultural citizenship, but instead should be seen as more globalized and less identifiably Latin American urban entities, creating an "urbanship" rather than a "citizenship." This view links with wider notions of the megalopolis, not least those espoused by such intellectuals as Manuel Castells, whose notion of the "space of flows" (Castells 1989) defined the globalized modern Third World megalopolis, globally connected but locally disconnected. Other theorists, following the "theaters of accumulation" model (Armstrong and McGee 1985), would of course argue that the local connection exists, but in a necessarily dependency-creating way, diffusing an exploitative "development" to the locality and the subcities but channeling resources (including cultural resources) from the periphery to the colonizing metropolitan countries.

However, it is clear that Havana does not quite fit any of these paradigms. Certainly, Havana as an urban space seems not to correspond to the Martín-Barbero notion of urbanía, since the city is far from the amorphous and commercialized Latin American metropolis and much closer to a multipolar urban space, each pole being either a definable barrio or a separate city center. This characteristic reflects Havana's traditional evolution rather than any post-1959 policy of urbanism, the roots lying in a century-long movement of residential patterns and commercial development out from the traditional core (Habana Vieja) southward to Cerro and westward, first to Centro Habana and after 1902 to the then-new suburb of Vedado (eventually, in the 1950s, the focal point for attempts to create a new civic center). Hence, by 1959, there was not a single recognizable center, but at least three (Segre et al. 1997, 2). After 1959, two processes exacerbated this amorphousness: the deliberate process of denial—denial of resources in favor of the provinces, but also the implicit denial of a city identity—and, contradictorily, a process of socialist centralization that concentrated power, decision making, and political mobilization in the capital, the new civic center around the Plaza de la Revolución and the Malecón (the post-1902 seafront promenade) becoming the public spaces for rallies.

Moreover, Havana can hardly be termed a megalopolis in Castells' terms, since the years of "siege" and isolation, plus the city's patterns of economic and social life since 1959, have conspired to make Havana into a city neither as globalized as, say, Mexico City, Rio, or Buenos Aires, nor as most Latin American capitals. Indeed, culturally and commercially, however much the post-1990 years may have imported elements of the market and capitalism, Havana, as the capital of a defiantly socialist Cuba, continues to act as a bulwark against globalization. Further, when one examines the patterns, purpose, and thinking of the Feria, what becomes clear is that Havana (globally disconnected but locally connected) is the opposite of a megalopolis. The Feria is, after all, the cultural event that has turned its back on the commercial publishing definition of the book fair (whether through being shunned by the big publishers or by deliberate choice) and has decided both to reach to the provinces and to make enormous efforts to ensure that the reading public, rather than the book industry, participates.

All this does not mean that Havana (including the Feria) is in some sort of isolation-induced time warp, confirming stereotypical images of a Cuba as frozen in time as its once-famous 1950s American cars. Rather, what it actually demonstrates is another reality: that Havana as a changing urban cultural space is not so much backward vis à vis globalization as resistant to it, creating in the process of siege, revolution, and survival new paradigms of urbanism rather than a distorted version of an existing one.

Havana and the Feria, that is, may be a different, modernized, and even revolutionary version of Rama's *ciudad letrada*, in which the *letrados* (the lettered persons) are both the intellectual-cultural elite (which, for the Feria's duration, is given its moment of glory) and the reading public, who clearly flock in their millions to the Feria's activities and wait in line for access to books, aware of the book's intrinsic value and cultural capital for them, the readers, as much as for the writers. In that sense, the Feria seems both a momentary phenomenon (plugging literature and the writer briefly into the state's infrastructure of cultural prestige and the public's consciousness) and a reflection of a deeper reality of organic relationship among writers, state, publishers, and readers.

This difference arises because Martín-Barbero's notions (dissenting from Rama's concept) are essentially informed by the ideas of mass culture and mass media in the modern city (Martín-Barbero 1987); hence his *urbanía* concerns a city where culture is massified. However, at the Feria, what seems to happen is different, not least because the notion of mass media as a controlling, mediating, or opiate mechanism seems less relevant in contemporary Cuba than in, say, Mexico City or Buenos Aires. In fact, the Feria seems consciously to reject the massification of the media and to exalt the mass prestige of the book.

Certainly, in Cuba the book does seem to possess a symbolic capital absent in Britain or North America, a capital perhaps dating from the effects of the 1961 campaign and subsequent strategies.

Therefore, the question arises as to whether the public who go to the Feria in their millions and wait in line for books are the massified objects of a mass culture or actors striving to be *letrados* (lettered), to acquire, possess, display, and read books for their intrinsic value or "symbolic capital" (Bourdieu 1986). Since Rama deliberately chose the term *la ciudad letrada* rather than *la ciudad de los letrados* (city of the lettered), seeing the former as more exclusive (Chasteen 1996), it may be that the Feria is an instance of the latter, where the Havana public are objects of the "culture industry" (Adorno 2000, 164) of a revolution that values culture as part of the systems of socialization, yet also subjects of a process in which they value being and being seen as letrado. Indeed, the concept of letrado is central to the meaning-making processes that constitute the circuit around the artifact of the book. Whether the letrado is writer, reader, book consumer, or cultural intermediary, the Feria enacts a network of mutually constitutive relationships, and provides the opportunities for a range of identity positions.

This whole experience, therefore, raises fundamental questions, going beyond merely the theory of literary culture and returning to the question of identity, not least the underlying question of who precisely is being represented at the Feria and to whom. There is the question of whether the Feria reflects a drive to emphasize a local identity (and, if so, how local?) or a national identity, or both. If the former, the question becomes whether this identity is about the city of Havana (and especially Habana Vieja) or about Havana as a city space and also the nation's capital. If the latter, the question becomes whether the Feria is a matter of restoring and celebrating a Cuban rather than a Havana identity.

Given these changes in policy, it seems clear that the 2006 Feria is understood primarily by policymakers as an event that first represents and promotes the identity of the capital *to* the capital and then represents and promotes it to the nation, with a variety of local identities (from the *municipio* down to the local barrio and workplace) being contained within that. Perhaps before its "provincialization," the Feria might have stood as a national event, much like the Havana-based Festival del Nuevo Cine Latinoamericano. However, as the Feria has now become a nationwide event, and as its organizers invest considerable effort and resources in the two-way movement between the capital and the provinces, it seems clear that the unifocal nature of the Havana event has given way to something far more complex and multidimensional.

The local dimension is being stressed by the authorities, with the relocation to the Cabaña fortress representing the restoration of Habana Vieja, the recovery of Havana as a metonymic representation of the nation in post-crisis recovery mode, a sign of confidence to be communicated to the outside world (and especially to allies in Latin America), and especially a symbol of confidence for the capital itself. In this sense, given Havana's multipolarity and the inequality of opportunities that this might imply, the Cabaña location allows the event to be reinscribed by its users as a city phenomenon, bringing together sectors of the population from all over the city in a single happening celebrating a Havana identity. Certainly, the evidence of general participation in the event confirms that habaneros see it as a celebration for themselves.

In light of the increasing provincialization of the event, however, the Havana Feria could also be projected as the origin and prototype of the provincial version—that is, as a focus for activity that can be repeated at a regional level across the country, with each province developing over time its own network of activities between its capital and secondary cities, thus maintaining the preeminence of the capital but allowing for regional variation. Eventually, then, the Feria in each province would acquire its own regional identity, and the interactions between the capital and the provinces could bestow mutual prestige through the same multidirectional processes of identity construction that link writers and general public in the capital. This point suggests that Havana's Feria is based on the identity of the capital rather than of the nation at large, and that the promotion and amplification of the provincial events will eventually bestow each province with its own regional/city-based identity, thus creating new communities, identities, and levels of belonging, and at last reemphasizing Havana as an urban cultural space, after decades of neglect.

Zapatistas in Mexico City and the Performance of Ethnic Citizenship

ANDREA NOBLE

n early March 1999, five thousand delegates from the Ejército Zapatista de Liberación Nacional (Zapatista Army of National Liberation, or EZLN) set forth from the Lacandón jungle in Chiapas, southeast Mexico, en route to multiple points throughout the republic. The object of their journey was to promote the Consulta Nacional por los Derechos de los Pueblos Indios y por el Fin de la Guerra de Exterminio (National Consultation for the Rights of Indigenous Peoples and the End of the War of Extermination). Scheduled to take place on March 21, the Consulta, or referendum, asked Mexican citizens to cast their vote on four basic questions related to the rights and place of indigenous peoples in the space of the modern nation:

1. Do you agree that indigenous peoples should be included in all their diversity in the national project and take an active part in the construction of a new Mexico?
2. Do you agree that indigenous rights should be incorporated into the national Constitution in accordance with the San Andrés Agreement and the corresponding proposal of the Commission for Harmony and Pacification of the Congress of Union?
3. Do you agree that we should attain real peace by means of dialogue, demilitarizing the country with the return of soldiers to barracks, as established by the Constitution and its laws?
4. Do you agree that the people should organize and demand that the government "lead by obeying" in all aspects of national life?

Given the nationally inflected orientation of the questions and, concomitantly, the movement that formulated them, the capital was, as symbolic center of the nation, an important hub in activities related to the Consulta. Buses transporting EZLN delegates from Chiapas converged on the heart of Mexico City before fanning out to the more far-flung corners of the country; meanwhile, promotional events in the capital itself received considerable media coverage.

Reporting on one Tojolabal woman's experience of the metropolis, in the pro-Zapatista daily newspaper *La Jornada*, respected EZLN commentator Hermann Bellinghausen recorded the following reaction: "Accustomed to seeing cars very occasionally, one at a time, she found herself trapped in a traffic jam on the way to Magdalena Mixhuca, and asked with surprise: 'Why do they want so many cars?'" To the degree that the urban environment presented this indigenous woman with an array of unfamiliar and alien sensations, the Zapatistas in the city proved an equally strange sight to the capital's residents: "But the surprises that the Zapatistas get are equal to the surprises they give. Commotion on the corners of Iztacalco when a cattle truck passed by (which, for peasants, is for passengers) full of masked people looking at the passers-by who looked at them, stopped, pointed at them, commented on them to one another animatedly and greeted them with sympathy" (Bellinghausen 1999). To be sure, the encounter with real-life (rather than *mediated*) Zapatistas must have been disconcerting for these individual capitalinos, as evinced in the double-take described by Bellinghausen. The Zapatistas' masked faces and the simple detail of their mode of transport underlined the ideologically charged gap separating rural and metropolitan Mexico, and marked them as out-of-place in the urban environment.

Even as the capital was the site of this kind of fleeting eye-witness encounter, the presence of the Zapatistas in the city was also documented in a series of photographs, perhaps more accurately described as photo opportunities. Captured during the weeklong activities to promote the Consulta, and published in *La Jornada*, these photographs conform to an implicit set of rules that govern the relationship between photographer and photographed subject/s in the production of the photo opportunity, where the latter collaborate actively in the staging of made-for-camera events in public places.[1] That is, in these images, Mexico City is not simply a scenic backdrop to the Zapatista incursion into the "urban leviathan" (Davis 1994). Rather, it represents a densely layered and intensely mediated historical site in which to mount "performances of democratic participation" (Saldaña-Portillo 2002, 297) for the camera in state-sanctified spaces of civic ritual: Zapatistas salute opposite the Palacio Nacional; Zapatistas visit the Templo Mayor; Zapatistas visit the Museo Nacional de Antropología.[2]

Focusing on a selection of images made during the Consulta, this chapter traces the Zapatistas' photographic itinerary through the city. It explores the photographs' strategic performative force in the wider context of the struggles for democracy and what anthropologist Guillermo de la Peña (1999) has termed

FIGURE 12. Zapatistas in the Zócalo, *La Jornada*, 19 March 1999 (© 1999 Duilio Rodríguez)

FIGURE 13. A friendly football match (© 1999 Duilio Rodríguez)

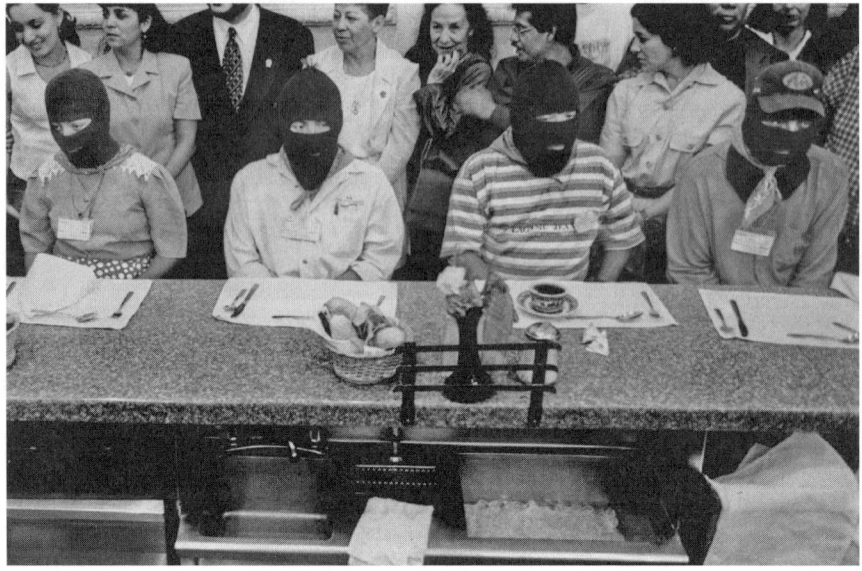

FIGURE 14. Zapatistas in Sanborns, 1999 (© 1999 Duilio Rodríguez)

FIGURE 15. Zapatista leaders in Sanborns, 1914 (Colección SINAFO-FN-INAH # 33532)

ethnic citizenship: an understanding of citizenship that encompasses both the right to equality before the law and the right to cultural specificity. If the sight of real-life Zapatistas in the city elicited reactions of surprise, then the meaning in these images also turns on the gesture of the double-take. Photographed occupying symbolically charged spaces in the capital, the Zapatistas stage acts of national identity that articulate at once their demand to occupy these places and by extension, to be included in the nation, and also their right to look out of place, their right to difference. This chapter is not simply centered on the spatial logic of the Zapatistas' presence in the city, however. As photographic performances involved in the demand for ethnic citizenship, drawing upon theoretical reflections on the idea of *presence*, the series also brings a temporal dynamic into play, a temporal dynamic that cuts to the quick of the Zapatistas' demand for "*coeval* participatory democracy" (Nash 2001, 244; emphasis added).

ZAPATISMO AND ITS CONTEXTS

The antecedents and trajectory of the Zapatista uprising are by now well documented in an abundant critical literature that includes the extensive writings produced by the EZLN itself, analyses by journalists, *cronistas*, political activists, and academics of varied disciplinary stripes, and internationally disseminated across a range of media: from the printed word and documentary films to the Internet. A few, albeit schematic, pointers are nevertheless expedient to signpost the analysis of the Zapatistas' photographic itinerary in the city.[3] As is well known, the Chiapas uprising took place on January 1, 1994, when armed and masked rebels, in their majority comprising indigenous peasants, occupied seven towns in eastern and central Chiapas, declaring war on the Mexican government. With its historical roots in the ethnic divisions established as a result of Spanish colonization, and more recently in the Mexican government's relentless pursuit of neoliberal reform, the rebellion occurred in one of Mexico's poorest states, home to a diverse Mayan population of Tzetzals, Tzotzils, Chols, and Tojolabals (to name but the largest groups).

The classification "Indian," as Alan Knight has argued in an influential essay, was born with the Spanish conquest and "remained part of Spanish rather than Indian usage. It defined those who were not Spanish or mestizo and it lumped together the wide range of Indian groups, languages, and communities" (1990, 76). As a homogenizing category, it has also been mobilized at various points in the historical trajectory of the entity that we now know as Mexico, in attempts to fashion successive Creole, postindependence, and postrevolutionary identities. With Chiapas populated by myriad ethnic groups, the events beginning in 1994 must be framed within the broader context of such hegemonic projects to appropriate elements of indigenous identity, and most particularly the context of the *indigenista* discourses that emerged in the aftermath of the 1910 revolution. The postrevolutionary period ushered in a program of intense social reform, spearheaded by influential anthropologists-cum-missionaries of the Mexican state such as Manuel Gamio and Moíses Saénz, who called for the assimilation of the Indian into the nation. Through educational, social, and cultural projects, these reformists' aim was to foster a national community in which "the old Indian/European thesis/antithesis [would give] rise to a higher synthesis, the mestizo, who was neither Indian nor European, but quintessentially Mexican" (Knight 1990, 85). This was to be achieved by promoting and thereby installing select, folkloric elements of indigenous culture as foundational in the myth of national origin. In the final analysis, then, *indigenismo* was in no sense about incorporating a complex, pluralistic notion of the multiple indigenous ethnicities within national culture; rather, as David Brading puts it in powerfully blunt terms: "The ultimate and paradoxical aim of official *indigenismo* in Mexico was thus to liberate the country from the deadweight of its native past or, to put the case more clearly, finally to destroy the native culture that had emerged during the colonial period. *Indigenismo* was therefore a means to an end. That end was cultural *mestizaje*" (1988, 85).[4]

If the postrevolutionary project of cultural mestizaje thus provides the broader framework in which to situate the Zapatista uprising, this must also be understood in relation to specific socioeconomic factors at work in Chiapas over two crucial periods: on the one hand, the economic boom related to the oil industry (1970–1982), and, on the other, the 1982 crash and its aftermath. The increased revenues associated with the expansion of the oil industry brought significant changes to the indigenous peasant communities of Chiapas. Support for traditional, small-scale agricultural production by the governments of Luis Echeverría (1970–1976) and José López Portillo (1976–1982) went hand in hand with programs that encouraged the diversification of the peasant economy, thereby integrating small landholders into the wider pattern of national and international market forces. The diversification of small-scale agricultural production—to include coffee, meat, and specialty fruits and vegetables, in addition to the more traditional beans and corn—brought with it the migration of significant numbers of indigenous peasants from the Chiapanecan highlands to the state's lowland Lacandón jungle. As a result, and of consequence in the formation of the EZLN, the jungle was colonized by newly formed pluriethnic communities, in which Tojolabals, Tzotzils, Chols, and so forth lived alongside one another.

Based precariously on borrowing set against future income, the boom inevitably led to bust when, in 1982, international oil prices fell precipitously. In response to the crisis, President Miguel de la Madrid (1982–1988), implemented the structural adjustments counseled by the World Bank and International Monetary Fund. These dramatically reversed the populist and protectionist government policies that were put in place after the revolution, privatizing state-owned industry and eliminating agricultural subsidies, making way for foreign investment and free enterprise. In the process, the strongly corporativist relationship that had existed between the Partido de la Revolución Institucional (PRI) and the peasantry, which had held firm since the 1930s, was abandoned overnight. Nowhere was the withdrawal of the social contract between state and peasantry more keenly felt than among the colonists of the Lacandón jungle, who were even more severely affected by the intensification of neoliberal reform during the presidency of Carlos Salinas de Gortari (1988–1994). Fixed on a course to insert Mexico into the global economy through the North American Free Trade Agreement (NAFTA), Salinas made dramatic changes to Article 27 of the nation's constitution, allowing the privatization of communally held peasant holdings (or *ejidos*). In the eyes of the modernizing technocrats who now governed Mexico, small-scale production, which the state had hitherto supported, was "backward," inefficient, and no longer economically viable. They therefore set out to eliminate the peasantry as an economic formation out of place in (and more to the point, outside) the time frame of the modern nation. Even as neoliberal reform constituted an attack on the peasantry as an economic category, it nevertheless coincided with a revitalized indigenismo, or what De la Peña terms a "peculiar (neo-liberal) defense of cultural diversity which emphasises the need for governments to 'transfer functions' to ethnic organisations and accept certain minority rights (such as bilingual education), yet to do all this without touching the political structure of the nation" (2006, 281).

While the government forged ahead with neoliberal reform, over the ten-year period between 1984 and 1994, far from the center of power, in Chiapas the EZLN took shape as a movement propelled by serious social grievances, with membership rising sharply during the Salinas *sexenio*. During the economic boom, with the influx of colonists, the demographic make-up of the Lacandón jungle had changed irrevocably. Left destitute by the onset of economic crisis, these colonists came to assert a reconfigured, overarching identity as indígenas (rather than as members of specific indigenous groups): an identity grounded in a sense of shared poverty. In other words, if Indians had traditionally been the objects rather than subjects of indigenismo, the formation of the EZLN involved a radical reappropriation of indigenous difference. The assertion of a shared indigenous identity now became an avatar for political protest and agency, a vehicle via which to establish these ethnic subjects' legitimacy and rights in the national public sphere. The EZLN was a complex phenomenon; nevertheless, its demands, as articulated in the first Declaración de la Selva Lacandona in January 1994, were straightforward. The rebels called for work, land, housing, food, health, education, independence, liberty, democracy, justice, and peace. In so doing, and as the movement gathered momentum, aided and abetted by extensive national and international media attention, their demands captured the imagination and came to reflect and refract concerns that were simultaneously local and national—and, indeed, international.

BETWEEN CHIAPAS AND MEXICO CITY

Although remote from the epicenter of the rebellion, Mexico City has been, as the nexus of power, the media, and national and international communities, an important strategic coordinate in the EZLN's struggle from the outset. It is widely acknowledged, for example, that thanks to the actions of the approximately ten thousand people who, on January 7, 1994, marched on Mexico City's main square, the Zócalo, representing the Zapatistas in absentia, a massacre by government troops was averted. With the rebels' cause placed in the media spotlight, the government had no choice but to call a ceasefire with the Zapatistas and start negotiations. When, in February 1995, government agents unmasked the EZLN's spokesperson, Subcomandante Marcos on national television, revealing his privileged, middle-class background, the anti-Zapatista publicity stunt backfired. Civil society mobilized in the Zócalo once again, chanting the slogans "¡Todos somos Marcos!" and "¡Todos somos indios!" ("We are all Marcos!"/ "We are all Indians!").[5]

The Zapatistas have not only been represented in the city in absentia by their most effective ally, civil society. In addition to the promotional activities associated with the 1999 Consulta, Zapatista representatives have made their way to, and staged their presence in, the nation's capital at a number of points during the movement's history. Between February and April 2001, after the historic defeat of the PRI and the election of Partido de Acción Nacional (PAN) candidate, Vicente Fox, to the presidency (2000–2006), twenty-four members of the EZLN embarked on the Caravana de la Dignidad Indígena (Caravan for Indian Dignity). Visiting a range of communities along the way, the Caravana—popularly dubbed the Zapatour—culminated in Mexico City, where Zapatista delegates made an historic address before the Federal Congress.[6] Then, on January 1, 2006, the EZLN launched La Otra Campaña (the Other Campaign). Timing their action to coincide with the launch of the official political parties' campaigns for the presidential elections of July 2006, delegates embarked upon the first leg of a six-month journey through the thirty-one states comprising the republic, during which they consulted with labor, peasant, indigenous, student, and civil organizations, with the aim of forging a united opposition to neoliberal capitalism. Like the Caravana before it, La Otra Campaña culminated in Mexico City, just as the capital's residents went to the urns.[7]

It would, of course, be wrong to suggest that the Zapatistas' incursions into Mexico City have constituted a form of one-way traffic, or indeed that the capital in any sense overshadows Chiapas in its significance in the struggle. Erecting makeshift "convention centers," or Aguascalientes, named after the revolutionary convention of 1914, the EZLN has hosted a number of national and international gatherings in the heart of rebel-held territory deep in the jungle of Chiapas. The first Convención Nacional Democrática (CND), for instance, was held in Guadalupe Tepeyac in August 1994 and was attended by some seven thousand Mexican and international delegates, who engaged in debate on democracy, justice, the rights of indigenous peoples, and civil rights in Mexico more generally.[8] The importance of this event and others like it cannot be overestimated. Indeed, in a revealing footnote, María Josefina Saldaña-Portillo cites an interview with sociologist Sergio Sarmiento, in which the latter states "the CND symbolizes, for the first time in [Mexican history], the Indians summoning the rest of the nation, summoning us, the *ladinos*, to the project of remaking the nation, to form a new constituency together" (2003, 332). Nevertheless, if the Zapatistas are engaged in a "project of remaking the nation," in which they have proved themselves highly skilled and astute players in the politics of ritual and spectacle, it would be equally shortsighted to overlook their symbolic enactments of ethnic citizenship in the heart of the nation.

PERFORMING ETHNIC CITIZENSHIP IN THE CITY

In an essay published in the journal *Desacatos* in 1999, De la Peña defines ethnic citizenship as "the call to maintain a different cultural identity and social organization within a given state, which in turn should not only recognize but also protect and legally sanction those differences" (23). For this Mexican anthropologist, then, ethnic citizenship is a concept that holds in delicate equilibrium (1) the notion of universal citizenship and equality before the law alongside (2) an emphasis on cultural and social specificity as manifest, for example, in the right to maintain different languages, customs, religious, and medical practices.[9] The demand for ethnic citizenship also lies at the heart of the 1999 Consulta and the four simple questions posed by the referendum. Thus, when voters were asked whether they agreed "that indigenous peoples should be included in all their diversity in the national project and take an active part in the construction of a new Mexico," the weight of the question rested on the counterpoint between indigenous peoples' right to inclusion and participation in the nation, and, at the same time, having their right to difference recognized. Meanwhile, the second question, with its reference to the San Andrés Peace Agreement negotiated between the EZLN and the government in February 1996, inserts the indigenous right to difference within the legal framework of proposed changes to the national constitution. Finally, the third and fourth questions call for the rejection of intensified military activity, and for the kind of community-based, consensual democracy practiced by the Zapatistas—grounded on the principle of "mandar obedeciendo" (lead by obeying) —to be embraced at a national level. Crucially, where indigenous difference has traditionally been registered in temporal terms in official narratives, as at once integral to the definition of, and yet temporally behind, the modernizing nation, the Zapatistas call for a reconfigured understanding of the temporal and spatial status of indigenous identity: Indians exist inside the space, and are coeval with the time of the modern nation.

Analysis of the Zapatistas' itinerary in the city, above all else, reveals a keen sense of the photo opportunities that their presence in the capital had to offer. It is no coincidence that the Zócalo, at the heart of the Centro Histórico, marked their point of arrival and the strategic point of departure from which to launch the Consulta in the city and in the wider context of the nation. Writing of the Centro Histórico (the official name for the zone of some ten square kilometers, with a high density of monuments of historical significance, designated by presidential decree in 1980) Jerome Monnet notes: "When what is at stake is the center of the capital of a great country, all discourses and practices enter into the arena of national politics, putting into play and manifesting the tensions that underpin all Mexican society and its relations with the world" (1995, 25). The Zapatistas' route through the city demonstrates that they were clearly alert to the profoundly national resonances of the Centro Histórico, overlain successively with Mexica, colonial, and postindependence foundations. As June Nash observes, during the Consulta the Zapatistas "experienced what it was to join in the production of national popular spaces in the Zócalo . . . the huge public space that has been the center of many storms of protest especially since the debt crisis of 1982" (2001, 241).

The symbolic occupation and production of nationally inflected space is increasingly evident, as the Zapatistas circulated in a range of sites and situations in which they were photographed. Sometimes the resulting images are the products of contingency—the photographer and his/her subject happened to have been in the right place at the right time. Such is the case of a high-angle shot of masked visitors in the entrance to the Legislative Assembly, and of the photograph depicting a lone Zapatista snapped seated on the bus that has carried him or her (the *pasamontañas* or ski mask makes it impossible to determine) from Chiapas to the Zócalo, his/her masked face juxtaposed beside a reflection of the national flag, which occupies the right-hand two-thirds of the frame. Elsewhere, there is evidence of more active collusion between photographer and subjects. Such images include: the row of seven Zapatista men and women, their backs to the camera as they salute assembled delegates in the Zócalo, the Palacio Nacional visible in the background, with the silhouette of the Mexican flag outlined above the central balcony (see figure 12); the photograph of the opening ceremony of the football match against ex-professional players for the national team, featuring masked, saluting Zapatistas sporting matching tops emblazoned with a star and the initials EZLN, as well as outsized white shorts over mismatched footwear (see figure 13); and a posed photograph in the entrance to the Zapata metro station

That these performances for the camera are highly theatrical, bordering on the self-reflexive, though on one level self-evident, nevertheless requires further elaboration and, in the first instance, can be productively explored in relation to an image taken in Sanborns, Casa de los Azulejos on Calle 5 de Mayo (figure 14). This image documents the visit on March 16, 1999, by eight members of the EZLN to Sanborns, where they partook of light refreshment in the store's famous restaurant, the event captured by scores of waiting photographers and TV camera operators. This was no ordinary photo opportunity, however; it was the re-creation of one of the most enduring images of the Mexican revolution—itself a quintessential photo opportunity—recording the moment when troops from Emiliano Zapata's Ejército Liberador del Sur (Liberation Army of the South) similarly took their seats at the bar of Sanborns and were immortalized in sepia (figure 15). In a striking juxtaposition, the two photographs appeared together on the front cover of *La Jornada* on March 17, 1999.[10]

Made in early December 1914, during the brief historic occupation of Mexico City by Zapatista and Villista troops, this photograph, when viewed in light of the values of the time, clearly captures the transgressive irruption of indigenous peasants from the nearby state of Morelos into the "civilized" and sacred space of the legitimate order represented by Sanborns. The 1914 incursion into the capital city was not something that the Zapatistas undertook with relish; their distrust and fear of urban values is well documented. Nor did the capitalinos greet the visitation by the armed rural masses with gusto, for their purported savagery and violent exploits had been vividly reported in the Mexico City press, in which the Zapatistas and particularly Zapata himself were consistently vilified throughout the armed conflict. We can read this 1914 photograph, then, as visual evidence of the Zapatistas' encounter with the city: their lack of élan is clearly legible in the troops' faces; their rural apparel and demeanor are incongruous in the gentrified ambience of the North American "soda fountain" Sanborns, which at this time would have been a favorite haunt of the capital's elite.[11] Equally, viewed through the ideological lens of the metropolitan photographers who documented the conflict, the image filters the disquiet of the city dwellers, finally confronted with the much-heralded "barbarians." In fact, what arguably made the sight of Zapatistas in Sanborns such a compelling photo opportunity at the time of the production of this iconic image is its representation of a world turned (briefly) upside down: in the turmoil of the revolution, the rightful occupants of the space behind the bar, frock-coated urban gentlemen, were usurped by gun-toting indigenous peasants. Crucially, if the original Zapatistas look out of place in Sanborns, that incongruity is predicated as much on a sense of temporal as spatial displacement: the city as bastion of modernity is no place for "backward" indigenous peasants from the provinces.

By referencing the iconic (photographic) space occupied by their 1910 revolutionary namesakes and forebears, the contemporary Zapatistas engage in a complex rhetorical play of meaning. To metropolitan viewers in 1914, images in the "Zapatistas in Sanborns" sequence connoted the irruption of the racial *other* into the "civilized" space of the modern city. In the aftermath of the conflict, however, the meanings associated with such images shifted fundamentally. The triumph of the conservative Constitutionalists brought with it the rehabilitation of both Emiliano Zapata and Pancho Villa, together with their popular, radical politics, as the postrevolutionary regime set out to establish (or, more to the point, invent) its revolutionary credentials.[12] With the redemption of these historical figures, and particularly Zapata, also came the valorization of indigenous Mexico as a source of historical pride in the project of official indigenismo, which, as already noted, was, between about 1920 and 1940, merely a means to an end: cultural mestizaje. In line with the official discourses of the postrevolutionary state, the meanings that accrued to images such as "Zapatistas en Sanborns" came to turn on a celebration of the popular forces unleashed by the revolution. What is more, nowhere was this visual rhetoric writ larger than across key public spaces of the capital, where the walls of the Palacio Nacional, for example, were filled to saturation with Diego Rivera's murals representing the nation's historical development: from the idyllic pre-Hispanic past, through the dark years of the conquest, to the progress and bright future to be produced in the popular revolutionary struggle.

To reference "Zapatistas in Sanborns" in 1999 is, then, to reappropriate an emblematic photographic image of the revolution and to inject it with radical meaning. Temporarily taking the place of their wealthy, urbanite compatriots, the contemporary Zapatistas skillfully signal that, despite the intervening eighty-five years between the production of the 1914 and 1999 photographs, they themselves still, like the original Zapatistas, as indigenous peasants (albeit masked indigenous peasants) look out of place at the bar of Sanborns. In so signaling, the reenactment of this instantly recognizable photograph not only alludes to the fact that the issue of social justice in Mexico is far from resolved; it calls into question, at the same time, the postrevolutionary project of official indigenismo, revealing it to be a discourse of teleological development in which "Indians may be Mexico's ideal ancestors, but mestizos are Mexico's ideal citizens. . . . Indian difference is an essential precedent for this mestizo nation, even as Indians, with their difference, are the continuing targets of educational and cultural reform" (Saldaña-Portillo 2002, 295).

POLITICS OF PHOTOGRAPHIC METONYMY IN MEXICO CITY

The contemporary Zapatistas invariably still look out of place in Sanborns and, what is more, wherever they go in the city. This is, in part, their point. Their struggle is about the simultaneous right to inclusion *and* to ethnic specificity within the space of the modern nation. If indeed the "out-of-place-ness" of the original Zapatistas is both spatial and temporal, then the incongruity of the contemporary Zapatistas is an emphatically spatial displacement. Or, put differently, the photographs produced during the Consulta are images that work performatively against the temporal logic inherent both in the photographic act and in the city as a densely layered historical environment. There is, then, more to be said about the terms and conditions of the Zapatistas' incongruity in the city—that sheds light not only on the spatial dimensions of their staged photo opportunities, but also on the temporal dynamics of these performances. These dynamics come into focus through an exploration of the concept of metonymy and its relationship to photographic representation, and are crystallized in an essay by Eelco Runia, "Presence." Arguing against the dominance of metaphor in recent historiography, this philosopher of history asserts that presence, "the unrepresented way the past is present in the present" (Runia 2006, 1), as it is stored in metonymy may in fact constitute an equally compelling conceptual paradigm for thinking about what is at stake in the narration of history. Although a theoretical meditation on historiography, Runia's reflections yet offer an insight into the ontology of the photographic image and, in particular, the relationship between space and time, presence and absence, inherent in photographic images. In turn, his reflections will illuminate our understanding of the Zapatistas' photographic performances in Mexico City.

Runia situates his analysis as part of the contemporary turn to memory, remembrance, and trauma, arguing that metonymy, the trope of "presence in absence" (2006, 6) may prove an appropriate tool with which to grasp how the past continues to inhabit the present.[13] Although a detailed gloss of his argument is beyond the scope of this chapter, it is essential to briefly consider what exactly is meant by metonymy as "presence in absence," and how and where this phenomenon might be manifest. In the first instance, Runia offers a dictionary definition of metonymy as "a figure in which the name of an attribute or adjunct is substituted for that of the thing meant" (15), providing a range of standard, specifically linguistic examples (e.g., scepter for authority). However, he quickly clarifies that metonymy is not an exclusively linguistic occurrence, but can also inhere in objects—for example, in monuments or indeed cities themselves, in which "[s]ome parts are carefully restored, others are dilapidated. There are areas that once were destroyed by war (of which traces may or may not remain), areas that have been completely transformed by public works, areas in which 'time has stood still'" (Runia 2006, 9). (Mexico City is a prime example of such a metonymic urban environment, manifesting traces of the Mexica and colonial pasts, as well as bearing the scars of conflict and, indeed, natural disasters—specifically, the 1985 earthquake.) To grasp the play of metonymy is thus to reconsider historical time not in linear terms, but rather in terms of "'[c]ontinuity' and 'discontinuity,' that is not in a historical, temporal, 'vertical' sense, but in the spatial, 'horizontal' sense of 'being thoroughly interwoven' and 'radically contiguous'" (9). It is ultimately to translate time into space. Further, context is crucial to an understanding of the way metonymy functions, a way describable as the "'willfully inappropriate transposition of something from one context to another' and is, in its new context 'slightly out of place'" (16).

With one brief exception, Runia has nothing explicitly to say about photography. That exception is an allusion to the work of the late German writer W. G. Sebald, in whose novel's illustrations, in the form of photographs, train tickets, receipts, postcards, and so forth, looking strangely incongruous on the printed page, represent "[c]urious specimens of nonverbal metonymies in a linguistic context [where they] function as fistulae or holes through which the past discharges into the present" (16).[14] Although Runia says, then, nothing directly on photography, it is striking that his analysis of metonymy or "presentism" could almost be a description of the ontology of the photographic image, in which the past lies in the object, whereby the photograph materializes presence in absence. Indeed, in his essay, Runia invokes fossils and relics (16) as examples of the kind of phenomena under his scrutiny, phenomena that, like photographs, are precisely indexical signs, the trace of contact with the real inscribed on their surfaces. This is, of course, a terrain well trodden by photography theorists from Bazin (1967) to Barthes (1983) and beyond. But where Runia's reflections on metonymy and its relationship to photography have particular explanatory force here is, first, in his emphasis on the translation of time into space; second, on his understanding of the city as a densely layered space; and third, on his notion of metonymy as incongruity. This leads to how Runia's reflections on the trope of metonymy may have a bearing on what is at stake in the Zapatistas' production of photographic space in the city.

Among the imaged destinations on the Zapatistas' schedule in the capital are two not yet commented upon fully here: visits to the Templo Mayor and to the Museo Nacional de Antropología. As even the casual visitor to Mexico City will recognize, these repositories of national cultural heritage are key sites not only on the tourist circuit but also of civic ritual. The ruins of the foundations of Tenochtitlán's ceremonial center, and the national museum dedicated to the indigenous peoples of Mexico, respectively, are prime examples of sites that manifest Indians' status in national culture as Mexico's "ideal ancestors" (Saldaña-Portillo 2002, 295), a status that does not, however, confer any right to coeval citizenship. This dichotomy, as critics have noted, is reinforced in the Museo Nacional de Antropología's layout, where the displays have: "consistently stressed the grandeur of the pre-Conquest past on the ground floor while promoting a stagnant, superficial profile of present-day indigenous communities on the top floor." This has "served to reinforce the notion that living indigenous communities are stuck in a cycle of reproducing a fixed 'traditional' and 'authentic' set of cultural practices, instead of actively producing culture" (Taylor 2005, 76). That is to say, the museum reproduces a temporal understanding of contemporary indigenous peoples as inhabiting a pre-modern space, one prior to the present of the nation. In short, it denies their presence as coeval subjects within that national space.

During the Consulta, the city, represented at the capital's key locations of cultural heritage, becomes a site in which the Zapatistas photographically perform the absence of contemporary Indians from the official spaces of the modern nation—which has, so to speak, only room for an idealized, archaic construction of indigenous difference. What is more, the Zapatistas register this absence and the right to inclusion through the masked incongruity of their presence at these sites. What, after all, is a photo opportunity by one definition, if not a sight worthy of recording for posterity for its unique or unusual quality? Presence, absence, and indeed incongruity are, as noted, key attributes not only of metonymy but also of photography. The photographic image, with its properties of preservation, fixes its referents in a time always prior to the click of the shutter.[15] In the context of the dominant teleological understanding of reality, the trace of an encounter with the real that is materialized as a presence in absence in the photograph is always incongruous. We just don't see it as such. This is because metonymies, as Runia points out, have "careers": "These careers come in two modalities. In most cases metonymy is absorbed by the context in which it is placed. What starts as an eye-catching, disconcerting, and ineluctable presence ends up as something so inconspicuous that it cannot even be called a cliché" (2006, 17). Here again, in modern culture, a photograph by one definition may be the ultimate inconspicuous object.

But there is also metonymy's second career. A conspicuous metonymy, says Runia, "disturbs places. When fresh, it questions meanings, awakens us from what we take for granted, and draws attention to what we don't like to be reminded of: that the implicit rules of the place are far from natural and self-evident, are indeed a system of habits and conventions" (19). Herein lies the key to understanding the Zapatistas' photographic performances in the city, and particularly to comprehending another inflection of their incongruity in that environment. If photography, like metonymy, functions by materializing presence in absence, at a discursive level, the performative thrust of these images works *against* this logic. The Zapatistas signal absence in presence: being photographed incongruously in the city, they simultaneously foreground their absence from this space and assert their right to presence in the nation as coeval citizens. That is, these images strategically reverse the temporal logic of the photographic image and, in so doing, insist not on temporality, but on spatiality. The Zapatistas may be out of place in the city—because they belong in another space—but they are not out of the city's time.

To close, let us return to Bellinghausen's description of the eyewitness encounter between the Zapatistas and the passersby in the city: "But the surprises that the Zapatistas get are equal to the surprises they give. Commotion on the corners of Iztacalco when a cattle truck passed by (which, for peasants, is for passengers) full of masked people looking at the passers-by who looked at them, stopped, pointed at them, commented on them to one another animatedly and greeted them with sympathy" (Bellinghausen 1999). Ultimately, perhaps what Bellinghausen captures here is an ideal encounter between citizens of the modern Mexican nation that also is played out in the photographs that have been the focus of this chapter: an encounter in which indigenous difference is understood not temporally but, rather, spatially.

Afterword The Dialectics of Identity in the Latin/o American Global City

ABRIL TRIGO

The chapters in this volume address, directly or indirectly, the problematic configuration (adulteration, negotiation, reinvention) of social subjectivities in contemporary Latin/o American urban milieus. They explore conflictive spaces, ravaged by neoliberal policies and plundered by transnational capital, contested by emergent social actors and imploded by new cultural practices, where most of the population lives ensnared in a global imaginary that condenses the cosmopolitan fantasies of universal happiness, unbridled individual freedom, and multicultural harmony in an ultratechnological world without borders, powers, or inequalities. In other words, these chapters, which focus on a wide array of topics, subjects, and social practices, portray vividly the exacerbation of the dialectics of identity formation between memory and performance, the imaginary and the imagination, subjectivity and citizenship, the world of affects and the realm of praxis. Or, as Gisela Cánepa sustains in regard to the reenactment of Andean festivals in Lima, they display a manifold geopoetics and geopolitics of identity intimately linked to a new kind of performative citizenship in such a way that economic, social, and political rights are obtained through the public performance of cultural difference.

CONSUMING CITIZENSHIP

Today, under the terms imposed by globalization, this dialectic is tensed to its very limits in Latin/o American cities, where 80 percent of the population live, and this is the ultimate reason for the widespread feeling of psychological anxiety and social instability so candidly captured by Geoffrey Kantaris's snapshots of personal and collective shipwrecks in Buenos Aires, shipwrecks that can no longer be explained as a byproduct of the postmodern shift. Globalization is in fact a misnomer for a new regime of capital accumulation that combines the exploitation of alienated work and alienating consumption with the industrial production of material goods and the cultural consumption of symbolic goods; a regime in which economy, politics, society, and culture are integrated into a totality that blurs the difference between the material and the symbolic, the base and the superstructure, the real and the ideological—insofar as ideology is embedded in the commodity-sign form that permeates and regulates the system.

Consumption, and particularly the consumption of symbolic goods and cultural services, has become the engine of the economy as well as its main indicator. Consequently, consumption has acquired a primordial political and cultural function, because we do not consume objects but messages, symbols, meanings, which tell us how much we are worth and who we are, as Rodolfo Torres and Juan Buriel so clearly demonstrate in their analysis of the symbolic economy of multiculturalism by which the global elites of Los Angeles commodify the culinary practices of a migrant community as ethnic nouvelle cuisine. Consumption, and particularly cultural consumption, works through the production and reproduction, creation, incitation, and manipulation of desires, by constantly pushing the threshold of pleasure, stirring additional consumption, and reinforcing consumerism as a "natural" way of life. Cultural consumption is the core of a politico-libidinal economy in which commodities are produced primarily as signs and signs are produced as commodities: a system in which everything that can be exchanged (objects, services, bodies, sex, information, pleasures) has a symbolic value and consequently can always be translated into the ultimate sign, money. This is the case of the city of Lima, whose cultural and economic development, according to Cánepa, is framed by globalization, insofar as the whole city is transformed into a scenographic, exotic, and touristic object of consumption. In the same way that Lima has become a brand name in the tourist global marketplace, the poverty of the Brazilian Northeast is aestheticized in global Brazilian cinema through a stylish "cosmetics of hunger" (a reversal of Glauber Rocha's "aesthetics of hunger"), as Angela Prysthon so aptly proves in her chapter.

Undoubtedly, the conflation of the culture of consumerism with the consumption of culture consummates in Latin/o American cities the more insidious, surreptitious, and overwhelming cultural symptom of globalization, exacerbated by the most perverse form of global exploitation: the asynchrony between expectations and possibilities suffered by the locally excluded, condemned to a systematic unevenness between the slow or even regressive pace of socioeconomic integration and their accelerated ideological integration to the global market of desires and symbolic consumption. This "disintegrative integration," in Martin Hopenhayn's terms (1994), only aggravates the material and symbolic stratification between those who enjoy the banquet as full members of a cosmopolitan elite, and those who, dazzled by transnational pop culture, are condemned to peep through the window.

Therefore, consumption is a field of cultural and political struggle, not only for direct access to, and the social distribution of, goods, but because consumption, and particularly the symbolic value provided by both material and cultural goods, creates the illusion of democracy. Or, as Antony Kapcia and Par Kumaraswami expound in their study on the Havana Feria del Libro, consumption can become a springboard for a new experience of citizenship that, following Jesús Martín-Barbero, they call "urbanship": a new form of participatory cultural consumption that rejects media mass-ification and exalts the prestige of the cultural object, thus resisting globalization. And this can happen because alongside the attrition of the nation-state and other modern political and social institutions, consumption subsumes, under the commodity form, the role, the rights, and the responsibilities of citizens, who are made more and more into consumers, the same way identities, especially in urban milieus, are shaped more and more by consumption.

Latin/o American subjects, as consumers, are atomized individuals, exchangeable and disposable like any commodity, subjected to the global symbolic economy exposed by Torres and Buriel, and massively integrated into a society of loners in which loneliness and encapsulation avert any form of solidarity that would make the individual's emancipation possible. No doubt consumption makes us think, as Néstor García Canclini (1995) believes, following Douglas and Isherwood (1979), but not think critically. This is so, in the end, because consumption is where desires, the desires that drive both the political and the libidinal economy, promise full satisfaction, and not only in the First World consumer societies of plenty where immediate satisfaction, in principle guaranteed, is permanently postponed (thus boosting desire) (Deleuze and Guattari 1985, 35; Bauman 1998, 82–83). In urban Latin/o America, the subject, as consumer, tormented by the anxiety of unattainable desires, becomes the sublimated pursuer of an impossible object of desire (Salecl 2005). Providing a satisfaction that is never enough and many times impossible, symbolic consumption molds subjects that cannot be fulfilled. This explains the profound instability of social identities and the shifting ground of citizenship in Latin/o American urban societies, where everything is for sale, translatable, exchangeable, where the contradictions of globalization reach their maximum intensity.

Moreover, this explains too the emergence of the new social movements, as well as the demands for ethnic citizenship and the staging of performative citizenship, such as the Zapatistas' forays into Mexico City analyzed by Andrea Noble, and the Andean festivals with which the indigenous and mestizo migrants seize the city of Lima, as studied by Cánepa.

SUBJECTED SUBJECTS

If identity is paradoxical, it is so even more in the periphery. It is always individual, but is realized only in the social, in the intersubjective relationship between the individual and society, as mediated by language and everyday life. Identity— that is, the feeling of *being apart from others* and *a part of others*—is the uncertain result of a process of socialization that begins during the Lacanian "mirror phase," when the child elaborates her own corporeal image and her emotions toward the Other(s). For this reason it materializes solely in the individual, which means that any collective identity is always the fallacious, retroactive effect of a discursive intervention. Therefore, in spite of being produced in the dialectical spinning of the individual in the social, identity is both psychological and social, and neither. Its true realm is culture, of course, that evasive, viscous, sumptuous texture that interweaves the libidinal and the political, practice and symbols, necessity and contingency. The subject, constituted through a convoluted process of identification in which s/he projects herself onto the Other (the *Ideal-Ego* of the Lacanian Imaginary), and introjects the Other as her own Self (the *Ego-Ideal* of the Lacanian Symbolic), is a psychosocial ideological effect, a virtual image woven into the network of imaginary-symbolic relations of power. Deprived of this spatial, temporal, and social network, there is no subject. Thus, identity is the product of a tautological process of inscription within an empty place, a tautological economy that not only is ideology at its best but also reveals identity's ultimate "substanceless subjectivity," similar to that of the commodity form. This means that the "value" of identity lies nowhere, since the subject's identity results from the structure of exchange and is actually nothing but an empty sign whose value entirely depends upon relational, universally contingent circumstances (Žižek 1991, 28–29).

The clue to this paradox, displayed with ironic detachment in César Aira's novels, analyzed by Richard Young, is found in the process of identification itself, whose intricate mirroring is made more intelligible by way of the Althusserian concept of ideological interpellation, which has a dual function: to establish and (re)produce ideological hegemony, and to transform the individual into a subject, a subjected, heteronomous subject who identifies herself with the discursive formation (see Althusser 1971). At heart, ideological interpellation designates a process of psychosocial recognition based upon the misrecognition of its performative nature. Such is the case of the processes of symbolic production and ideological interpellation found by Prysthon in the manipulation of the images of poverty in Brazilian contemporary cinema, and by Torres and Buriel in the cosmopolitan consumption of Latina/o difference in multicultural Los Angeles.

To recognize herself as a subject, the individual feels as if she had been chosen by the call of the social imaginary (ideology, nationality, religion), while, on the contrary, it is she who sanctions the social imaginary in order to conceal the banal contingency that she is actually identifying with the sheer act of identification. However, as Héctor Fernández L'Hoeste demonstrates regarding the transformation of the TransMilenio mass transit system into the imaginary national template of a modern, global Colombia, it is the subject herself who, by consenting to the authority of the social imaginary, authorizes it; as Balibar once said, "as *subditi*, the subjects will their own obedience" (1991, 41). And they do so because the feeling of belonging produces enjoyment, and the subject is fulfilled only through enjoyment (Žižek 1993, 280). Allusive and elusive, in constant deferment, always luring and avoiding the subject, *jouissance* constitutes, therefore, the substance of ideology, because "'Ideological' is not the 'false consciousness' of (social) being but this being itself, in so far as it is supported by 'false consciousness'" (Žižek 1989, 21). This accepted, it would be wrong to conclude that ideology is only an illusion masking the real, and that we can simply suspend this illusion and see things as they really are. The crucial point, superbly made by Prysthon, is that these images structure the way we live our lives, walk our cities, and enact our fantasies, to the point that their disintegration would import a "loss of reality" (Žižek 1991b, 71).

This is the realm of the social imaginary, which according to Prysthon does not furnish us with an image of reality, but with reality itself, an effect of the real that molds cultural identity, sometimes resorting to social engineering (Fernández L'Hoeste), sometimes to avant-garde aesthetics of the abject (Brooksbank-Jones), sometimes to the mythopoetics of mourning and nostalgia (Holmes). The social imaginary is structured around "imaginemes," empty floating signifiers which roughly correspond to Castoriadis' "imaginary significations" (1987, 364), Lacan's "point de capiton" (Žižek 1989, 98), Laclau and Mouffe's "nodal points" (1985, 105): sorts of mooring for meaning that, at the symbolic level, consolidate the identity of the (subject in the) social imaginary and structure and produce social, political, and cultural reality. This is obviously the symbolic function of the TransMilenio transit system in the newly remodeled Colombian national imaginary. The social imaginary names that which cannot be named but is "lived as even more real than the real, yet not known as such, precisely *because* it is not known as such" (Castoriadis 1987, 103); therefore, the identification with that "Thing" stimulates libidinal fantasies and bonds together the members of a given community around enjoyment incarnated (Castoriadis 1987, 127; Žižek 1993, 201).

The paradox of the social imaginary is that, although it does not exist exclusively at the level of reality or of the real, it articulates them both. It designates a kernel that precedes and resists symbolization and, consequently, can only be apprehended through its effects at the symbolic level. The social imaginary encapsulates, thus, the paradoxical substance of enjoyment (*jouissance*, the Freudian *das Ding*, the Lacanian *objet petit a*, the object of desire that is posed by desire) (Lacan 1998: II, 635–36 and 773), and the surplus of enjoyment (the *plus-de-jouir*, an excessive and impossible remainder) generated at the symbolic level by the subject's libidinal investment, which eventually bursts into the radical imagination. Thus, the identification with the social imaginary (at the Symbolic level) is complemented by the malleability of the process of symbolization, which enables us to adapt to the contingent by adopting new identities. This dialectics between fixity and plasticity explains the strength and durability of the collective "we" constructed by the social imaginary, a construction that is nothing but an empty signifier built upon the intentional amnesia of its traumatic origins. The Zapatistas' struggle to uncover the national imaginary's original sins and reinscribe themselves as Mexican citizens and the silenced *other* of modern civil society is captured with accuracy by Noble's analysis of their performance of ethnicity in Mexico City.

But the subject, who becomes a subject by identifying with the social imaginary, resists identification by resorting to tactical maneuvers that allow her to imagine alternative and alternating, heterogeneous and frequently contradictory, subject positions (Smith 1988, 84; Bhabha 1994, 185). Agency, as a result, ensues when the subject questions the authority of the imaginary and assumes the responsibility of becoming a being-for-herself while standing for-others. Autonomy consists, in this regard, in the subject's becoming a sovereign agent who resists her control by the Law of the Other and the social imaginary, the *Other in me speaking through me*. But autonomy does not arise solely from an act of self-awareness; it must be achieved through the antagonistic performance of the radical imagination, as in the Nueva Trova postrevolutionary reappropriation of Cuban musical traditions, analyzed by Robin Moore; the postapocalyptic critique of globalized urban violence in Mexico City that Anny Brooksbank-Jones finds in Teresa Margolles's neoconceptual necro-art; the cultural re-cognition and political remapping of urban space realized by Detroit's Latin/o migrants through the tactical uses of virtual media, as documented by Catherine Bena-mou; the symbolic takeover of the streets of Lima by Peru's internal migrants, described by Cánepa; the recovery of the symbolic value of the book as a cul-tural artifact through which Habaneros resist patterns of global consumption, as indicated by Antoni Kapcia and Kumaraswami; or the Zapatistas' ironic contestation of iconic national *lieux de mémoire*, according to Noble. In other words, antagonism gives rise to a sovereign subject that confronts society as an enclosing containment established by the social imaginary, and that opens the gates to the excess of the social and of social praxis (Laclau and Mouffe 1985, 96), which install the political against the grain of politics (Lechner 1988; Arditi 1988).

Autonomy, therefore, is the work of the radical imagination, a centrifu-gal performative praxis that destabilizes the centripetal pedagogy of the so-cial imaginary (Castoriadis 1987, 369). The alterity of the radical imagination emerges from the enjoyment that identification with the social imaginary can-not possibly fulfill, and manifests itself as a surplus of desire, as an excess of the process of identification triggered by the performative praxis of the sovereign subject. The radical imagination is the political dimension of the social where the subject builds its sovereignty by pursuing autonomy through antagonistic practices. This is demonstrated by the iconoclastic representation of the glo-balized city in the novels of César Aira studied by Young, the contemporary Argentine cinema revisited by Kantaris, or the necropolitan Mexican body art sculpted by Brooksbank-Jones; by the cannibalistic cosmopolitanism of cul-tural consumption of the citizens of Havana as described by Kapcia and Ku-maraswami, or the exoticism for export of the Brazilian Northeast as described by Prysthon; by the antagonistic performance of Andean ethnic identities as reported by Cánepa, and the daring appropriation of Mexican identity by Zap-atistas, analyzed by Noble. It is the fluid dimension where the sovereign subject navigates, thus making possible its analogy to the Lacanian *plus-de-jouir*, a pure desire and productivity of desire which, as residue of jouissance, returns to the symbolic level in the form of a symptom that resists domestication and persists as absolute loss. Because *plus-de-jouir* connotes, in French, "surplus of enjoy-ment" as well as "no more enjoyment," it is a double entendre that verifies the moment when plus-de-jouir is produced at the limit of jouissance and as the limit that makes jouissance possible. It is thus the excess of the Zapatistas chal-lenging Mexican civil society, the Andean migrants re-conquering the City of Kings, the transnational migrants demanding their global citizenship. *Plus-de-jouir* is a surplus, an excess that cannot be named, cannot be apprehended, and as such is the very stuff of the sublime, emerging when the symbolic representation of this Loss gives rise to a pleasure of its own, a pleasure found when the impossibility of presentation is rendered into the presentation of impossibility (Žižek 1997, 47). Here lies the ultimate productivity of the radical imagination, as is dramatically represented in the daily performance of identity in urban Latin/o America.

PERFORMING MEMORIES

What is behind this complex dialectic? Identity is a disputed zone, an edifice shakily crafted between identification with the social imaginary (which provides the comfort of the familiar) and the performance of the radical imagination (which promises the adventure of the unknown), between the fulfillment of jouissance and the anxiety of the plus-de-jouir, between the subjected subject and the sovereign subject. Affirmation and negation, home and prison, identity is the boundary of certainty and the horizon of the possible. Truly, as Stuart Hall said, "Identity is formed at the unstable point where the 'unspeakable' stories of subjectivity meet the narratives of history, of a culture. And since s/he is positioned in relation to cultured narratives which have been profoundly expropriated, the colonized subject is always 'somewhere else'" (1993, 135).

Identities are performed, but they are made out of memories, as the contributors in this collection profusely demonstrate. Since several authors, like Moore, Benamou, Torres, and Buriel, for instance, employ concepts inherently problematic, it is useful to distinguish, as a point of departure, Maurice Halbwachs' classical notion of social or collective memory, a daily oral fabric of traditions produced by, and producer of, a given community, from historical memory, an oxymoron, in fact, since history does not begin except at the moment when tradition ends and collective memory starts to fade away (Halbwachs 1950, 68). The transition from collective memory to historical memory records, according to Ferdinand Toennies' classic distinction, the passage from communal life (Gemeinschaft) to contractual society (Gesellschaft), and consequently, if the former designates a realm of presence, immediacy, and plenitude, the latter, in contrast, is the mediated reconstruction, compulsory and dubious, of that which is no longer. Collective memory, a memory without past that is permanently renewed in the form of myths, is organic and holistic, concrete and plural, but historical memory is analytical and critical, abstract and particular. Despite the devious essentialism that pervades the dichotomy between Gemeinschaft and Gesellschaft, Richard Terdiman is correct in pointing out that it grasps the crisis of modernity with unparalleled candor (1993, 6). This crisis was momentarily resolved with the invention of national historical memories and literary memories, built upon the ruins of intrinsically a-historic collective memories with the explicit purpose of erasing their traces, of emptying history of its *Jetztzeit*, while erecting a cumulative, homogeneous, empty temporality whose corollary would be the modern nation-state (Benjamin 1969, 261).

In order to avoid this modern ruse, I prefer to use the more subtle notions of cultural memory and instrumental memory, proposed by Jesús Martín-Barbero (1987), which resonate with the postcolonial concepts of the performative and the pedagogical, employed by Homi Bhabha (1994). According to Martín-Barbero, cultural memory, in contrast to instrumental memory (which feeds on information and has a cumulative, linear nature), holds the opacity of experience and the thickness of events. This is the kind of memory that Moore refers to as collective memory, or Benamou as collective urban memory. It is not a memory we can use, but the memory of which we are made. On the other hand, instrumental memory is a historical, literary, and pedagogical narrative, an apparatus of ideological homogenization and social exclusion put at the service of the nation-state under the pretense of preserving endangered collective memories. Indeed, the modern discipline of history, a refined mechanism of identity building, carried out the most brutal disciplining of social, performative, cultural memories, and in order to reinvent origins, dehistoricized memory. Later on, with the advent of mass consumer society and global capitalism, those national historical and literary memories were progressively overlaid by a transnational pop memory, no longer enforced by educational institutions but instilled by mass media, global corporations, stylish consumption, and advertisement. In the same way that historical memory suppressed, appropriated, and disciplined cultural memories in order to homogenize heterogeneous societies and capitalize on the temporal surplus extracted through the economic administration of social time (Debord 1995, 129), global pop memory implements an even more radical suppression of local, regional, and national memories in order to establish the autistic, oblivious present of consumer happiness and symbolic seduction. These are contradictions magnificently displayed in the peculiar situation of contemporary Cuba, analyzed by Moore, where a proudly nationalist culture resists globalization wearing the rags of a socialist society. Whereas national historical memories were produced and reproduced by the ideological state apparatus and consequently driven by a primordially national teleology, global pop memory, a multimedia "desiring machine" for the symbolic and material reproduction of social consumption, is produced and distributed by transnational mass media and hence in concert with global capitalism. Such is the case of the global transformation of local cultures into exoticism for export, like the cosmopolitanism of the poor exploited by Brazilian cinema, in Prysthon's subtle employment of Silviano Santiago's apt expression.

Cultural memories, however, torn apart by urban cataclysm and the temptations of cosmopolitan consumption, are entwined in lived experience and everyday life. Cultural memories, thus, should not be confused with collective memory: whereas the latter is concerned with the preservation of an idealized status quo, cultural memories are pregnant with contradictions, always staged in social performance and put to test in political praxis, as the Indianization of Lima, foretold by José María Arguedas and chronicled by Cánepa, vividly shows. Of course, cultural memories are as contaminated by political contingency and the struggle for power as any, since any memory is a cognitive field culturally constructed, socially embedded, and emotionally embodied. Even so, cultural memories contain the repressed residues of subaltern practices, whose intermittent, interstitial eruption destabilizes the homogeneity of both national historical and global pop memories. This explains the intense dispute for the control of both the historical and pop memories so intense in Buenos Aires and other globalized cities of Latin/o America, as Kantaris and others reveal, and the struggle for recovering tattered cultural memories, to the extent that the definitive configuration of society, the freeing of the radical imagination, and the construction of alternative counterimaginaries always depend upon the appropriation and manipulation of memories, as shown in the photographic series *Zapatistas in Sanborns* studied by Noble. But, when, how, and where does one recover those other, submerged cultural memories? This is where forgetting comes in, since forgetting is a way of remembering.

Of the three kinds of history acknowledged by Nietzsche—the monumental, the antiquarian and the critical—the monumental is the one of interest here, inasmuch as it relates to the kind of foundational historiography involved in the construction of nationalist social imaginaries. It is to this historiography à la Carlyle ("a heroic past, great men, glory . . . the social capital upon which one bases a national idea") that Renan resorts in his classic piece "What is a nation?" (1990). The amnesia inherent to this monumental history, which Renan discards in favor of "a rich legacy of memories," constitutes for Nietzsche a traumatic loss (1957). If, according to Nietzsche, the will to forget is indispensable for life, action, and freedom, the amnesia constitutive of monumental history feeds paralysis and entranced ecstasy. It is more a compulsory oblivion (or genesis amnesia, in Bourdieu's terms [1977]) than a voluntary forgetfulness. Forgetting thus functions differently according to the kind of memory, so that if the pedagogy of historical memory is based upon social amnesia (the induced or imposed oblivion of its historical genesis), radical forgetfulness activates a proactive memory that abolishes the monumentality of History and stimulates the daily, social, performative practice of cultural memories. In a word, social amnesia is to the social imaginary what radical forgetfulness is to the radical imagination. In contrast to the pedagogical erasure of history instrumented by social amnesia, as so well described by Kantaris, radical forgetfulness (forgetting to remember) promotes the historicizing of history, the unveiling of historical discourse, the writing, in Foucaultian terms, of a documental narrative (1969). For this reason, "we must know the right time to forget as well as the right time to remember," as Nietzsche stated (1957, 8).

Radical forgetfulness is at the core of the subject's most basic psychosocial equilibrium, and amounts to a device that works like a gear between the individual and the social. What at the social level remains an abstract rationalization, in the individual's psyche is dramatically real. Like those ruins of the past that emerge unexpectedly from oblivion, fragments of the Real folded in the imaginary that suddenly shatter our reality into pieces: traces of memories we have chosen to forget, simply because they are too painful, but that once they come to surface must be rationalized so we may put them to rest and keep going. Such is the experience of *unheimlich* that drives the relentless, desolate search for the *desaparecidos* and the demand for truth raised by the Mothers of the Plaza de Mayo, HIJOS, and other human rights organizations, as candidly expressed by Alejandro Agresti in Kantaris's quotation. Their anamnesis is, in fact, a claim for radical forgetfulness as well as a rejection of the officially imposed social amnesia, an urgent demand to be able to mourn and only subsequently administer therapeutic forgetfulness. As Argentinians have learned, the disappeared haunt us as "living dead" because they have not been properly buried, and their return indicates that the trauma of their disappearance has not been adequately integrated into historical memory. Their return is the symptom of an open sore in society's symbolic fabric. They and we, will only rest when assured that, in spite of being dead, they will continue to live with us in our cultural memory.

There is no doubt about the overall importance of memory in the process of identity formation, but what is the articulation between memory and the performing body, time and space, the individual, society, and the urban stage? This is a central issue in many of these contributions, concerned with bringing to light the location, recovery, and performance of manifold "urban memories," as Holmes, Prysthon, and Benamou explicitly claim. The sites of national historical memory—museums and archives, cemeteries and festivals, monuments and sanctuaries, that is, any monument invested with a symbolic aura and dedicated to the cult of the dead, the preservation of the national patrimony, and the revival of the past—are posed as *les lieux de mémoire* which substitute for the decayed milieux of a supposedly authentic collective memory. They are the sacred rituals of a society that desecrates everything. Now, if the sites of memory are the loci that guarantee the pedagogy of historical memory, where could we find the loci of cultural memories? This issue is addressed by Amanda Holmes's study on the nostalgic reminiscence of the barrios of Asunción. Perhaps it could be that cultural memories would not need any sort of ideological location or mnemonic anchorage, and would work "naturally" in their own social milieu, as Nora (pace Halbwachs) purports of true collective memory (1984).

The successive modernizations that chart the history of capitalism have definitely induced formidable transformations in the way memory works, particularly regarding the articulation of temporal and spatial categories. Despite their constant, random slippage, present, past, and future, here, there, and no-where have always been the substance and the justification for the induction of productive sites of memory. Any kind of memory operates on the assumption and the inception of specific places, which function simultaneously as its locus and its milieu, as the appropriation and rewriting of the contested urban stage by ethnic minorities and transnational migrants, from Mexico City to Lima, from Los Angeles to Detroit, dramatically demonstrates. In that sense, there is no naturally given or organic memory, because memory is not just the recollection of the traces of the past but its writing under conditions and constraints determined by the present. Autobiographical or social, pre-modern, modern, or postmodern, memory is thus simultaneously analeptic and proleptic, in such a way that the past is necessarily a retroactive effect of the present: "Memory is neither something preexistent and dormant in the past nor a projection from the present, but a potential for creative collaboration between present consciousness and the experience or expression of the past; . . . memory is not only constantly disintegrating and disappearing but constantly being created and elaborated" (Frow 1997, 228). Thus, memories are the effect of "intersubjective practices of signification, neither given nor fixed but constantly re-created within the framework of marginally contestable rules for discourse" (Boyarin 1994, 22). This is why any city, like the city of Asunción studied by Holmes, is an urban palimpsest, a notion proposed by Andreas Huyssen (2003) to describe how memories (cultural memories, but also instrumental memories, such as historical and global pop memories) are embedded in the city and mediate the individual's psychological and social experience of time and space. Thus, subjectivity, either individual or social, is formed at the intersection of time and space, not so much as abstract categories but rather materialized in the performance of social praxis (here-now) and the exercise (recollection and forgetfulness) of memory (then-there).

REIMAGINING SPACE

According to David Harvey (1995), the history of Western modernity is marked by successive time-space compressions intrinsically associated with the development of capitalism and its internal logic of creative destruction. Every time-space compression has occurred through technological modernization and as a political response to the periodic economic crises of accumulation that bring to a close the historical cycles of capitalist expansion. Driven by its relentless necessity to open new markets, accelerate the distribution of commodities, and strengthen the international division of labor, capitalism implemented a radical rationalization in the use of space and time, a continuous historical reduction of the ratio between time and space that resulted in the unrelenting colonization of space and commodification of time by the logic of money. Concomitantly to the passage from communal life (*Gemeinschaft*) to modern society (*Gesellschaft*), and the suppression of collective memories by historical memory, social space was detached from actual cultural places, becoming as abstract, homogeneous, and empty as historiographic time. Velocity, driven by fashion and consumption, as Kantaris argues, following Fredric Jameson, swallowed time, in the same way that style swamped lived experiences. To put it bluntly, globalization could be the ultimate space-time compression, a regime of accumulation and a new cultural formation where the rampant reification of time colludes with the brutal fetishization of space.

Accordingly, contemporary, postmodern global space could be considered, in line with Marc Augé, a non-place, a strictly functional, instrumental space devoid of the personal, historical, and intersubjective texture that makes of spaces the locus of identity (1995): the purely economic urban spaces emptied out of human substance, as discussed by Kantaris, in the films of Pablo Trapero. Augé elaborates this notion from Martin Heidegger's existential conception of *dwelling* in his ontology of being (1977). For Augé, a place is a space historically and relationally stipulated that "is formed by individual identities, through complicities of language, local references, the unformulated rules or living know-how" (Augé 1995, 101). Therefore, following Marcel Mauss and his anthropological tradition, a place is the scene of existence, material and symbolic, where a culture is localized in time and space, both a product of lived experiences and where lived experiences are produced. This last point returns to the proposition, so conspicuous in contemporary Latin/o American cities, that individual subjectivity and social identity materialize at the temporal-spatial intersection between social praxis (here-now) and the fluency of memory (then-there). As Young remarks, cities are lived through memories and affects, so the imagined city could be even more "real" than the real city. Social praxis and memory articulate themselves, according to Henri Lefebvre, in three interconnected experiences of space: as spatial practice (by virtue of perception and the sensorium, "the spatial practice of a society secretes that society's space; it propounds and presupposes it, in a dialectical interaction"), as representations of space ("conceptualized space, the space of scientists, planners, urbanists, technocratic subdividers and social engineers . . . the dominant space in any society") and as representational space ("space as directly *lived* through its associated images and symbols, and hence passively experienced—space which the imagination seeks to change and appropriate") (Lefebvre 1991, 38–39). According to Lefebvre, space is simultaneously experienced in three ways: as practical space, produced in the physical and material flows that ensure its reproduction (markets, modes of transportation and communication, territorial demarcations, police); as strategic-hegemonic space, conceptualized as science and technology, ideology and social imaginary; and as tactical-subaltern space, lived through culture and transformed by the radical imagination (family, household, *pagus*; rituals, traditions, everyday life). Even though the limits among these categories seem fuzzy and arbitrary, it is possible to speculate that practical space—constituted by and constitutive of social practices—is the basis upon which strategic-hegemonic space (domain of the social imaginary, the state and capital) and tactical-subaltern space (domain of the radical imagination, the citizen and the worker) perform and struggle. The city, the modern city and, even more, the globalized city, is the arena where this drama is acted out.

In this regard, all the chapters in this volume deal one way or another with different and conflictive experiences of practical space. Among them, the studies on the Colombian TransMilenio (Fernández L'Hoeste), the commodification of the Brazilian Northeast (Prysthon), and the "feasting on Latina/o labor in multicultural Los Angeles" stand out as splendid examples of the workings of strategic-hegemonic space, and the investigation on the necropolitan art in Mexico City (Brooksbank-Jones), the Zapatista contestation of civil national space (Noble), and the contamination of the conqueror's city by Andean migrants (Cánepa) show remarkable instances of tactical-subaltern spaces brought to life through memory and performance. This is why, redolent with imaginary and symbolic elements, tactical-subaltern spaces are intrinsically historical and have always an affective kernel: bed, bedroom, dwelling house, square, church, graveyard. It is always the pagus: the village or the city, a kernel comprising the loci of passion, action, and lived experience, and so, necessarily, memory and time, as Young reminds us (see also Lefevbre 1991, 41–42).

Lefevbre's notion of time-space coincides with the notion of home-memory so central to Gaston Bachelard's poetics of space (1983). According to Yi-Fu Tuan (1977), what really matters in global society is the experience of space, since time no longer enlivens memory, and thus there is need for what Bachelard called topoanalysis, because, though time is the substance of memory, it is a dematerialized time, a time lacking duration, density, and texture, only apprehensible through its anchoring in space. "This is the mysterious power of memory—the power to generate nearness. A room we inhabit whose walls are closer to us than to a visitor. This is what is homey about home," wrote Walter Benjamin (1999a, 248). It can be, as Holmes reminds us in her elegant analysis on urban remembrance, a house, a street, or a neighborhood, always associated with a face or an object, a taste or a smell, perhaps a voice, where the real sense of identity lies. It is the pagus—the hometown, the village, the *Heim*, any locus where affects are invested: "The nostalgic object is the land of our childhood, the past that happened and the past that didn't happen, the fantasies we dreamed of, that dreamed us, and that still live there" (Gil 1993, 9).

As Holmes, Cánepa, Young, and Prysthon underscore in their respective contributions, nostalgia is a widespread contemporary feeling, particularly acute in urban milieus traumatized by hasty modernizations and global cosmopolitism. Asunceños' balancing act between restorative nostalgia and reflective nostalgia, described by Holmes, finds its counterpart in the ersatz nostalgia that Prysthon discovers in contemporary Brazilian filmmaking, as well as in the economy of nostalgia that supplies Latina/o immigrants with the raw ingredients to nurture and elaborate their vibrant culinary identity, as seen in Torres and Buriel's Los Angeles. In spite of Bachelard's metaphysical thrust, his actual descriptions of the home-memory refer to everyday experiences whose psychological dimension rests upon physical texture. In effect, if identity dwells in the space lodged in memory, Bachelard's poetics of space nevertheless projects itself into the present through memories that are materially inscribed in the body and knitted in language, as the chapters by Brooksbank-Jones, Cánepa, Noble, and Benamou illustrate. I am not referring just to physical memories, but also to the recognition of space realized in the body, as well as the transformation that space brings about through bodily kinetics and proxemics, or, in Bachelard's own word, through "habits," a concept obviously homologous to Pierre Bourdieu's sociocultural *habitus* and Bertolt Brecht's theatrical *gestus* (Bourdieu 1977; Brecht 1970).

These are the cultural memories inscribed in the skin, in the senses, in the resonance of what is absent to the body—the smells, textures, and sounds that Kantaris and Young are able to recover in the filmic and literary rendition of

Argentinean historical trauma (Viñar and Viñar 1993, 88). It is precisely this interpellation of cultural memories by the actual circumstances of the here-now that activates the calling up of the experiences of the then-there, thus producing Benjamin's "dialectical images": "It's not that what is past casts its light on what is present, or what is present its light on what is past; rather, image is that wherein what has been comes together in a flash with the now to form a constellation. In other words, image is dialectics at a standstill. For while the relation of the present to the past is a purely temporal, continuous one, the relation of what-has-been to the now is dialectical: is not progression but image, suddenly emergent" (1999b, 462).

This is the dialectics of identity under discussion here. It is precisely in the confluence of Benjamin's "presence of the now" (*Jetztzeit*) with the past of accumulated experiences (*Erfahrung*) that *lived experience* (*Erlebnis*) is produced as "becoming in duration": that is, as a concrete present, right now, as I write these words, with one foot in my childhood and one foot in the grave. Clearly, duration in this sense does not pertain to a strictly personal memory or a solipsistic experience. Just as the most solitary experience is conditioned by and grafts itself onto a specific sociocultural context, a jumble of experiences converge in memory, along with individual and social discourses, contemporary and ancient, really imagined and imaginedly real. Daily lived experiences are tantamount to the duration of memory in the presence of the now: the confluence of being (the past that is inescapably identical to itself) with becoming (the constant flow of difference). The issue is that when memory is swallowed by sheer velocity, identities flatten out, lose historical depth, and become bizarrely spatialized, as Kantaris points out. Even lived experiences and the human body, Brooksbank-Jones makes clear, become commodified in the global regime of capital accumulation, and commodities, by nature, leave no room for any kind of memory not instrumental for the production of economic and libidinal surplus. Commodities, as demonstrated by Torres and Buriel's analysis of the commodification of Latin/o traditional cooking as cosmopolitan nouvelle cuisine, fulfill some sort of ersatz, self-referential memory, and thrive in the absolute, autistic present of consumptive amnesia. This explains why cultural memories, as well as national memories, are an obstacle to hedonistic consumption and the intoxicating circulation of images and desires articulated to the global imaginary and staged and contested in globalized cities, insofar as cultural memories reconnect the subject to symbolic and affective networks that make consumption irrelevant or at least subsidiary. This also explains the political, epistemological, and even ontological importance that the struggle for memory and identity has taken on around the world, most evident in the globalized urban context of Latin/o American cities from Buenos Aires to Detroit, from Mexico City to Havana, from Los Angeles to Asunción, from Recife to Lima, and from Salvador to Bogotá, where the contradictions between memory and performance, the imaginary and the imagination, subjectivity and citizenship, the world of affects and the realm of praxis, exacerbated by cultural globalization and economic neoliberalism, shape everyday life and mediate new identities.

Notes

INTRODUCTION: MEDIATING URBAN IDENTITIES

1. Studies in urban anthropology include the work of James Holston on Brasilia (1989), Teresa Caldeira on São Paulo (2000), and Setha Low on San José, Costa Rica (2000). From more humanistic perspectives, the Mexico City studied by David William Foster (2002) is drawn from representations of the Mexican capital in contemporary cinema, and the New York explored by Juan Flores (2000) is concerned with Puerto Rican constructions of identity, mainly through popular music.

2. See, for example, Susana Rotker's edited volume on urban violence (2002), or the volumes in Spanish edited by Mabel Moraña (2002) and by Boris Muñoz and Silvia Spitta (2003), although representations of the city in literature predominate in the latter two.

3. See, for example, several of the essays in Moraña (1997). Rama's book has also become something of a watershed, with a need to move beyond the "lettered city," both conceptually and historically (Rama's analysis stops at the early twentieth century), signaled by more recent publications (see Franco 2002 and Muñoz 2003).

4. Notable urban *cronistas* from various periods of twentieth-century Latin America include: Enrique Gómez Carrillo and Roberto Arlt for Buenos Aires; Salvador Novo, Elena Poniatowska, and Carlos Monsiváis for Mexico City; Pedro Lemebel for Santiago de Chile; and Enrique Bernardo Núñez for Caracas.

5. This use of *performance* comes, of course, from the linguistic theory of speech acts (see Austin 1975, 1–11) and has acquired wider currency in social discourse, notably through studies such as Judith Butler's inquiries into representations of gender and identity (see Butler 2000).

HAVANA IN THE *NUEVA TROVA* REPERTOIRE OF GERARDO ALFONSO

This chapter reprints lyric excerpts with the stated permission of Gerardo Alfonso.

1. For further information on the many cultural/musical changes associated with the revolution of 1959, see Moore 2006 and Pacini Hernández and Garofalo 2004.

2. The majority of basic biographical information on this artist has been gleaned from Web sites listed in the references, as well as verbal commentary from Alfonso on his *Recuento* album.

3. See Portalatino.com at http://www.portalatino.com/platino/website/ew/alternativo/acerca.jsp?fvuid=600952052280&secid=716042659280&ptitle=Acerca%20de.

4. During the food shortages associated with the Special Period, Havana became known for its *paladares,* or clandestine restaurants that served food in an underground black market economy. Some of these home restaurants have been legalized in more recent years, but they tend to be taxed so heavily by the state that many have become clandestine again.

5. This refers to the fact that motorized transportation is in very short supply in much of Havana and that bicycles are thus used for nonconventional activities such as transporting a family of four (using extra seat attachments) or moving a mattress and box spring to a new apartment across town.

6. For more information on López Lledín, see http://www.cubagenweb.org/misc/paris .htm.

7. Alfonso wore dreadlocks for many years, though he has since cut them off.

LAST SNAPSHOTS/TAKE 2: PERSONAL AND COLLECTIVE SHIPWRECKS IN BUENOS AIRES

1. I describe these experiences as *haptic* (associated with feeling and touch as opposed to the visual) because they translate visual epithets, rendering them metaphors for a nonvisual sensorium.

2. Baudelaire is self-consciously cited by one character.

3. *Fags* is British slang for cigarettes, corresponding to the slang term *faso.*

4. This fantasmatic circulation represents perhaps the haunted flip side of another, more visible circulation that also abolishes time—that of the commodity, as suggested by Sarlo: "Time has been abolished in the market commodity, not because the commodity is in any way eternal, but because it is *entirely transitory*" (1994, 31).

5. The interview cited in this chapter appears in written form on the Spanish DVD edition of the film.

BUENOS AIRES AND THE LITERARY CONSTRUCTION OF URBAN SPACE

The analysis of *El sueño* included in this chapter is a revised version of a text first published in Hart and Young, ed. (2003), 301–4, and is reprinted by permission of Edward Arnold (Publishers) Ltd.

BODY ART AND THE REMAKING OF MEXICO CITY

1. This visual "practicing" of space recalls Michel de Certeau (1988), but also Salvador Novo's insistence, in the 1940s, on the need to *ejercer* or "practice" the city in order to understand it (cited in Gallo 2005, 36). Armando Silva goes further, suggesting that the city as a whole needs to be approached in primarily visual terms, "as a form of art" (2004, 297).

2. Martin Jay offers an astute account of this long history. For a flavor of Spanish and

Latin American debates around the rise of visual culture, see Sarlo (1994), Hopenhayn (2000), Martín-Barbero (2000), and Brea (2005).

3. It is not suggested that globalization or international art exhibitions began in the 1980s, but both changed their character importantly during this period. See Brooksbank-Jones (2007, chapter 2).

4. A video exhibited in Vienna and showing the conservation of a still-born baby was described by members of the local council as "sickening, perverse, and inhuman" (Nungesser 2003, 3).

5. Most relevantly here, certain global art curators have used decontextualized elements from his work to yoke together heterogeneous art practices. See, for example, the catalogue accompanying *Mexico City: An Exhibition about the Exchange Rates of Bodies and Values* curated for P.S.1, New York, in 2002 by Klaus Biesenbach. This presents México City as "a place of extremes—polluted, corrupt, dangerous and crowded . . . overstimulating, hyperbolic" (Dailey 2002, 1). Monsiváis's work has also been used to ground the car-crash aesthetics that brackets Enrique Metinides's photographs of traffic accidents with films such as *Amores perros* (Love's a Bitch; Alejandro González Iñarritu 2000), and normalizes them as "lo mexicano" (Springer 1).

6. Parallels with the case of Anthony Noel Kelley are striking. This formally trained British artist and former abattoir worker bribed a technician at the Royal College of Surgeons to smuggle out severed heads and other body parts as the basis for plaster casts that he would then decorate and exhibit. He was arrested in 1997, the year that Margolles began working independently. See http://news.bbc.co.uk/1/hi/uk/68877.stm (accessed 4 March 2006).

7. Margolles's words here are taken from a dated but unattributed quotation cited on the label of a 1997 video by SEMEFO, shown at the *Eco: Arte Contemporáneo Mexicano* exhibition in the Museo Nacional Centro de Arte Reina Sofia, Madrid, in 2005.

8. This is part of a wider trend in which visual culture, and Mexico, are playing a prominent part. The global circulation of Margolles's work is one aspect of the trend; so, too, are films like *The Three Burials of Melquíades Estrada* (Tommy Lee Jones 2005), produced and directed in the United States but written by a Mexican (Guillermo Arriaga), which are helping to internationalize a nonpathological, if not yet homely, understanding of the corpse as an organic part of life. The contrast with Cold War parables of the living dead is instructive.

9. For this and other images of Margolles's work, see http://images.google.com/images ?q=teresa+margolles&hl=en&lr=&rls=GGLD,GGLD:2004–39,GGLD:en&sa=N&tab=wi& sourceid=tipimg (accessed March 4, 2006). The author is grateful to Teresa Margolles for permission to reproduce one of her photographs in this chapter, and to Cynthia Krell of Peter Kilchmann Gallery, Zurich, for her kind assistance in obtaining them.

10. It should be said that, although Mexico City streets are at the heart of her preoccupations, Margolles does not restrict her activities to the capital. The murders of more than three hundred women in Ciudad Juárez have given a new focus to questions concerning globalization's role in attracting transnational business (especially maquiladoras), in accelerating local inequities, and in escalating drug-trafficking and associated violence.

Margolles has participated in these debates by making bricks from sand collected where the bodies of victims were found, and by displaying installations made from them. In Cali, widely viewed as one of Latin America's most violent cities (still more so now, in the absence of the drug cartel and its brutal enforcers), she distributed flyers asking residents whose friends and family members had been victims of violence to bring along mementos for burial in a hole in the pavement alongside the Parque Panamericano. Filled with these mementos and sealed, this hole became an *escultura negativa* (negative sculpture), as Roca (2003) puts it, something between a womb, a tomb, and a monument, a way of returning to public space those violently removed from it and of making death present without rendering it either spectacular or banal.

11. The rendering of the body part as artwork was completed in 2000. The coffin exchanged was apparently one that Margolles had used to smuggle bodies from the morgue in order to make plaster casts of them.

12. SEMEFO's suggestion that political readings of their work might be a strategy on the part of the spectator "to justify a taste for macabre images" indicates that they were alert to tensions in its reception, if not its production (Roca 2003, np, n.10).

13. This is not to suggest that Mexican visual culture is wholly globalized; globalization *everywhere* is a project yet to be achieved (Moreiras). As García Canclini observes, the work of some artists remains an expression of national iconographic traditions that circulate only within the national space. However, a significant proportion of this work's creation, diffusion, and reception takes place today with an eye to larger contexts (1999, 146–47).

14. My use of the term *globalization* in this chapter is informed by Garcá Canclini's *La globalización imaginada* (1999). For a compelling critical discussion of the term, see also Bourdieu and Wacquant (1999) and Friedman's (2000) response.

15. From the late 1600s, with the emergence of the anatomical specimen, the human body would increasingly serve as a quasi-sculptural medium, as body parts were preserved and colored, or replicated in wax and other materials. Contemporary art has seen a strong revival of interest in body-part art since the mid-1990s, much of it based on close copies. But the anatomical tradition resonates most famously, perhaps, in the Body Worlds exhibition of German anatomist Gunther von Hagens, with its display of plastinated and dissected human corpses and clear performance art dimension. The best-known explicitly artistic interpretations of the anatomical tradition, however, are probably the cows, sheep, and sharks pickled in formaldehyde by British artist Damien Hurst. These are not human remains, however. Arguably closer to Margolles's practice in this respect is Anthony Noel Kelley (see my note 6 here).

The origins of Margolles's own materials, especially before she began working at the Central Morgue, remain obscure: some corpses appear to have been smuggled out with the complicity of morgue staff, and there are contradictory accounts of whether parts were purchased from relatives (technically illegal in Mexico), or donated by them. These questions are complicated by the fact that the majority tend to be poor and vulnerable families whose sons or (less often) daughters are the victims of murder. The fact that Margolles's work includes not only plaster casts but also plastinated body parts brings her closer to the work of von Hagens, whom she professes to admire. What chiefly distinguishes her work from that of, for example, U.S. photographer Joel-Peter Witkin, who visits "medical schools, morgues, and insane asylums around the world" in search of "human spectacles including hermaphrodites, dwarfs, amputees, androgynes, carcasses, people with odd physical disabilities, fetishists," is the disturbingly sexualized poses in which he arranges these usually female elements and his "scratching and piercing" of their images (Edelman Gallery 2005, np). A specifically Mexican geneaology links Margolles to the therapeutic or propitiatory use of representations of affected body parts in popular religion. By contrast, Witkin's work seems driven by more explicitly pathological energies.

FEASTING ON LATINA/O LABOR IN MULTICULTURAL LOS ANGELES

1. The "big Other," as opposed to the "small other," is commonly used in psychoanalysis to refer to a fundamental modality of otherness wherein language, or the Symbolic order, always functions as a wall that prevents a self-same understanding of others. As Jacques Lacan claims, "Language is as much there to found us in the Other as to drastically prevent us from understanding him [or her]" (244). Thus in this article we recurrently utilize the "big Other" to emphasize the symbolic density of multicultural discourses that paradoxically prevent an understanding of ethnic and minority others despite the fact that the intention of such discourses is to know, to understand, an "exoticized" Other.

2. This is a concept utilized by Sharon Zukin in *Landscapes of Power* (1991) to refer to a broad spectrum of knowledge workers and cultural service workers typically identified with the cultivation of urban taste. Knowledge service workers might include artists and performers, whereas chefs and museum curators might constitute cultural service workers.

3. Peter McLaren writes that liberal multiculturalists believe that there is a certain "intellectual 'sameness' among the races, on their cognitive equivalence or the rationality imminent in all races that permits them to compete equally in a capitalist society" (51). He admits that this view "often collapses into an ethnocentric and oppressively universalistic humanism in which the legitimating norms which govern the substance of citizenship are identified most strongly with Anglo-American cultural-political communities" (51).

MEDIATING THE PUBLIC SPHERE IN LATINA/O DETROIT: HEART AND MARGIN OF AN EMBATTLED METROPOLIS

I wish to thank Kristy Rawson, PhD candidate in Screen Arts and Cultures, University of Michigan–Ann Arbor, for her excellent assistance with the gathering of local demographic data and English-language news sources, Michael Casas, PhD candidate in Communication Studies, University of Michigan, for his helpful collaboration during the early stages of the Detroit viewer survey, Leo Ogata for his expert assistance with cartographic accuracy, and Bruce Daniel for designing the digital maps in Figures 4 and 6. Funding for the Detroit field research was provided in part by a grant from the College of Literature, Science, and the Arts and the Horace G. Rackham School of Graduate Studies at the University of Michigan–Ann Arbor (2005–2007), as well as the School of Humanities, University of California–Irvine (2008).

1. See "Table 3: Population Change by Community, 2000–2006" (Muller 2006) and "Population by Race and Ethnicity: City of Detroit and Detroit's Planning Cluster 5" (*American Community Survey Profile* 2007). Statistics in the latter are probably conservative, given the tendency for Hispanics to be undercounted.

2. Arjun Appadurai has defined *mediascape* as "the distribution of the electronic capabilities to produce and disseminate information (newspapers, magazines, television stations, and film-producing studios) . . . and . . . the images of the world created by these media" (Appadurai 1997, 35). Note that, along its full spectrum, the Detroit mediascape includes, by dint of border location, a smattering of Francophone and mainstream Canadian radio and television channels, along with a handful of other foreign-language programs and stations, most in Arabic or Spanish.

3. A recent nationwide study by the Furman Center for Real Estate and Urban Policy at New York University found that subprime mortgage lending has been "unusually concentrated in black and Hispanic neighborhoods," with Hispanics "twice as likely" to obtain high-cost loans as "whites" in 2006 (Lee 2008).

4. This dual formulation of enfranchisement is closely related to the notion of cultural citizenship. For a range of views on the importance of cultural citizenship in dynamic contrast with more traditional, political forms, see Stevenson (2001).

5. For more on the renewed significance of a sense of place as a criterion in urban planning (and its historical analysis), see Herzog 2006, 7–9 and *passim*.

6. Rivera worked on the murals between 1932 and 1933, and claims in his autobiography to have assisted many Mexicans who were returning to Mexico during this period (Rivera 1991, 124).

7. For more information on these subsequent waves, and on the differences in settlement patterns and civic relations among them in the Detroit context, see Hoffnung-Garskof 2008, 415–20.

8. See Muller 2006, "Table 2, 2005 Hisp. Pop. Xls," and "Population by Race and Ethnicity: City of Detroit and Detroit's Planning Cluster 5," in *American Community Survey Profile* 2007 (attachments to e-mail correspondence from Sirisha Uppalapati, SEMCOG Planning Analyst, to Kristy Rawson, August 21, 2007).

9. This last figure was cited in an e-mail communication to the author from a WUDT reporter, September 3, 2007. An American Community Survey conducted in 2005 and focusing only on households revealed that the Hispanic/Latina/o population living in Wayne County alone was close to 90,995, out of a total county population of 1,966,909 (U.S. Census Bureau, "Wayne County Michigan–Fact Sheet–American FactFinder," http://factfinder.census.gov/servlet/ACSSAFFFacts?_event=Search [accessed July 23, 2007]).

10. This is according to the Michigan Metropolitan Information Center at Wayne State University, as reported in Mexicantown International Welcome Center and Mercado, "Southwest Detroit Area Residents" (2007, 4).

11. For example, a "Midwest Market Profile" of Hispanic newspapers published in *Portada* only mentions the regional (Michigan and Ohio) paper *La Prensa* and the Grand Rapids-based *El Vocero Hispano*, in its report on "Michigan: the Water Wonderland" (see

Midwest Market Profile 2007, 30); neither of these papers are primary sources of news for Detroit Latinas/os.

12. The survey was part of a multisite study of the transmission of Spanish-language media and its significance for Latina/o audiences in the United States and Spain initiated at the University of Michigan under IRB approval #B05–00008004-M1 (2005–2006). The Detroit viewer survey was designed with the collaboration of Michael Casas and administered with the assistance of Michael Casas, Ricardo Ramos, and José Nevarez.

13. *¡Informando!*, hosted by Gustavo Potes and Gloria Guerra, WUDT-Univisión Detroit, December 8, 2007.

14. The FSN Detroit and FSN Plus coverage featured commentary by sportscaster Clemson Smith Muñiz and by sports historian Adrian Burgos (see del Valle 2008).

15. Examples of Detroit portrayals include *Out of Sight*, directed by Steven Soderbergh (1998), and *8-Mile*, directed by Curtis Hanson (2002), notwithstanding Eminem's creative participation in the latter.

16. See "Detroit Michigan Census and Demographic Information" at http://www.hellodetroit.com/Census.Cfm; and "Quick Facts from the U.S. Census Bureau, Livonia, Michigan" at http://www.infoplease.com/us/census/data/michigan/livonia/. See also "Percentage of the Three-County Metropolitan Population Living in the City of Detroit: 1900 to 2000" at http://www.detroit1701.org/Percent%20in%20Detroit.html, and Brookings Institute, "Detroit in Focus: A Profile from Census 2000" (November 2003 executive summary) at http://www.brookings.edu/reports/2003/11_livingcities_detroit.aspx.

17. Note that those claiming "Some Other Race Alone" in the Non-Hispanic or Latino/a population grew by 128.5 percent between 2000 and 2005 in the city of Detroit, and by 147.6 percent in Planning Cluster 5, a predominantly Hispanic/Latino district (see *American Community Survey Profile* 2007).

18. According to the 2005 American Community Survey, over 2,000 Latinas/os chose "Black or African American Alone," 682 claimed "American Indian" identity, over 1,000 claimed "Two or More Races," and over 27,000 claimed "Some Other Race Alone" (other than "white"), from an overall citywide Latino/a population of 46,993 (see *American Community Survey Profile* 2007).

19. My thanks to Windsorite Christopher McNamara for sharing his personal recollections of these exchanges.

20. This was corroborated by my 2005 media survey, which revealed that roughly half of the respondents who viewed television were receiving satellite transmissions directly from Chile and Central America, or special networks like TV Azteca and Telemundo, available only via satellite.

21. As pointed out by Canadian authorities interviewed on WUDT, only about 13 percent of those who apply for residency status in Canada are granted visas.

22. These are anonymous responses to a question in my 2005 survey, "Preferences and Opinions of the Latina/o Community Regarding Communications Media," University of Michigan IRB approval #B05–00008004-M1 (2005–2006), drafted in collaboration with Michael Casas.

TEXTUAL REVISIONS OF IDENTITY: NOSTALGIA AND MODERNITY IN ASUNCIÓN

1. Cities have been touted as the "ideal crossroads" for the expression of certain principal dichotomies, among them "longing and estrangement, memory and freedom," and "nostalgia and modernity" (Boym 2003, 76).

2. Carlos R. Miranda (1990) notes, in reference to the Stroessner leadership, that "few other governments claimed credit for so many civic and public works, even works that were somehow remote from the actual sphere of government" (69).

3. Aníbal Quijano (1990) noted this modernization process as a general tendency for Latin America (149).

4. The term was coined by the Swiss doctor Johannes Hofer, who derived it from a combination of the Greek *nostos* (to return home) and *algos* (pain) (Piason Natali 2006, 10).

5. This approach to modernity underscores the exceptional differences between Paraguay and the rest of Latin America. According to Jorge Larraín, who identifies five stages in the Latin American trajectory toward modernity, the era from 1990 onward marked a diminution of industrial production and a new attention toward democracy and human rights (Larrain 2000, 23). Paraguay has not yet been industrialized, and these contemporary political concerns have only begun to be expressed there within the last two years. Although Prieto and Rubiani still pay particular attention to comparisons with European forms of modernity, this attitude has been replaced by more local models in other parts of the region.

6. This is not to mention Augusto Roa Bastos' earlier powerful depictions of military and social oppression, albeit they are mostly set against the backdrop of rural Paraguay.

7. The much-discussed cultural group founded in the late 1970s, C.A.D.A. (Colectivo de acciones de arte), introduced new subtle, but potent, images to confront the codes produced by Pinochet's redefinition of the city. Cofounders of the group, the authors Diamela Eltit and Raúl Zurita, artists Lotty Rosenfield and Juan Castillo, and sociologist Fernando Balcells, sought to overcome the fictional constructions produced by the dictatorship through the exposure of the marginalized body in public space. For example, Eltit's novel *Lumpérica* (1983), which obliquely recounted the experience of a homeless woman during one night on a public plaza in downtown Santiago, escaped censorship because of its complexity.

8. These include *Ignacia* (1905) by José Rodríguez Alcalá and *Aurora* (1920) by Juan Stefanich.

9. For a detailed account of contemporary literary representations of Asunción, see José Vicente Peiró Barco's chapter on the city in fiction in his dissertation (2001).

10. Susana Rotker identifies a difference between these late twentieth-century chronicles and those of the *costumbrista* writers: "Unlike the case of the costumbrista chroniclers of the nineteenth century, these chronicles of violence do not organize a system of coherence. Even in giving a voice to those who normally do not have one, they do not manage to normalize them or appropriate them into the orders of writing and thought" (220).

11. See Aníbal González (1993) and Julio Ramos (1989) for analysis of the chronicle during Modernismo.

12. "Reconstrucción *literaria* de sucesos o figuras, género donde el empeño formal domina sobre las urgencias informativas" (Monsiváis 1980 , 13).

13. See Boris Muñoz for a study of the escatological image of Mexico City in the work of these chroniclers. Muñoz observes a change in perception of the city based on the two major incidents affecting the D.F. in the last decades of the twentieth century: the Massacre at Tlatelolco in 1968 and the earthquake in 1983. Whereas the chronicles of Mexico City following 1968 characterize the urban center as apocalyptic, after the earthquake—here, Muñoz cites the example of *Los rituales del caos*—the images become, rather, "post-apocalyptic."

NORTHEASTERN IMAGES: RECIFE AND SALVADOR IN CONTEMPORARY BRAZILIAN CINEMA

1. We could also associate this hybridity and peripheral cosmopolitanism with previous multicultural phenomena in Brazilian culture such as the Semana de Arte Moderna in 1922 or the Tropicália movement of the late 1960s. See Prysthon (2002a) for the connections between Oswald de Andrade's *Antropofagia* and musical Tropicalism, and Dunn (2001) for a more specific discussion of Tropicália. See Stam (1997) for an analysis of Brazilian cinema through the lenses of race and for the concept of Tropical multiculturalism.

2. Lampião was the nickname of Virgulino Ferreira da Silva, the most notorious leader of the Cangaço (bands of outlaws who terrorized the Northeast in the 1920s and 1930s). *Baile Perfumado* took its inspiration from a real episode in which Lampião and his band were filmed by the Lebanese peddler Benjamin Abrahão.

3. The change from traditional to modern societies in the context of the neocolonial relationship of Latin America to the European and North American centers of capitalism has been studied by Sarlo (1988) and Sevcenko (1992), who offer a detailed understanding of the complex processes of modernization and urban growth at the beginning of the twentieth century in Latin America, specifically with respect to Buenos Aires and São Paulo (respectively).

4. The expression *árido movie* was not only the title of the film, but was coined by a journalist and circulated in Recife's cultural press, some years before the film was made, to refer to the growing production of films from Pernambuco.

5. There is a significant group of films in the 1990s and 2000s that adhere to the *carioca* clichés of white sand beaches, beautiful women in swimsuits, dark people playing soccer, and the relative bourgeois security of the Zona Sul *bairros*. Sandra Werneck's *Pequeno dicionário amoroso* (*Little Book of Love*; 1997) and *Amores possíveis* (*Possible Loves*; 2000), Bruno Barreto's *Bossa Nova* (2000), Mara Mourão's *Avassaladoras* (*Overwhelming Women*; 2002), and Daniel Filho's *A partilha* (*The Inheritance*; 2001) and *E se eu fosse você* (*If I Were You*; 2006) are all examples of an effort to show the normal urban life of the middle class in Rio de Janeiro, in a very deliberate attempt to serve as a counterweight to the reports of urban violence in Rio.

6. *Manguebit* or *manguebeat* are two names given to the pop music movement (later extended in a more or less fashionable manner to the visual arts, cinema, and a mode of behavior) that emerged in Recife in the early 1990s. One of the basic principles of this aesthetic is hybridism, a mix of elements from global culture with clearly vernacular aspects (Fonseca 2005). In fashion, for instance, the recurrence of adornments, patterns, and prints from manifestations of popular culture and folklore was especially evident.

PERFORMING CITIZENSHIP: MIGRATION, ANDEAN FESTIVALS, AND PUBLIC SPACES IN LIMA

This chapter was translated from the Spanish by Richard Young. It is part of a larger research project, "Geopoética y geopolítica de la danza: migración, identidad, y lugar en el Perú," undertaken with the support of the CLACSO-Asdi program of grants for senior researchers in Latin America and the Caribbean (2000–2002).

1. See Altamirano (1984) for the role of religious festivals in the process of cultural insertion in the city.

2. Berg and Paerregaard (2005) have approached the study of Andean festivals in the context of transnational migration.

3. In October 2002, President Alejandro Toledo ended a twelve-year paternity suit by recognizing Zaraí Toledo as his daughter, an event interpreted in commentaries circulating on the radio and in other media as a miracle performed by El Señor de los Milagros to restore calm to a complicated political situation.

4. See Cánepa (2007) for a more extensive discussion of how Lima's centralism is contested in particular contexts through the configuration of a new geography of identity promoted by the recontextualization of Andean festivals in Lima, and how, in most instances, centralism is reinforced.

THE TRANSMILENIO EXPERIENCE: MASS TRANSIT IN BOGOTÁ AND NATIONAL URBAN IDENTITY

1. For a comparable account of the relation in Buenos Aires between urban space and the inhabitants of the city, one that also considers public transportation and the movement of the citizenry, see Adrián Gorelik's *La grilla y el parque: Espacio público y cultura urbana en Buenos Aires, 1887–1936* (1998).

THE FERIA DEL LIBRO AND THE RITUALIZATION OF CULTURAL BELONGING IN HAVANA

As this article is part of a larger project, funded by the Leverhulme Trust, the authors would like to acknowledge the support of the Trust in carrying out their research for it.

1. *Instructores de arte* were intensively trained cultural educators who were dispatched nationwide to enact a program of mass cultural participation; the aficionados (amateur performers) were those members of the public who responded to this program by developing their cultural skills in a nationally organized movement; the Casas de Cultura grew out of this movement and were municipio-based cultural centers.

2. Casa de la Américas is the prestigious cultural center and publishing house that, since 1959, has disseminated Latin American culture in Cuba and Cuban culture in Latin America; ICAIC is the post-1959 cinema institute, responsible for all film production and distribution in Cuba; UNEAC is the post-1961 Union of Cuban Writers and Artists.

3. From the early 1990s, two currencies have operated in Cuba: hard currency (initially the U.S. dollar and then, after 2004, the substitute peso convertible); and the peso cubano, which was exchangeable at 24:1 for the peso convertible in 2010.

4. In fact, more such opportunities were available to nonliterary cultural forms (especially music, dance, and the visual arts) than to literature.

5. In 1960, limited U.S. economic sanctions on Cuba were first imposed, and by 1963 this was a full-blown embargo, supported by all Latin American nations except Mexico.

6. The entire issue of the journal was dedicated to Havana, with contributions by Leal and other prominent intellectuals.

7. Italy, France, and Germany were named in 2000, 2001, and 2003, respectively, with a subsequent shift from Europe toward Latin America: 2005 was dedicated to Brazil, 2006 to Venezuela, and 2007 to Argentina, each reflecting new regional friendships and political shifts.

8. In 2006, sales fell to 3.1 million (*www.cubaliteraria.com/evento/filh/2007/espa/convoca. htm* [accessed May 2, 2007]), but these were back to 5.2 million in 2007 (*www.granma.cu/ espanol/2007/marzo/lun12/feria.html* [accessed April 30, 2007]).

9. One may speculate that this refocusing was also to save money or to make a virtue of necessity, given a reduction in publishers' interest, although there is no firm evidence of either.

10. This was the six-month-long campaign for the return of the six-year-old boy who, left stranded in the Florida straits after his mother's death on their makeshift boat, was held by her Miami family against the father's wishes.

11. The text that follows is based on a fieldwork study of the Feria in February 2–9, 2006, followed up by interviews with twenty participating writers and publishers.

12. Seventeen Havana bookshops throughout the city (at least one in each municipio and more in the central districts) also act as satellites for those unable or unwilling to travel, as does the small Vedado-based exhibition site, Pabellón Cuba, where the Feria consists of two second-hand peso cubano bookstalls, one large shop for children's books (also in pesos cubanos), several stationery shops, and a musical performance or competition event, with entry costing half that of the main Feria.

13. It is possible that some were also buying in bulk to resell to second-hand bookshops, although this would still suggest the existence of a large market.

14. In 2006, although some literary lectures addressed only about ten people, historians' events regularly attracted some forty to fifty, and one event attracted over one hundred.

15. The interviews that form the evidence for this section sought to elicit writers' general reactions, in particular with regard to the Feria's importance for the public and for themselves as writers and how the 2006 iteration compared with previous events.

16. We are indebted, for information on media coverage, to the work of Laura Betancourt, of the ICL.

17. A more recent study of the literary field is offered by Pascale Casanova (2004). Her notion of the "republic of letters" in some senses takes Rama's model further, exploring the mechanisms of canonization and prestige operating between center and periphery, and by underlining the complex relationship between the literary and political fields in national and international contexts.

18. This appeared in a paper presented at the University of Cambridge.

ZAPATISTAS IN MEXICO CITY AND THE PERFORMANCE OF ETHNIC CITIZENSHIP

1. Coverage of the Consulta can also be found in a range of national dailies, including *Excélsior, El Universal,* and *Reforma.*

2. Photographs with these captions were among several published in *La Jornada.*

3. The contextualizing section that follows is indebted to the work of De la Peña (2006), Harvey (1998), Nash (1995 and 2001), and Saldaña-Portillo (2003).

4. In addition to Knight (1990) and Brading (1988), Dawson (2004) provides an excellent account of the efforts to integrate the Indian into postrevolutionary society, and Lomnitz (2001) offers a critical history of the development of anthropology in Mexico.

5. See Guillermoprieto (2002) for an account of the unmasking.

6. The Caravana is documented in words and images in *El Otro Jugador* (2001). For an account of Comandanta Esther's address to congress, see Carbó (2003).

7. See La Otra Campaña (2006) and Williams (2007) for analysis.

8. For chronicles of the 1994 CND, see Monsiváis (1994) and Poniatowska (1994); for an analysis of these chronicles, see Jörgensen (2004). See also Saldaña-Portillo (2002) for an excellent account of the meanings associated with silence in the first Encuentro Intercontinental por la Paz y contra el Neoliberalismo / Intercontinental Meeting for Humanity and against Neoliberalism, at the 1996 Aguascalientes at Oventic. In August 2003, the EZLN Command announced the end of the Aguascalientes and the creation of Caracoles. A continuation of the communitarian, consensus-based model of democracy espoused by the Zapatistas and enshrined in the notion of "mandar obedeciendo" (lead by obeying), Caracoles involved the formation of like-minded localities and communities into autonomous governments that, in turn, conjoined with similar networks to form wider networks of autonomous rule (see González Casanova 2005).

9. See also Leyva Solano (2005).

10. A number of images were made of this event in 1914, significantly going on to become some of *the* photographic icons of the revolution, reproduced and disseminated to this day. Similarly, a number of photographs were made and disseminated of the 1999 incursion into Sanborns.

11. The real haunt of the elite at this time was the Jockey Club, but as this photograph clearly depicts, Sanborns would have had a similar status. Sanborns was founded in 1903 as a soda fountain and American-style drugstore by the North American brothers Frank and Walter Sanborn. See Noble (1998) for an analysis of the gendered relations of *looking* established in the Sanborns series.

12. See O'Malley (1986) and Benjamin (2000) for an account of postrevolutionary myth making; on Zapata, see Brunk (2008). See Rajchenberg and Héau-Lambert (1998) on the relationship between the contemporary Zapatistas and revolutionary symbolism.

13. See also the special 2006 issue of *History and Theory* for further critical reflection on the notion of presence for our understanding of the past. "The idea of presence," as Keith Moxey puts it in a more recent essay on the iconic turn in visual culture, "has entered the precinct of the humanities and made itself at home" (2008, 131).

14. The work of W. G. Sebald has become a ubiquitous touchstone in contemporary

theoretical debate, where, beyond the sphere of strictly literary analysis, it has acquired an emblematic status in scholarship concerned with questions of memory and trauma. This is certainly the status of Sebald's novel, *Austerlitz,* in Runia's essay. For a serious, critical analysis of Sebald's work that acts as a corrective to this tendency, see Long (2008).

15. I am adapting here Catherine Russell's (1999, 5) notion regarding the relation between film and James Clifford's definition of the "salvage paradigm." Where the latter is a denial of coevalness of the ethnographic subject, for Russell this denial is "especially true of film, which feeds on photographic properties of preservation, fixing its referents in the prior time of shooting. In the cinema, the pastoral allegory becomes exaggerated by the role of technology in the act of representation, further splitting the 'modern' from 'the premodern.'"

References

A toda máquina. 2004. *Cambio,* no. 586 (September 20): 46–49.

Acosta, Leonardo. 1991. The Rumba, the Guaguancó, and Tío Tom. In *Essays on Cuban Music: North American and Cuban Perspectives,* ed. Peter Manuel, 51–73. Lanham, MD: University Press of America.

Acuña, Claudia. 1999. El neorrealista bonaerense. *El amante.* http://www.elamante.com.ar/nota/0/0001.shtml (accessed October 19, 1999).

Ades, Dawn. 1989. *Art in Latin America.* New Haven, CT: Yale University Press.

Adorno, T. 2000. The Culture Industry Reconsidered. In *The City Reader,* ed. Malcolm Miles and Tim Hall, with Iain Borden, 163–68. 2nd ed. London and New York: Routledge.

Agresti, Alejandro. 1996. *Buenos Aires vice versa.* Screenplay by Alejandro Agresti. Argentina. 122min. 35mm/color.

Aira, César. 1998. *El sueño.* Buenos Aires: Emecé.

———. 2001. *La villa.* Buenos Aires: Emecé.

Alfaro, Santiago. 2005. Las industrias culturales e identidades étnicas del huayno. In *Arguedas y el Perú de hoy,* 57–76. ed. Carmen María Pinilla. Lima: SUR.

Alfonso, Gerardo. 1997. *Sábanas blancas.* Bis Music compact disc 126. Havana: ARTEX.

———. 2001. *El ilustrado caballero de París.* EGREM cassette C-686. Havana: EGREM.

———. 2002. *Momentos.* Unicornio cassette UN-KCT7017. Havana: Abdala Studios.

———. 2003. *Las cosas que te cuento.* Bis Music compact disc 257. Havana: ARTEX.

Altamirano, Teófilo. 1984. *Presencia andina en Lima metropolitana: Estudio sobre migrantes y clubes de provincianos.* Lima: Fondo Editorial de La Pontificia Universidad Católica del Perú.

Althusser, Louis. 1971. Ideology and Ideological State Apparatuses (Notes towards an Investigation). In *Lenin and Philosophy,* trans. Ben Brewster, 127–86. New York: Monthly Review Press.

Álvarez, Sonia, Evelina Dagnino, and Arturo Escobar. 1998. Introduction: The Cultural and the Political in Latin American Social Movements. In *Cultures of Politics / Politics of Culture: Re-Visioning Latin American Social Movements*, ed. Sonia Álvarez, Evelina Dagnino, and Arturo Escobar, 1–29. Boulder: Westview Press.

American Community Survey Profile, Michigan, 2005. 2007. Southfield and Detroit: Southeast Michigan Census Council (SEMCC) and Southeast Michigan Council of Governments (SEMCOG).

Anderson, Benedict. 1983. *Imagined Communities: Reflections on the Origin and Spread of Nationalism.* London: Verso.

Appadurai, Arjun. 1997. *Modernity at Large: Cultural Dimensions of Globalization.* Minneapolis: University of Minnesota Press.

———. 2004. The Capacity to Aspire: Culture and the Terms of Recognition. In *Culture and Public Action*, ed. Vijayendra Rao and Michael Walton, 59–84. California: Stanford University Press.

———, and Carol Breckenridge. 1995. Introduction: Public Culture in India. In *Consuming Modernity: Public Culture in a South Asian World*, ed. Carol Breckendrige, 1–20. Minneapolis: University of Minnesota Press.

Arditi, Benjamín. 1988. La sociedad a pesar del Estado. In *Imágenes desconocidas: La modernidad en la encrucijada postmoderna*, ed. Fernando Calderón, 161–71. Buenos Aires: CLACSO.

Arellano Cueva, Rolando, and David Burgos Abugattas. 2004. *Ciudad de los Reyes, de los Chávez, los Quispe . . . Una visión social y de mercado de la nueva urbe latinoamericana.* Lima: Empresa Periodística Nacional.

Armstrong, A., and T. G. McGee. 1985. *Theatres of Accumulation: Studies in Asian and Latin American Urbanization.* London: Methuen.

Augé, Marc. 1995. *Non-Places: Introduction to an Anthropology of Supermodernity.* London: Verso.

Austin, John L. 1975. *How to Do Things with Words.* 2nd ed. Cambridge, MA: Harvard University Press.

Avelar, Idelber. 1999. *The Untimely Present.* Durham, NC, and London: Duke University Press.

Ávila, Javier. 2002. Regionalismo, religiosidad y etnicidad migrante trans/nacional andina en un contexto de 'glocalización': El culto al Señor de Qoyllur Ritti. In *Interculturalidad y política: Desafíos y posibilidades*, ed. Norma Fuller, 209–46. Lima: Red Para el Desarrollo de las Ciencias Sociales en el Perú.

Bachelard, Gaston. 1964. *The Poetics of Space.* New York: Orion Press.

Balderrama, Francisco E., and Raymond Rodríguez. 1995. *Decade of Betrayal: Mexican Repatriation in the 1930s.* Albuquerque: University of New Mexico Press.

Balibar, Etienne. 1991. Citizen Subject. In *Who Comes after the Subject?* ed. Eduardo Cadava, Peter Connor, and Jean-Luc Nancy, 33–57. London: Routledge.

Barber, Stephen. 2002. *Projected Cities: Cinema and Urban Space.* London: Reaktion Books.

Barthes, Roland. 1983. *Camera Lucida: Reflections on Photography.* Trans. Richard Howard. London: Vintage.

———. 1984. O efeito de real. In *O rumor da língua,* 131–36. Lisbon: Edições 70.

———. 1997. The Eiffel Tower. In *Rethinking Architecture: A Reader in Cutural Theory,* ed. Neil Leach, 172–80. New York: Routledge.

Bataille, Georges. 1991. *The Accursed Share: An Essay in General Economy.* Vol. 1, *Consumption.* Trans. Robert Hurley. New York: Zone Books.

Bauman, Zygmunt. 1998. *Globalization. The Human Consequences.* New York: Columbia University Press.

Bauza, Margarita, 2006. Local Activists Want Impact, Not Backlash. *Detroit Free Press,* April 28 (accessed through *Access World News*).

Bazin, André. 1967. The Ontology of the Photographic Image. In *What is Cinema?* trans. Hugh Gray, 9–16. Berkeley and Los Angeles: University of California Press.

Beausse, Pascal. 2005. Teresa Margolles: Primordial Substances. *Flash Art International,* July–September: 106–9.

Bellinghausen, Hermann. 1999. Engullidos en el caos citadino, los zapatistas promueven la consulta. *La Jornada,* March 16. http://www.jornada.unam.mx/1999/03/16/promueven.html.

Benjamin, Thomas. 2000. *La Revolución: Mexico's Great Revolution as Memory, Myth, and History.* Austin: University of Texas Press.

Benjamin, Walter. 1969. Theses on the Philosophy of History. In *Illuminations: Essays and Reflections,* 253–64. New York: Schocken Books.

———. 1991. *Para una crítica de la violencia, y otros ensayos: Iluminaciones 4.* Madrid: Taurus Humanidades.

———. 1996. *Selected Writings,* vol. 1, 1913–1926, ed. Marcus Bullock and Michael W. Jennings. Cambridge, MA: The Belknap Press of Harvard University Press.

——— 1999a. The Great Art of Making Things Seem Closer Together. In *Selected Writings,* 2, 1927–1934, ed. Michael W. Jennings, Howard Eiland, and Gary Smith, 248. Cambridge, MA, and London: The Belknap Press of Harvard University Press.

———. 1999b. *The Arcades Project.* Trans. by Howard Eiland and Kevin McLaughlin. Cambridge, MA, and London: The Belknap Press of Harvard University Press.

Bentes, Ivana. 2001. Da estética à cosmética da fome. *Jornal do Brasil,* July 8.

Berg, Ulla, and Karsten Paerregaard. 2005. *El quinto suyo, transnacionalidad y formaciones diaspóricas en la migración peruana.* Lima: Instituto de Estudios Peruanos.

Bergero, Adriana. 2008. *Intersecting Tango: Cultural Geographies of Buenos Aires, 1900–1930.* Trans. Richard Young. Pittsburgh: University of Pittsburgh Press.

Berman, Marshall. 1982. *All That Is Solid Melts into Air.* London: Verso.

Bhabha, Homi K. 1994. *The Location of Culture.* London: Routledge.

Bielinsky, Fabián. 2001. *Nueve reinas.* Argentina. 35mm/color.

Biesenbach, Klaus. 2002. *Mexico City: An Exhibition about the Exchange Rates of Bodies and Values.* New York: P.S.1 Contemporary Art Center/KW–Institute for Contemporary Art.

Bodipo-Memba, Alejandro. 2005. Minority Media Outlets; Station Reaches Out to Hispanics (WUDT-TV 23 Univision/Detroit). *Detroit Free Press*, June 9 (accessed at http://www.highbeam.com/DocPrint.aspx?Docid=1G1:133095095)

Borges, Jorge Luis. 1969. *Fervor de Buenos Aires*. Buenos Aires: Emecé.

Borja, Jordi, and Zaida Muxi. 2003. *El espacio público: Ciudad y ciudadanía*. Barcelona: Electa.

Bourdieu, Pierre. 1977. *Outline of a Theory of Practice*. Cambridge: Cambridge University Press, 1977.

—— 1986. The Forms of Capital. In *Handbook of Theory and Research for the Sociology of Education*, ed. John G. Richardson, 214–58. New York: Greenwood Press.

—— and Loïc Wacquant. 1999. On the Cunning of Imperialist Reason. *Theory, Culture, and Society* 16, no. 1: 41–58.

Boyarin, Jonathan. 1994. *Remapping Memory. The Politics of Timespace*. Minneapolis: Minnesota University Press.

Boym, Svetlana. 2003. *The Future of Nostalgia*. New York: Basic Books.

Brading, David. 1988. Manuel Gamio and Official *Indigenismo* in Mexico. *Bulletin of Latin American Research* 7: 75–89.

Brea, José Luis, ed. 2005. *Estudios visuales*. Madrid: Akal.

Brecht, Bertolt. 1970. *Escritos sobre teatro*. Buenos Aires: Nueva Visión.

Brooksbank-Jones, Anny. 2007. *Visual Culture in Spain and Mexico*. Manchester, Manchester University Press.

——, and Ronald Munck, eds. 2000. *Cultural Politics in Latin America*. London: Macmillan.

Brunk, Samuel. 2008. *The Posthumous Career of Emiliano Zapata: Myth, Memory, and Mexico's Twentieth Century*. Austin: University of Texas Press.

Buck-Morss, Susan. 2005. Estudios visuales e imaginación global. In Brea (2005), 145–59.

Burbano Valente, Johanna, and Luz M. Carvajal Marín. 2005. Empresas de transporte: Entre TransMilenio y la incertidumbre. *Universitas Psycologica*, no. 003 (October–December): 317–24.

Butler, Judith. 2000. Critically Queer. In *Identity: A Reader*, ed. Paulk du Gay, Jessica Evans, and Peter Redman, 108–17. London and Thousand Oaks, CA: SAGE Publications/The Open University.

Caetano, Adrián, and Bruno Stagnaro. 1997. *Pizza, birra, faso*. Argentina. 90mins. 35mm/color.

Caldeira, Teresa. 2000. *City of Walls: Crime, Segregation, and Citizenship in São Paulo*. Berkeley and Los Angeles: University of California Press.

Candidatos Hispanos en Contienda en 38 de los 50 Estados de EEUU. 2006. *El Central* (Detroit), November 2: 1, 4.

Cánepa, Gisela. 2007. Geopoética de identidad y lo cholo en el Perú: Migración, geografía y mestizaje. In *Crónicas urbanas: Análisis y perspectivas urbano-regionales* (Cusco-Perú: Centro Guamán Poma de Ayala) 11, no. 12: 29–42.

Carbó, Teresa. 2003. Comandanta Zapatista Esther at the Mexican Federal Congress. *Journal of Language and Politics* 2, no. 1: 131–74.

Carrión, M. F. n.d. Valoración del experto de la UNESCO. http://www.habananuestra.cu/page.asp (accessed May 9, 2007).

Casanova, P. 2004. *The World Republic of Letters*. Cambridge, MA: Harvard University Press.

Casey, Edward. 1996. How to Get from Space to Place in a Fairly Short Stretch of Time: Phenomenological Prolegomena. In *Senses of Place*, ed. Steven Feld and Keith H. Basso, 13–52. Santa Fe and Mexico City: School of American Research Press.

Castells, Manuel. 1989. *The Informational City: Information Technology, Economic Restructuring, and the Urban Regional Process*. Oxford and Cambridge, MA: Blackwell.

———. 1996. The Space of Flows. *The Rise of the Network Society (The Information Age: Economy, Society and Culture)*, 1: 376–428. Malden, MA, and Oxford: Blackwell.

Castillo Faílde, Osvaldo. 1964. *Miguel Faílde, creador musical del danzón*. Havana: Editora del Consejo Nacional de Cultura.

Castoriadis, Cornelius. 1987. *The Imaginary Institution of Society*. Cambridge: Polity Press.

Celorio, Gonzalo. 2005. Mexico, ciudad de papel. In Gallo (2005): 39–58.

Chasteen, John Charles. 1996. Introduction. In Angel Rama, *The Lettered City*, vii–xiv. Durham, NC, and London: Duke University Press..

Chatterjee, Partha. 2004. *The Politics of the Governed: Reflections on Popular Politics in Most Parts of the World*. New York: Columbia University Press.

Chow, Rey. 1998. *Ethics after Idealism: Theory, Culture, Ethnicity, Reading*. Bloomington: Indiana University Press.

Cirules, E. 1999. *El imperio en La Habana*. Havana: Letras Cubanas.

Clendinnen, Inga. 2002. The Cost of Courage in Aztec Society. In *The Mexico Reader: History, Culture, Politics*, ed. Gilbert M. Joseph and Timothy J. Henderson, 61–78. Durham, NC, and London: Duke University Press.

Comaroff, John, and Jean Comaroff. 2001. Naturing the Nation: Aliens, Apocalypse, and the Postcolonial State. *Journal of Southern African Studies* 27 no. 3: 627–51.

Conley, Tom. 2003. The City Vanishes. In *After-images of the City*, ed. Joan Ramón Resina and Dieter Ingenschay, 209–23. Ithaca, NY, and London: Cornell University Press.

Cresswell, Tim. 2004. *Place: A Short Introduction*. Oxford: Blackwell Publishing.

Dailey, Meghan. 2002. Mexico City: An Exhibition about the Exchange Rates of Bodies and Values. http://www.findarticles.com/p/articles/mi_m0268/is_3_41/ai_95122702# (accessed November 6, 2005).

Dávila, Arlene. 2004. The Marketable Neighborhood: Commercial Latinidad in New York's East Harlem. In *Mediaspace: Place, Scale, and Culture in a Media Age*, ed. Nick Couldry and Anna McCarthy, 95–113. London: Routlege.

Davis, Diane, E. 1994. *Urban Leviathan: Mexico City in the Twentieth Century*. Philadelphia: Temple University Press.

Davis, Mike. 2000. *Magical Urbanism: Latinos Reinvent the U.S. City*. London: Verso.

Dawson, Alexander S. 2004. *Indian and Nation in Revolutionary Mexico*. Tucson: University of Arizona Press.

de Certeau, Michel. 1988. *The Practice of Everyday Life*. Trans. Steven Rendall. Berkeley and Los Angeles: University of California Press.

De la Peña, Guillermo. 1999. Territorio y ciudadanía étnica en la nación globalizada. *Desacatos*, Spring: 13–27.

———. 2006. A New Mexican Nationalism? Indigenous Rights, Constitutional Reform, and the Conflicting Meanings of Multiculturalism. *Nations and Nationalism* 12, no. 2: 279–302.

De Soto, Hernando. 1987. *El otro sendero*. 6th ed. Lima: Instituto de Libertad y Democracia.

Dear, Michael, ed. 1996. *Atlas of Southern California. Prepared for the USC Presidential Roundtable*. Los Angeles: University of Southern California, Southern California Studies Center. November 12.

Debord, Guy. 1995. *The Society of the Spectacle*. New York: Zone Books.

Debroise, Olivier 2005. Fin de temporada: Saldos. In *Eco: Arte contemporáneo mexicano*, 181–87. Madrid: Museo Nacional Centro de Arte Reina Sofia/Conaculta.

Degregori, Carlos Iván. 1994. Dimensión cultural de la experiencia migratoria. *Páginas* 19, no. 130 (Dec.): 18–29.

———, Cecilia Blondet, and Nicolas Lynch. 1986. *Conquistadores de un nuevo mundo: De invasores a ciudadanos en San Martín de Porres*. Lima: Instituto de Estudios Peruanos.

Del Valle, Elena. 2008. Watch Video—Detroit Station to Offer First Spanish Language Baseball Presentation. *Hispanic Marketing and Public Relations*, August 6 (accessed at http://www.hispanicmpr.com/2008/08/06/watch-video-detroit-station-to-offer-first-spanish-language-baseball-presentation/).

Deleuze, Gilles, and Felix Guattari. 1985. *El Anti-edipo: Capitalismo y esquizofrenia*. Trans. Francisco Monge. Barcelona: Editorial Paidos.

Díaz del Castillo, Bernal. 1963. *The Conquest of New Spain*. Harmondsworth, UK: Penguin Books.

Douglas, Mary, and Baron Isherwood. 1979. *The World of Goods*. New York: Basic Books.

du Gay, Paul, ed. 1997. *Production of Culture, Cultures of Production*. London: Sage/Open University.

———, et al. 1997. *Doing Cultural Studies: The Story of the Sony Walkman*. London: Sage/Open University.

Duncan, James S. 1996. Me(trope)olis: Or Hayden White among the Urbanists. In *Re-Presenting the City: Ethnicity, Capital, and Culture in the 21st-Century Metropolis*, ed. Anthony D. King. New York: New York University Press.

Dunn, Christopher. 2001. *Brutality Garden: Tropicália and the Emergence of a Brazilian Counterculture*. Chapel Hill: University of North Carolina Press.

Edelman Gallery. 2005. Joel-Peter Witkin. http://edelmangallery.com/witkin.htm (accessed May 3, 2006).

Edgar, Andrew. 2006. *Habermas: The Key Concepts*. London: Routledge.

El conflicto: Los buses rojos. 2008. *Cambio*, no. 791 (August 28): 10.

El otro jugador: La Caravana de la Dignidad Indígena. 2001. Mexico City: Ediciones *La Jornada.*

Es cuestión de justicia social. 2006. *Semana,* no. 1,163 (August 16): 124–25.

Fagen, R. R. 1969. *The Transformation of Political Culture in Cuba.* Stanford, CA: Stanford University Press.

Farley, Reynolds. 2003. "Detroit in 2003: Racial, Economic, and Geographiuc Trends in a Polarized Metropolis." In *Racial Liberalism and the Politics of Urban America,* ed. Curtis Stokes and Theresa Meléndez, 295–319. East Lansing: Michigan State University Press.

Feria Internacional del Libro 15. 2006. Official Program. La Habana: (no publisher).

Fernández, James. 1986. *Persuasions and Performances: The Play of Tropes in Culture.* Bloomington: Indiana University Press.

Flores, Juan. 2000. *From Bomba to Hip-Hop: Puerto Rican Culture and Latino Identity.* New York: Columbia University Press.

Fonseca, Nara Aragão. 2005. Reapropriação urbana e ruptura estética: A ótica mangue em *Conceição.* In *Simulacros e espetáculos,* ed. Paula C. Cunha Filho, 97–114. Caderno de esboços. Recife: Bagaço.

Foster, David William. 2002. *Mexico City in Contemporary Mexican Cinema.* Austin: University of Texas Press.

Foucault, Michel. 1969. *L'Archéologie du savoir.* Paris: Gallimard.

Franco, Jean. 2002. *The Decline and Fall of the Lettered City: Latin America in the Cold War.* Cambridge, MA, and London: Harvard University Press.

Friedman, Jonathan. 2000. Americans Again, or the New Age of Imperial Reason? Global Elite Formation, Its Identity and Ideological Discourses. *Theory, Culture, and Society* 17, no. 1: 139–46.

Frow, John. 1997. *Time and Commodity Culture: Essays in Cultural Theory and Postmodernity.* Oxford: Clarendon Press.

Gallo, Rubén. 2004. *New Tendencies in Mexican Art: The 1990s.* New York and Basingstoke: Palgrave.

———, ed. 2005. *México DF: Lecturas para paseantes.* Madrid: Turner.

———. (n.d.). Interview with Sylvère Lotringer. http://www.echonyc.com/~trans/ Telesymposia3/Lotringer/Slotringer.html (accessed October 22, 2005).

Gandhi, Leela 1998. *Postcolonial Theory: A Critical Introduction.* New York: Columbia University Press.

Gané, porque la ciudadanía estuvo conmigo. 2006. *Semana* 1, 253 (May 8): 60–62.

García Canclini, Néstor. 1995. *Consumidores y ciudadanos: Conflictos multiculturales de la globalización.* México City: Grijalbo.

———. 1995. *Hybrid Cultures.* Trans. Christopher L. Chippari and Silvia L. López. Minneapolis: University of Minnesota Press.

———. 1997. *Imaginarios urbanos.* Buenos Aires: Editorial Universitaria de Buenos Aires.

———. 1999. *La globalización imaginada.* Buenos Aires: Paidós.

———, Alejandro Castellanos, and Ana Rosas Mantecón, eds. 1996. *La ciudad de los viajeros: Travesías e imaginarios urbanos: México, 1940–2000.* Mexico City: Grijalbo.

Gil, Daniel. 1993. Memorias del horror. Prologue to Maren Viñar and Marcelo Viñar, *Fracturas de memoria: Crónicas para una memoria por venir,* 5–11. Montevideo: Trilce.

Goldstein, Daniel M. 2004. *The Spectacular City: Violence and Performance in Urban Bolivia.* Durham, NC, and London: Duke University Press.

Golte, Jürgen. 2001. *Cultura, racionalidad y migración andina.* Lima: Instituto de Estudios Peruanos.

———, and Norma Adams. 1987. *Los caballos de Troya de los invasores: Estrategias campesinas en la conquista de la Gran Lima.* Lima: Instituto de Estudios Peruanos / Minneapolis and London: University of Minnesota Press.

González, Aníbal. 1983. *La crónica modernista hispanoamericana.* Madrid: José Porrúa Turanzas, S.A.

———. 1993. *Journalism and the Development of Spanish American Narrative.* New York: Cambridge University Press.

González Casanova, Pablo. 2005. The Zapatista 'caracoles': Networks of Resistance and Autonomy. *Socialism and Democracy* 19, 3: 79–92.

González Iñárritu, Alejandro. 2000. *Amores perros.* Screenplay Guillermo Arriaga. México. 120min. 35mm/color.

Gorelik, Adrián. 1998. *La grilla y el parque: Espacio público y cultura urbana en Buenos Aires, 1887–1936.* Buenos Aires: Universidad Nacional de Quilmes.

Governor Granholm Statement on Cinco de Mayo. 2007. *El Central* (Detroit), May 3: 1.

Gregory, Derek. 1994. *Geographical Imaginations.* Oxford: Blackwell.

Gruzinski, Serge. 2001. *Images at War: Mexico from Columbus to Blade Runner (1492–2019).* Trans. Heather MacLean. Durham, NC: Duke University Press.

Gugler, J. 1980. A Minimum of Urbanisation and the Maximum of Ruralism: The Cuban Experience. *International Journal of Urban and Regional Research* 4, 4 (December).

Guillermoprieto, A. 2002. The Unmasking. In *The Zapatista Reader,* ed. Tom Hayden, 33–45. New York: Thunder's Mouth Press/Nation Books.

Habermas, Jürgen. 1991. *The Structural Transformation of the Public Sphere: An Inquiry into a Category of Bourgeois Society.* Trans. Thomas Burger, with Frederick Lawrence. Cambridge: Massachusetts Institute of Technology.

Halbwachs, Maurice. 1950. *La Mémoire collective.* Paris: Presses Universitaires de France.

Hall, Stuart. 1993. Minimal Selves. In *Studying Culture,* ed. Ann Gray and Jim McGuigan, 133–35. London: Edward Arnold.

Hart, Stephen, and Richard Young, eds. 2003. *Contemporary Latin American Cultural Studies.* London: Arnold.

Hartmann, Alia Lira. 2002. Teresa Margolles exhibe "la niebla del horror" en Mex-artes Berlín. *La Jornada,* October 30.

Harvey, David. 1989. *The Urban Experience.* Oxford: Blackwell.

———. 1990. *The Condition of Postmodernity: An Enquiry into the Origins of Cultural Change.* Cambridge, MA, and Oxford: Blackwell.

Harvey, Neil. 1998. *The Chiapas Rebellion: The Struggle for Land and Democracy.* Durham, NC, and London: Duke University Press.

Heidegger, Martin. 1977. Building Dwelling Thinking. In *Basic Writings,* ed. David Farrell Krell. New York: Harper and Row.

Hernández, Felipe. 2005. Introduction: Transcultural Architectures in Latin America. In *Transculturation: Cities, Spaces and Architectures in Latin America,* ed. Felipe Hernández, Mark Millington, and Iain Borden, ix–xxv. Amsterdam: Rodopi.

Herzog, Lawrence A. 2006. *Return to the Center: Culture, Public Space, and City Building in a Global Era.* Austin: University of Texas Press.

History and Theory. 2006. Forum: On Presence, 45, no. 3 (October): 305–74.

Hoffnung-Garskof, Jesse. 2008. Michigan. In *Latino America: A State-by-State Encyclopedia.* Vol. 1, *Alabama–Missouri.* Series ed. Mark Overmyer-Velásquez. Westport, CT: Greenwood Press.

Holston, James. 1989. *The Modernist City: An Anthropological Critique of Brasilia.* Chicago: Chicago University Press.

hooks, bel. 1992. *Black Looks: Race and Representation.* Boston: South End Press.

Hopenhayn, Martín. 1994. *Ni apocalípticos ni integrados: Aventuras de la modernidad en América Latina.* Santiago de Chile: Fondo de Cultura Económica.

———. 2000. Globalization and Culture: Five Approaches to a Single Text. In Brooksbank-Jones and Munck (2000): 142–57.

Huyssen, Andreas. 2000. *Seduzidos pela memória: Arquitetura, monumentos, mídia.* Rio de Janeiro: Aeroplano.

———. 2003. *Present Pasts: Urban Palimpsests and the Politics of Memory.* Stanford, CA: Stanford University Press.

Infraestructura víal. 2003. *Cambio,* no. 527 (August 4): 72.

Iznaga, Diana. 1986. Prólogo. In Fernando Ortiz, *Los negros curros.* Havana: Editorial de Ciencias Sociales.

Jameson, Fredric. 1971. *Marxism and Form: Twentieth-Century Dialectical Theories of Literature.* Princeton, NJ: Princeton University Press.

———. 1981. *The Political Unconscious: Narrative as a Socially Symbolic Act.* Ithaca, NY: Cornell University Press.

———. 1992. *The Geopolitical Æsthetic: Cinema and Space in the World System.* London: British Film Institute.

———. 1994. *The Seeds of Time.* New York: Columbia University Press.

Jauregui, Gabriela. 2004. Necropolis: Exhuming the Works of Teresa Margolles. In *Teresa Margolles: Muerte sin fin,* ed. Ugo Kittelmann and Klaus Görner, 175–90. Frankfurt: Museum für Kunst/Hatje Verlag/Ostfildern-Ruit.

Jay, Martin. 1993. *Downcast Eyes: The Denigration of Vision in Twentieth-Century French Thought.* Berkeley and Los Angeles: University of California Press.

Jörgensen, Beth E. 2004. Making History: Subcomandante Marcos in the Mexican Chronicle. *South Central Review* 21, no. 3: 85–106.

Judd, Dennis R., and Susan S. Fainstein, eds. 1999. *The Tourist City.* New Haven, CT: Yale University Press.

Kantaris, Elia Geoffrey. 1996. The Last Snapshots of Modernity: Argentine Cinema after the "Process." *Bulletin of Hispanic Studies* [Glasgow] 73, no. 2 (April): 219–44. http://www.cus.cam.ac.uk/~egk10/notes/PD-ArgCinema.htm.

Kapcia, Antoni. 2005. *Havana: The Making of Cuban Culture*, Oxford: Berg Publishers

Kilchmann, Peter. 2005. Teresa Margolles (accessed March 12, 2006, at http://www.kilchmanngalerie.com/exhibition.php?exi_id=19).

King, Anthony D. 1996. Introduction: Cities, Texts and Paradigms. In *Re-Presenting the City: Ethnicity, Capital, and Culture in the 21st-Century Metropolis,* ed. Anthony D. King, 1–19. New York: New York University Press.

Kismaric, Susan. 2004. *Héctor García*. Madrid and Mexico City: Turner/DGE-Equilibrista/Conaculta.

Knight, Alan. 1990. Racism, Revolution, and Indigenismo: Mexico, 1910–1940. In *The Idea of Race in Latin America, 1870–1940,* ed. Richard Graham. Austin: University of Texas Press.

Lacan, Jacques. 1991. Introduction of the Big Other. In *The Seminar of Jacques Lacan. Book 2: The Ego in Freud's Theory and in the Technique of Psychoanalysis, 1954–1955,* ed. Jacques-Alain Miller, trans. Sylvana Tomaselli, 235–47. New York: W. W. Norton and Co.

———. 1998. *Escritos*. México: Siglo XXI.

Laclau, Ernesto, and Chantal Mouffe. 1985. *Hegemony and Socialist Strategy: Towards a Radical Democratic Politics.* London: Verso.

LaGanga, Maria L. 1997. At a Career Crossroads? Try the Kitchen. *Los Angeles Times*, March 2: Section A.

La grasa de los muertos mexicanos gotea en Francia. 2005. *El Ciudadano,* http://archivo-elciudadano.co.ar/04–03–2005/cultura/grasa/php (accessed October 9, 2005).

La onda trans. 2005. *Cambio.* no. 617 (April 25): 76–78.

La Otra Campaña. 2006. *Contrahistorias: La otra mirada de Clío* 3, no. 6.

Lapique Becali, Zoila. 1979. *Música colonial cubana tomo 1 (1812–1902).* Havana: Editorial Letras Cubanas.

Larraín, Jorge. 2000. *Identity and Modernity in Latin America.* Cambridge: Polity Press.

La troncal del sur. 2005. *Cambio,* no. 603 (January 17): 40.

Lechner, Norbert. 1988. El desencanto postmoderno. In *Imágenes desconocidas: La modernidad en la encrucijada postmoderna,* ed. Fernando Calderón, 129–38. Buenos Aires: CLACSO.

Lee, Jennifer S. 2008. Study Notes Fewer Loans to Hispanics and Blacks. *New York Times*, October 28 (accessed at: http://www.nytimes.com/2008/10/28/nyregion/28mortgage.html).

Lefebvre, Henri. 1991. *The Production of Space.* Trans. Donald Nicholson-Smith. Oxford: Blackwell.

Leite Neto, Alcino. 2003. Produção brasileira atual é "cinema ONG. *Folha de S. Paulo,* November 22.

Le Pera, Alfredo. 1934. Mi Buenos Aires querido. http://www.todotango.com (accessed May 13, 2010).

Les llegó el turno. 2005. *Semana,* no. 1225 (October 24): 102–3.

Leyva Solano, Xochitl. 2005. *Indigenismo, Indianismo,* and "Ethnic Citizenship" in Mexico. *Journal of Peasant Studies* 32, no. 3–4: 555–83.

Lomnitz, Claudio. 2001. *Deep Mexico, Silent Mexico: An Anthropology of Nationalism.* Minneapolis: University of Minnesota Press.

———. 2005. *Death and the Idea of Mexico.* New York: Zone Books.

Long, J. J. 2008. *W.G. Sebald: Image, Archive, Modernity.* Edinburgh: Edinburgh University Press.

López, Ana M. 2000. Early Cinema and Modernity in Latin America. *Cinema Journal* 40, no. 1: 48–78.

López Cuenca, Alberto. 2005. El desarraigo como virtud: México y la deslocalización del arte en los años 90. *Revista de Occidente* (accessed July 20, 2005, at http://www.ortegaygasset.edu/revistadeoccidente/artículos/(285)Alberto_Lopez.pdf).

Low, Setha M. 1999. Introduction: Theorizing the City. In *Theorizing the City: The New Urban Anthropology Reader,* ed. Setha M. Low, 1–33. New Brunswick, NJ: Rutgers University Press.

———. 2000. *On the Plaza: The Politics of Public Space and Culture.* Austin: University of Texas Press.

Lowe, Lisa 1996. *Immigrant Acts: On Asian American Cultural Politics.* Durham, NC: Duke University Press.

Lummis, Charles Fletcher. 1989. *Letters from the Southwest, September 20, 1884, to March 14, 1885.* Ed. James W. Byrkit. Tucson: University of Arizona Press.

Maak, Niklas. 2005. Memento mori: Del culto al cuerpo y de la cultura del placer: acerca de "Secreciones" de Teresa Margolles (accessed April 13, 2006, at http://www.elinterpretador.net/17NiklasMaak-MementoMori.htm).

Marcuse, Herbert. 1991. *One-Dimensional Man: Studies in the Ideology of Advanced Industrial Society.* Boston: Beacon Press.

Margulis, Mario. 1994. *La cultura de la noche: La vida nocturna de los jóvenes en Buenos Aires.* Buenos Aires: Editorial Biblos.

Martín-Barbero, Jesús. 1987. *De los medios a las mediaciones: Comunicación, cultura, y hegemonía.* Barcelona: Ediciones G Gili.

———. 1993. *Communication, Culture, and Hegemony. From the Media to Mediations.* Trans. Elizabeth Fox and Robert A. White. London: Sage.

———. 2000. Art/Communication/Technicity at Century's End. In Brooksbank-Jones and Munck (2000): 56–73.

Marzal, Manuel. 1983. *La transformación religiosa peruana.* Lima: Fondo Editorial de la Pontificia Universidad Católica del Perú.

Massey, Doreen. 1997. A Global Sense of Place. In *Reading Human Geography: The Poetics and Politics of Enquiry,* ed. Trevor Barnes and Derek Gregory, 315–23. London: Arnold.

———. 2005. *For Space.* London: Sage Publications.

McKenzie, Jon. 2001. *Perform or Else: From Discipline to Performance.* London: Routledge.

McLaren, Peter. 1994. White Terror and Oppositional Agency: Towards a Critical Multi-culturalism. In *Multiculturalism: A Critical Reader,* ed. David Theo Goldberg, 45–74. Cambridge: Blackwell.

Medina, Cuahtémoc. 2005a. Notas para una estética del modernizado. In *Eco: Arte contemporáneo mexicano,* 13–18. Madrid: Museo Nacional Centro de Arte Reina Sofia/Conaculta.

———. 2005b. SEMEFO: La morgue. In Gallo (2005): 341–56.

Mendonça Filho, Kleber. n.d.. Freak show de pudor e perversão. In *Cinemascópio.* http://www.cf.uol.com.br/cinemascopio/criticasf.cfm?CodCritica=841 (accessed September 2007).

Mendoza, Zoila. 1999. *Shaping Society through Dance: Mestizo Ritual Performance in the Peruvian Andes.* Chicago: University of Chicago Press.

Mexicantown International Welcome Center and Mercado. 2007. *Opening Our Door,* 4–5. Detroit: Mexicantown Community Development Corporation.

Meyer, Josh. 1997. County Crackdown on Dirty Restaurants OK'd. *Los Angeles Times,* November 26: Section B.

Michigan. Secretary of State. 2008. State Driver's License Requirements Now Include Permanent Legal Presence in U.S. Press release, January 21 (accessed at http://www.michigan.gov/0,1687,7-127-1640_9150-183894--,00.html).

Midwest Market Profile: Hispanic Print in the Nation's Heartland. 2007. *Portada* 5, no. 25 (April–May): 29–32.

Miranda, Carlos R. 1990. *The Stroessner Era: Authoritarian Rule in Paraguay.* Boulder, CO: Westview Press.

Mockus, Antanas. 1999. Cambio cultural voluntario hacia la paz. In *Educación para la paz: una pedagogía para consolidar la democracia social y participativa,* ed. Fabio Ospina, Sara Alvarado, and Ligia López Moreno. Bogotá: Cooperativa Editorial Magisterio.

———. 2003. Resistencia civil y ciudadanía. *Universidad Nacional Periódico,* no. 52 (November 23). http://unperiodico.unal.edu.co/ediciones/52/10.htm

Monnet, Jerome. 1995. *Usos e imágenes del Centro Histórico de la Ciudad de México.* Departamento del Distrito Federal: Centro de Estudios Mexicanos y Centroamericanos.

Monroy Nasr, Rebeca. 2003. *Historias para ver: Enrique Díaz, fotorreportero.* Mexico: UNAM/INAH.

Monsiváis, Carlos. 1980. *A ustedes les consta: Antología de la crónica en México.* Mexico City: Ediciones Era.

———. 1994. Crónica de una convención (que no lo fue tanto) y de un acontecimiento muy significativo. In *EZLN: Documentos y comunicados* 1. Mexico City: Ediciones Era.

———. 1995. *Los rituales del caos.* Mexico City: Ediciones Era.

———. 2004. Architexture and the City. In Mosquera and Samos (2005): 268–90.

Moore, Robin. 2006. *Music and Revolution: Cultural Change in Socialist Cuba.* Berkeley and Los Angeles: University of California Press.

Moraña, Mabel, ed. 1997. *Ángel Rama y los estudios latinoamericanos.* Pittsburgh: Instituto Internacional de Literatura Iberoamericana.

———. 2002. *Espacio urbano, comunicación, y violencia en América Latina*. Pittsburgh: Instituto Internacional de Literatura Iberoamericana.

Moreiras, Alberto. 2001. *The Exhaustion of Difference: The Politics of Latin American Cultural Studies*. Durham, NC: Duke University Press.

Morin, Edgar. 1997. *O cinema ou o homem imaginário*. Lisbon: Relógio D'Água.

Mosquera, Gerardo, and Jean Fisher, eds. 2004. *Over Here: International Perspectives on Art and Culture*. New York: New Museum of Contemporary Art / Cambridge, MA: MIT Press.

———, and Adrienne Samos, eds. 2005. *Multiple City, Panama, Urban Art, and Global Cities: An Experiment in Context*. Amsterdam: Kit Publishers.

Moxey, Keith. 2008. Visual Studies and the Iconic Turn. *Journal of Visual Culture* 7, no. 2: 131–46.

Mraz, John. 2003. *Nacho López: Mexican Photographer*. Minneapolis and London: University of Minnesota Press.

Mucho caos. 2005. *Semana*, no. 1221 (September 26): 60–62.

Muller, Delores. 2006. *Population and Households in Southeast Michigan, 2000–2006*. Detroit: Southeast Michigan Council of Governments (SEMCOG).

Muñoz, Boris. 2003. La ciudad de México en la imaginación apocalíptica. In *Más allá de la ciudad letrada*, 75–98.

———, and Silvia Spitta, eds. 2003. *Más allá de la ciudad letrada: Crónicas y espacios*. Pittsburgh: Instituto Internacional de Literatura Iberoamericana.

Museo Nacional Centro de Arte Reina Sofia/Conaculta. 2005. *Eco: Arte contemporáneo mexicano*. Madrid: Museo Nacional Centro de Arte Reina Sofia/Conaculta.

Nash, June. 1995. The Reassertion of Indigenous Identity: Mayan Responses to State Intervention in Chiapas. *Latin American Research Review* 30, no. 3: 7–41.

———. 2001. *Mayan Visions: The Quest for Autonomy in an Age of Globalization*. New York and London: Routledge.

Nietzsche, Fredrich. 1957. *The Use and Abuse of History*. Indianapolis-New York: Bobbs-Merrill Co.

Noble, Andrea. 1998. *Zapatistas en Sanborns* (1914): Women at the Bar. *History of Photography* 22, no. 4: 366–70.

Nora, Pierre, ed. 1984. *Les Lieux de mémoire*. Paris: Gallimard.

Noriega, Chon. 1996. Birth of the Southwest: Social Protest, Tourism, and D. W. Griffith's *Ramona*. In *The Birth of Whiteness: Race and the Emergence of U.S. Cinema*, ed. Daniel Bernardi, 204–26. New Brunswick, NJ: Rutgers University Press.

Noriega, Gustavo. 2001. Historia de una búsqueda. *El amante* (November 22). http://www.elamante.com/nota/1/1436.shtml (accessed May 3, 2002).

Nungesser, Michael. 2003. Via the Dead to Life: Teresa Margolles Sierra. http://www.culturebase.net/artist.php?1013 (accessed March 3, 2006).

O'Malley, I. 1986. *The Myth of the Revolution: Hero Cults and the Institutionalization of the Mexican State: 1920–1940*. New York: Greenwood Press.

Oboler, Suzanne. 1995. *Ethnic Labels, Latino Lives: Identity and the Politics of (Re)Presentation in the United States*. Minneapolis: University of Minnesota Press.

Obrist, Hans Ulrich. 2001. Conversation with Minerva Cuevas. http://www.nettime.org/Lists-Archives/nettime-l-0107/msg00160.html (accessed January 26, 2006).

Office of the Wayne County Executive. 2005. Greater Detroit Foreign Trade Zone. In *Wayne County Economic Resource Guide*, 24. Detroit: American Images Publishing.

———. 2005. Ports. In *Wayne County Economic Resource Guide*, 36. Detroit: American Images Publishing.

Orlove, Benjamin. 1993. Putting Race in its Place: Order in Colonial and Postcolonial Peruvian Geography. *Social Research* 60, no. 2: 301–36.

Pacini Hernández, Deborah, and Reebee Garafalo. 2004. Between Rock and a Hard Place: Negotiating Rock in Revolutionary Cuba, 1960–1980. In *Rockin' Las Américas: The Global Politics of Rock in Latin/o America*, ed. Deborah Pacini Hernández, Héctor Fernández L'Hoeste, and Eric Zolov, 43–67. Pittsburgh: University of Pittsburgh Press,

Paz, Octavio. 1973. *El laberinto de la soledad*. Mexico: Fondo de Cultura Económica.

Peiró Barco, José Vicente. 2001. Literatura y sociedad: La narrativa paraguaya actual (1980–1995). Diss. Universidad Nacional de Educación a Distancia. http://www.cervantes virtual.com/FichaObra.html?Ref=6999&ext=pdf.

Pérez de Mendiola, Marina. 2004. Mexican Contemporary Photography: Staging Ethnicity and Citizenship. *Boundary 2*, 31, no. 3: 125–53.

Piason Natali, Marcos. 2006. History and the Politics of Nostalgia. *Iowa Journal of Cultural Studies* 5: 10–25. http://www.uiowa.edu/~ijcs/nostalgia/nostfe1.htm.

Pike, Burton. 1996. The City as Image. In *The City Reader*, ed. Richard T. LeGates and Frederic Stout, 242–49. London and New York: Routledge.

Poniatowska, Elena. 1994. La CND: De naves mayores a menores. In *EZLN: Documentos y comunicados 1*. Mexico City: Ediciones Era.

Poole, Deborah. 1988. Landscapes of Power in a Cattle-Rustling Culture of Southern Andean Peru. *Dialectical Anthropology* 12, no. 4: 367–98.

Portocarrero, Gónzalo. 1998. *Las clases medias: Entre la pretensión y la incertidumbre*. Lima: TEMPO, SUR.

Pred, Allan. 1984. Place as Historically Contingent Process: Structuration and the Time-Geography of Becoming Places. *Annals of the Association of American Geographers* 74, no. 2: 279–97.

Preston, Julia. 1997. In Mexico City's War on Crime, Citizens Are Armed and Angry. *New York Times*, November 7, 1997. http://www.owlnet.rice.edu/~poli354/Mexico_pages/971107_Mexico_crime.html (accessed April 12, 2006).

Prieto, Juan Manuel. 2004. *La ciudad en que vivimos*. Asunción: Intercontinental Editora.

Primera estación. 2004. *Cambio*, no. 579 (August 2): 32–33.

Prysthon, Angela. 2002a. *Cosmopolitismos periféricos: Ensaios sobre modernidade, pós-modernidade e estudos culturais na América Latina*. Recife: Bagaço/PPGCOM-UFPE.

———. 2002b. Rearticulando a tradição: Rápido panorama do audiovisual brasileiro nos anos 90. *Contracampo* (Rio de Janeiro), no. 7: 65–78.

———. 2003. A periferia fashion: Dois exemplos do cinema brasileiro contemporâneo. *Suplemento Diário oficial do Estado de Pernambuco,* suplemento cultural 2: 2–4.

———. 2005. Os conceitos de subalternidade e periferia nos estudos de cinema brasileiros. *A comunicação revisitada,* ed Sérgio Capparelli, Muniz Sodré, Sebastião Squirra, 233–47. Porto Alegre: Sulina.

Pulso de poderes. 2006. *Semana* 1, no. 254 (May 15): 74–75.

Quijano, Aníbal. 1993. Modernity, Identity, and Utopia in Latin America. Trans. John Beverly. *Boundary 2,* 20, no. 3: 140–55.

Radcliffe, Sarah, and Sallie Westwood. 1996. *Remaking the Nation: Place, Identity, and Politics in Latin America.* London and New York: Routledge.

Rajchenberg, Enrique, and Catherine Héau-Lambert. 1998. History and Symbolism in the Zapatista Movement. In *Zapatista! Reinventing Revolution in Mexico,* ed. John Holloway and Eloína Peláez, 19–38. London: Pluto Press.

Rama, Ángel. 1996. *The Lettered City.* Trans. John Charles Chasteen. Durham, NC, and London: Duke University Press.

Ramos, Julio. 1989. *Desencuentros de la modernidad en América Latina.* México: Fondo de Cultura Económica.

Ravaschino, Guillermo. 2002. *Pizza, birra, faso. Cineismo.* http://www.cineismo.com/criticas/pizza,%20birra,%20faso.htm (accessed May 3, 2002).

Relph, Edward. 1976. *Place and Placelessness.* London: Pion.

Renan, Ernest. 1990. What is a Nation? In *Nation and Narration,* ed. Homi K. Bhabha, 8–22. London: Routledge.

Richard, Nelly. 1996. Postmodern Decentrednesses and Cultural Periphery: The Disalignments and Realignments of Cultural Power. In *Beyond the Fantastic: Contemporary Art Criticism from Latin America,* ed. Gerardo Mosquera, 260–69. Cambridge: MIT Press.

Rieff, David. 1991. *Los Angeles: Capital of the Third World.* New York: Simon and Schuster.

Rivera, Diego, with Gladys March. 1991. *My Art, My Life: An Autobiography.* New York: Dover Press.

Roca, José, 2003. Columna de Arena/Columna 48: Ausencia/Evidence: José Alejandro Restrepo, Oscar Muños, Teresa Margolles. http://www.universes-in-universe.de/columna/col48/col48-print.htm (accessed October 7, 2005).

Rodríguez-Juliá, Edgardo. 2005. *San Juan, ciudad soñada.* Madison: University of Wisconsin Press.

Rodríguez Sotomayor, Daynet. n.d.. Estoy de pie. Interview with Gerardo Alfonso. http://www.trovacub.com/nuke/modules.php?name=News&file=article&sid=922

Rojas, Rafael. 1998. *El arte de la espera: Notas al margen de la política cubana.* Madrid: Editorial Colibrí.

Romero, José Luis. 2001. *Latinoamérica: Las ciudades y las ideas.* 5th ed. Mexico and Buenos Aires: Siglo XXI Editores.

Romero, Raúl. 2002. Popular Music and the Global City: *Huayno, Chicha,* and *Technocumbia* in Lima. In *From Tejano to Tango: Latin American Popular Music,* ed. Walter Aaron Clark, 217–39. New York and London: Routledge.

Rosaldo, Renato. 1991. *Cultura y verdad: Nueva propuesta de análisis social*. Mexico City: Grijalbo.

Rotker, Susana, ed. 2002. *Citizens of Fear: Urban Violence in Latin America*. New Brunswick, NJ: Rutgers University Press.

Rubiani, Jorge. 2002. *Postales de Asunción de antaño*. Asunción: Intercontinental Editora.

Runia, Eelco. 2006. Presence. *History and Theory* 45, no. 1: 1–29.

Russell, Catherine. 1999. *Experimental Ethnography: The Work of Film in the Age of Video*. Durham, NC: Duke University Press.

Saldaña-Portillo, María Josefina. 2002. Reading a Silence: The "Indian" in the Era of Zapatismo. *Nepantla* 3, no. 2: 287–314.

———. 2003. *The Revolutionary Imagination in the Americas and the Age of Development*. Durham, NC, and London: Duke University Press.

Salecl, Renata. 2004. *On Anxiety*. London: Routledge.

Sallnow, Michael. 1987. *Pilgrims of the Andes: Regional Cults in Cuzco*. Washington DC: Smithsonian Institute Press.

Sandoval, Edgar. 2001. La receta de Transmilenio. *Cambio*, no. 400 (February 19): 34.

Sandrós, Paraná. 1998. Filmar es algo apasionante, pero hace envejecer [entrevista a Bruno Stagnaro y Adrián Caetano]. *Ambitoweb*. http://www.ambitoweb.com/ediciones anteriores/afinancieroback/98–01–12/espectaculos001.htm (accessed August 16, 2004).

Santiago, Silviano. 2004. *O cosmopolitismo do pobre*. Belo Horizonte: Editora da UFMG.

Santos Cabrera, Kaloian. 2006. Conversando con Gerardo Alfonso. Rembranzas de un cuarto de siglo. http://oreja.trovacub.com/

Sarlo, Beatriz. 1988. *Una modernidad periférica: Buenos Aires, 1920 y 1930*. Buenos Aires: Ediciones Nueva Visión.

———. 1994. *Escenas de la vida posmoderna: Intelectuales, arte y videocultura en la Argentina*. Buenos Aires: Ariel/Espasa Calpe.

———. 1996. *Instantáneas: Medios, ciudad y constumbres en el fin de siglo*. Buenos Aires: Ariel/Espasa Calpe.

Schechner, Richard. 2002. *Performance Studies: An Introduction*. London and New York: Routledge.

Schelling, Vivian, ed. 2000. *Through the Kaleidoscope: The Experience of Modernity in Latin America*. London: Verso.

Sciscioli, Alejandro. 2009. Reviving the Guaraní Route. *Tierramérica: Environment and Development*, August 26. http://www.tierramerica.info-nota.php?lang=eng&idnews=559.

Scobie, James. 1964. *Argentina: A City and a Nation*. New York: Oxford University Press.

Seamon, David. 1980. Body-Subject, Time-Space Routines, and Ballet-Places. In *The Human Experience of Space and Place*, ed. David Seamon and Anne Buttimer, 148–65. New York: St. Martin's Press.

Segre, R., M. Coyula, and J. L. Scarpaci. 1997. *Havana: Two Faces of the Antillean Metropolis*. Chichester: John Wiley and Sons.

Sevcenko, Nicolau. 1992. *Orfeu extático na metrópole: São Paulo, sociedade e cultura nos frementes anos 20*. São Paulo: Companhia das Letras.

Shaw, Wendy. 2002. Art among the Myths of Globalism: The Istanbul Biennial. *Third Text* 58, 16, no. 1 (March): 94–102.

Shiel, Mark, and Tony Fitzmaurice, eds. 2001. *Cinema and the City: Film and Urban Societies in a Global Context.* Oxford: Blackwell.

Shields, Rob. 1991. *Places on the Margin.* New York: Routledge.

Shohat, Ella, and Robert Stam. 2002. *Multiculturalismo, cine y medios de comunicación.* Barcelona: Paidós.

Silva, Armando. 2000. *Imaginarios urbanos.* 4th ed. Bogotá: Tercer Mundo Ediciones.

———. 2004. Civic Urbanism: Toward an Anthropology of the Urban Phantom. In Mosquera and Samos (2005): 295–309.

Smith, Paul. 1988. *Discerning the Subject.* Minneapolis: University of Minnesota Press.

Sobre ruedas. 2001. *Semana,* no. 998 (June 18): 54–55.

Solanas, Fernando E. 1988. *Sur.* Argentina: Pacific Productions Cinesur Argentina / Canal Plus France. 115min. 35mm/color.

Souza, Gustavo. 2006. Traficantes, justiceiros, e rappers: A invasão dos setores da margem na produção de documentários. MA thesis. Rio de Janeiro: PPGCOM–UFRJ.

Springer, José Manuel. 2004. Mexican report: Crónica de un deslinde. *Replica 21.* http://www.replica21.com/archivo/articulos/s_t/348_springer_m_report.html (accessed October 9, 2005).

Stam, Robert. 1997. *Tropical Multiculturalism: A Comparative History of Race in Brazilian Cinema and Culture.* Durham, NC, and London: Duke University Press.

Stevenson, Nick, ed. 2001. *Culture and Citizenship.* Thousand Oaks: SAGE.

Stokes, Martin, ed. 1994. *Ethnicity, Identity, and Music: The Musical Construction of Place.* London: Berg.

Subiela, Eliseo. 1989. *Últimas imágenes del naufragio.* Argentina: Cinequanon–TVE, 127mins. 35mm/color.

Taylor, Analisa. 2005. The Ends of *Indigenismo* in Mexico. *Journal of Latin American Cultural Studies* 14, no. 1: 75–86.

Terdiman, Richard. 1983. On the Determination of Social Action in Time and Space. *Environment and Planning D: Society and Space* 1, no. 1: 23–57.

———. 1993. *Present Past: Modernity and the Memory Crisis.* Ithaca, NY: Cornell University Press.

Thrift, Nigel. 2008. *Non-Representational Theory: Space/Politics/Affect.* London and New York: Routledge.

Trapero, Pablo. 1999. *Mundo grúa.* Screenplay by Lita Stantic. Argentina. 90mins. 35mm/BW.

Trigo, Abril. 2004. General Introduction. In *The Latin American Studies Cultural Reader,* ed. Ana del Sarto, Alicia Ríos, and Abril Trigo, 1–14. Durham, NC: Duke University Press.

Trigo, Benigno. 2002. Introduction. In *Foucault and Latin America: Appropriations and Deployments of Discursive Analysis,* ed. Benigno Trigo, xi–xxi. New York and London: Routledge.

Tuan, Fu-Yi. 1974. *Topophilia: A Study of Environmental Perception, Attitudes, and Values.* Englewood Cliffs, NJ: Prentice-Hall.

———. 1977. *Space and Place: The Perspective of Experience.* Minneapolis: University of Minnesota Press.

Turner, Terence. 1999. Indigenous and Culturalist Movements in the Contemporary Global Conjuncture. In *Globalización, Fronteras Culturales y Política y Ciudadanía (Actas del VIII Congreso de Antropología, 1999),* 51–72. Santiago de Compostela: Federación de Asociaciones de Antropología del Estado Espanol/Asociación Galega de Antropoloxia.

Valle, Victor, and Rodolfo D. Torres. 2000. *Latino Metropolis.* Minneapolis: University of Minnesota Press.

Vía al desarrollo. 2004. *Semana,* no. 1169 (September 27): 136–39.

Viñar, Maren, and Marcelo Viñar. 1993. *Fracturas de memoria: Crónicas para una memoria por venir.* Montevideo: Trilce.

Vitali, Valentina, and Paul Willemen, eds. 2006. *Theorising National Cinema.* London: British Film Institute.

¿Volver al tranvía? 2004. *Semana,* no. 1151 (May 24): 44.

Ward, Peter M., and Elizabeth Durden. 2002. Government and Democracy in Mexico's Federal District, 1997–2001: Cárdenas, the PRD, and the Curate's Egg. *Bulletin of Latin American Research* 21, no. 1 (January): 1–39.

Watson, John G. 1992. Busboys' Night Out: Top Latino Restaurant Workers to Be Feted at Ceremony Jan. 17. *Los Angeles Times,* November 5: Nuestro Tiempo (section).

Williams, Gareth. 2007. The Mexican Exception and the "Other Campaign." *South Atlantic Quarterly* 106, no. 1: 129–51.

Yúdice, George. 2003. *The Expediency of Culture: Uses of Culture in the Global Era.* Durham, NC, and London: Duke University Press.

Žižek, Slavoj. 1989. *The Sublime Object of Ideology.* London: Verso.

———. 1991. *For They Know Not What They Do: Enjoyment as a Political Factor.* London: Verso.

———. 1993. *Tarrying with the Negative: Kant, Hegel, and the Critique of Ideology.* Durham, NC: Duke University Press.

———. 1997. *The Plague of Fantasies.* London: Verso.

Zukin, Sharon. 1991. *Landscapes of Power: From Detroit to Disney World.* Berkeley and Los Angeles: University of California Press.

———. 1995. *The Culture of Cities.* Cambridge: Blackwell.

Contributors

Catherine L. Benamou is associate professor of Film and Media Studies and of Chicano/Latino Studies at the University of California–Irvine. Her research interests in Latin American and Latina/o media arts include realist aesthetics and Spanish-language television and spectatorship. She is the author of *It's All True: Orson Welles's Pan-American Odyssey* (University of California Press 2007) and is at work on a book manuscript, *The Electronic Embrace: Transnational Television and Its Latina/o Diasporic Audiences.*

Anny Brooksbank-Jones was until November 2007 Hughes Professor of Spanish at the University of Sheffield. Her teaching and research centered on visual culture in Spain and Latin America. Her publications include *Cultural Politics in Latin America*, coedited with Ronaldo Munck (Macmillan/ Palgrave 2000), *Visual Culture in Spain and Mexico* (Manchester University Press 2007), *Latin American Women's Writing,* coedited with Catherine Davies (Oxford University Press 1996), and *Women in Contemporary Spain* (Manchester University Press 1997). She is a former cultural editor of the *Bulletin of Latin American Research* and member of the editorial boards of *International Journal of Iberian Studies: Intellect,* and the *Bulletin of Hispanic Studies.*

Juan R. Buriel is assistant professor of English at College of the Canyons in Valencia, California. He is a doctoral candidate in Comparative Literature at the University of California–Irvine (2010) and a Ford Foundation Diversity Fellow (2006–2007). His articles and book reviews appear in *Rio Bravo, 49th Parallel, Alud, Céfiro, Aztlán, Material Culture,* and *Southwestern Historical Quarterly.* His dissertation, which is in progress, examines some theoretical implications of subaltern representation in contemporary Chicano literature. He is specifically concerned with the Chicano as native informant, with power and representation during the Chicano Movement, and with the discursivity of Chicano voice.

Gisela Cánepa teaches in the Department of Social Sciences at the Pontificia Universidad Católica del Perú where she is coordinator of the Master's Program in Visual Anthropology. Her research interests include the formation of ethnic and regional identities, the politics of cultural representation and the public sphere, and visual anthropology. She is the author of *Máscara, transformación, e identidad en los Andes* (1998), *Identidades representadas: Performance, experiencia y memoria en los Andes* (2001), and *Mirando la esfera pública desde la cultura en el Perú* (2006). She has directed four ethnographic documentaries and a multimedia CD-ROM on music and ritual in the Andes.

Héctor Fernández L'Hoeste is associate professor of Spanish and director of the Center for Latin American and Latino/a Studies at Georgia State University, where he teaches Latin American Cultural Studies. He is the author of *Narrativas de representación urbana: Un estudio de expresiones culturales de la modernidad latinoamericana* (Lang, 1998) and coeditor of *Rockin' Las Americas* (University of Pittsburgh Press, 2004) and *Redrawing the Nation* (Palgrave Macmillan, 2009).

Amanda Holmes is associate professor and chair of the Department of Hispanic Studies at McGill University. She studies contemporary Latin American literature and has published on urban topics such as the circulation of metropolitan figures, political violence and the city, and the urban uncanny. In her book, *City Fictions: Language, the Body, and Spanish-American Urban Space* (Bucknell University Press 2007), she interprets generic and metaphoric modes of urban representation.

Geoffrey Kantaris is director of the Centre of Latin American Studies in the University of Cambridge and senior lecturer in the Department of Spanish and Portuguese. His current research is on contemporary urban cinema from Argentina, Colombia, and Mexico. He has published several articles in this area and is preparing a book provisionally titled Contemporary Latin American Cinema: The Urban Paradigm. He has also worked extensively on women's writing and on dictatorship in Argentina and Uruguay, and is the author of *The Subversive Psyche: Contemporary Women's Narrative from Argentina and Uruguay* (Oxford University Press 1996).

Antoni Kapcia is professor of Latin American History and director of the Centre for Research on Cuba at the University of Nottingham. He has researched Cuban history since 1971, publishing extensively since 1974, specializing on modern and contemporary Cuban political and cultural history. He is the author of *Havana: The Making of Cuban Culture* (Berg, 2005) and *Cuba in Revolution: A History Since the Fifties* (Reaktion, 2008).

Par Kumaraswami is a lecturer in Latin American Cultural Studies at the University of Manchester. She has taught and researched revolutionary Cuban culture for over ten years, completing a PhD in 2004 on the reception of women's testimonial writing from revolutionary Cuba. More recently, she has published several articles on revolutionary Cuban cultural policy and practice. She is currently completing, with co-researcher Tony Kapcia, a five-year project that examines the way literary activity has developed in theory and practice in Cuba over fifty years of revolution. The chapter included here is one of a series of case studies examining how literature functions for a range of actors and spaces within the Cuban Revolution.

Robin Moore is associate professor of Ethnomusicology at the University of Texas (Austin). His principal research interests include music and nationalism, music and race relations, popular music, and socialist art aesthetics. His publications include *Nationalizing Blackness* (University of Pittsburgh Press 1997), *Music and Revolution* (University of California Press 2006), *Music of the Hispanic Caribbean* (Oxford Press 2010), and articles on Cuban music in *Latin American Music Review, Cuban Studies, Ethnomusicology, Encuentro de la cultura cubana*, and other journals and book anthologies. He is currently editor of the *Latin American Music Review*.

Andrea Noble is professor of Latin American Studies at Durham University, where she is also associate director of the Durham Centre for Advanced Photography Studies (DCAPS). Her publications include *Tina Modotti: Image, Texture, Photography* (University of New Mexico Press 2000), *Mexican National Cinema* (Routledge 2005), and *Photography and Memory in Mexico: Icons of Revolution* (University of Manchester Press 2010), and two coedited volumes: with Alex Hughes, *Phototextualities: Intersections of Photography and Narrative* (University of New Mexico Press 2003); with Jonathan Long and Edward Welch, *Photography: Theoretical Snapshots* (Routledge 2009). Her research interests currently focus on the visual culture of human rights in Latin America, part of a broader project with colleagues in DCAPS, and the cultural history of tears and crying in Mexico.

Angela Prysthon is associate professor in the Department of Social Communication at the Federal University of Pernambuco, Brazil, where she is head of Cinema Studies. She is the author of *Cosmopolitismos periféricos: Ensaios sobre modernidade, pós-modernidade e estudos culturais na América Latina* (Edições Bagaço 2002) and editor of *Imagens da cidade: Espaços urbanos na comunicação e cultura contemporâneas* (Sulina 2006) and *Ecos urbanos: A cidade e suas articulações midiáticas* (Sulina 2009), among other works. Her writings on film, media, and literature have appeared in numerous books and journals, including *Brazil and the Discovery of America: Narrative, History, Fiction* (Edwin Mellen Press), *Cinema dos anos 90* (Chapecó), *Galaxia, Contemporanea,* and *Contracampo.*

Rodolfo D. Torres is professor of Urban Planning and Political Science at the University of California–Irvine. He has written widely on racism, class inequality, urban theory, and Marxist social theory. His previous books include *Latino Metropolis* (University of Minnesota Press 2000), *Savage State: Welfare Capitalism and Inequality* (Rowman and Littlefield 2004), and *After Race: Racism After Multiculturalism* (New York University Press 2004). He is editor of ten books and coeditor of the journal *Ethnicities* (published by Sage).

Abril Trigo is a professor in the Department of Spanish and Portuguese at Ohio State University, where he specializes in Latin American Cultural Studies. He has published widely on Latin American culture, including literature, music, and cultural theory. He is author of *Memorias migrantes: Testimonios y ensayos sobre la diáspora uruguaya* (Rosario/Montevideo: Beatriz Viterbo Editora/Ediciones Trilce, 2003), *¿Cultura uruguaya o culturas linyeras? Para una cartografía de la neomodernidad posuruguaya* (Montevideo: Vintén Editor, 1997), and *Caudillo, estado, nación: Literatura, historia, e ideología en el Uruguay* (Gaithersburg, MD: Ediciones Hispamérica, 1990). He coedited *The Latin American Cultural Studies Reader* (Duke University Press, 2004) and is currently writing *Crisis y transfiguración de los estudios culturales latinoamericanos* and *Crítica de la economía político-libidinal.*

Richard Young is emeritus professor of Spanish and Latin American Studies at the University of Alberta. He has published widely on Latin American Culture (literature, film, music) and currently focuses on cultural representations of Buenos Aires. He edited *Music, Popular Culture, Identities* (Amsterdam and New York: Rodopi, 2002) and coedited *Contemporary Latin American Cultural Studies* (London: Arnold, 2004). He is a former editor of *Revista Canadiense de Estudios Hispánicos* (1996–2003).

Index